# *Our Mark on This Land*

*Thank God for President Roosevelt. Without him, I
don't know what we would have done.*

— Ruben Keel, CCC Company 1459 NP-10
Great Smoky Mountains National Park, 1933

# *Our Mark on This Land*

A Guide to the Legacy of the
## Civilian Conservation Corps
in America's Parks

by
## Ren and Helen Davis

The McDonald & Woodward Publishing Company
Granville, Ohio

The McDonald & Woodward Publishing Company
Granville, Ohio
*www.mwpubco.com*

*Our Mark on This Land*
A Guide to the Legacy of the Civilian Conservation Corps in America's Parks
A McDonald & Woodward Guide to the American Landscape

All rights reserved
Printed in the United States of America by McNaughton & Gunn, Inc.,
Saline, Michigan, on paper that meets the minimum requirements of
permanence for printed library materials.

First printing December 2011

10 9 8 7 6 5 4 3 2 1
20 19 18 17 16 15 14 13 12 11


## Library of Congress Cataloging-in-Publication Data

Davis, Ren, 1951-
  Our mark on this land : a guide to the legacy of the Civilian Conservation
Corps in America's parks / by Ren and Helen Davis.
     p. cm.
  Includes index.
  ISBN 978-1-935778-18-9 (pbk. : alk. paper)
  1. Civilian Conservation Corps (U.S.)—History. I. Davis, Helen, 1951-
II. Title.
  S930.D38 2011
  333.78—dc23

                                                         2011036548

# "Who Are We?"

*We are the young men of the 1930s
who made up the Civilian Conservation Corps — 1933 to 1942.
We are the young men who mended the scarred land,
the eroded fields, the muddied waters of our creeks and rivers,
and the depleted woodlands of our country.
We replanted our forests from Maine to California.
We built the fire trails to protect the old and new forests;
cleared out the diseased deadwood to protect the healthy and new
trees;
and fought forest fires and floods.
We built lodges and campsites in our National Parks
so that people could enjoy our beautiful country.
We built the roads and trails in the parks — many of which are still
in existence today.
We worked the quarries to produce the building stone
needed to build the dams in our state and national parks,
the same dams that stand today creating the lakes that have given
recreation to campers,
fishermen, and family groups over the last 60 years.
We worked in quarries getting the rock to crush for limestone
to spread on the farmland to sweeten the overworked soil, which
helped restore productivity.
From other quarries came the building stone
needed for masonry dams and flumes which controlled the rapidly
eroding soil.
We were educated and given job opportunities,
honor, respect, and a purpose in life.*

*All over this country, the work we did with our hands,*
*our minds, and our bodies, still stands today*
*as a monument to the youth of the 1930s and what we*
*accomplished,*
*bearing in mind that 90% of what we did was done by hand,*
*pick, hoe, axe, shovel, mauls, drills, and wheelbarrows.*
***We put our mark on this land***
*and that mark will be seen for many more years to come.*
*As a generation, we have much to be proud of.*
*We have earned a place in history, and speaking as an individual,*
*I am grateful for having had the chance to be there.*

— Anonymous CCC veteran

# Table of Contents

# Foreword

From 1933 to 1942, more than three million men, most of them young and unemployed, answered President Franklin D. Roosevelt's call for volunteers to restore the nation's forests, enhance our National Parks, and create systems of state parks offering citizens unprecedented opportunities for healthful outdoor recreation. These men formed the "Civilian Conservation Corps," one of the New Deal's most popular programs.

During the Corps' nine years of operation, enrollees — often called "dollar-a-day-men" or "Roosevelt's Tree Army" — participated in what has been called the most comprehensive environmental restoration and protection program in the nation's history. The accomplishments of these men were astounding and enduring. They restored millions of acres of badly eroded woods and abandoned farmlands and planted nearly three billion trees in cut-over and denuded national and state forests. The healthy forests we see today are a tribute to their labors.

In my 40-year career with the National Park Service, I have seen, first hand, the handiwork of the CCC in both state and national

Robert Stanton was the Director of the National Park Service from 1997 to 2001.

parks, as profiled by Ren and Helen Davis in this book. I have never ceased being amazed at the accomplishments of the CCC enrollees — the thousands of miles of trails they blazed; the hundreds of lodges, cabins, shelters, and lakes they built; and the nearly endless opportunities they provided for all Americans to enjoy the outdoors. The statistics are remarkable. Working from over 3,000 camps in nearly every state and territory, CCC enrollees enhanced or improved facilities and trails at 71 National Park units, developed 405 state parks, and created 46 Recreational Demonstration Areas — parks intended for groups such as the Boy Scouts and Girl Scouts, 4-H Clubs, civic and church groups, and others — most of which are now state parks.

In their brief history of the CCC and its work under Park Service supervision, Ren and Helen provide readers with the context to better understand the scale of the Corps' achievements and why those achievements, profiled in subsequent sections of the book, are so deserving of celebration and preservation. It took visionaries to see, in the darkest days of the Great Depression, opportunities to protect our natural resources and address unmet needs for outdoor recreation. Fortunately, we were blessed with such leaders, from President Roosevelt and CCC director Robert Fechner, to National Park Service directors Horace Albright and Arno Cammerer. I would be remiss not to include among those leaders, Conrad Wirth, at the time director of the NPS Branch of Planning and State Cooperation. He guided the CCC's work in the state parks which, today, remain the backbone of America's parks systems.

When I began my forty-year career with the National Park Service in 1962 as a seasonal ranger at Grand Teton National Park, Conrad "Connie" Wirth was NPS Director, culminating a remarkable 33-year career of service to the parks and the nation. In his book, *Parks, Politics, and the People*, Wirth noted that "the work accomplished in the parks conservation field in the ten years of the CCC was equal to what might have been expected in 50 years without its assistance."

As a nation, we are blessed with a remarkable parks legacy handed down to us by the men of the CCC. We have an obligation to preserve and enhance it for generations to come.

Robert G. Stanton

# Preface

Each year, millions of Americans visit state, regional, and national parks. They hike trails, picnic by blue-water lakes, camp beneath towering trees, and relax in rustic lodges or cabins — often without giving a thought to the young men of the Depression-era Civilian Conservation Corps (CCC) who created or enhanced the parks they so much enjoy.

In one of the first initiatives of his administration, President Franklin D. Roosevelt, in March, 1933, called for the creation of the CCC, urging that more than a quarter-million unemployed young men be enrolled in only three months. With unprecedented cooperation among federal agencies, including the Labor, War (now Defense), Agriculture, and Interior departments, this effort — which succeeded — was the largest peacetime mobilization in our nation's history.

The superlatives did not end there. Over the next decade (1933–1942), from Maine to California, and Florida to Alaska, more than three million CCC workers carried out what has been described as the most effective large-scale environmental protection and restoration program ever undertaken in our country. During the program's existence, CCC enrollees planted billions of trees, erected hundreds of fire towers, restored worn out forests and farm lands, constructed lakes and dams, blazed thousands of miles of trails, and built rustic-style cabins, lodges, shelters, and other structures in hundreds of parks and recreation areas. Today, the Corps' work in our nation's parks during its nine years of existence remains the program's most tangible legacy. Through this guide, we hope to enhance awareness of, and appreciation for, the treasures entrusted to us by these men who were an integral part of what journalist Tom Brokaw called the "greatest generation."

The National Parks are the "crown jewels" of America's parklands and the CCC carried out projects of enduring value in nearly all that were in existence at the time, from Acadia in Maine and Big Bend in Texas to Wyoming's Yellowstone (the world's first national park) and Alaska's Mount McKinley (now Denali). In these magnificent parks, the CCC legacy is often subtle, complementing but not competing with the natural splendor. In the state parks, however, the handiwork of the CCC is more clearly evident in cabins, pavilions, lakes, and lodges crafted by hand in a characteristic, rough-hewn "rustic" style. For more than a dozen states, the CCC provided the resources to create parks systems where none previously existed. In others, they offered the means to improve and expand existing recreation areas, always operating under the supervision of trained engineers and architects of the National Park Service.

Our purpose in writing this short history and guide is to provide readers with an understanding of the era in which these men worked, of the hardships and deprivations of the Great Depression, and of the remarkable vision of the Roosevelt administration that saw an unparalleled opportunity both to put unemployed men to work on projects that restored and enhanced our nation's natural resources and to restore the men themselves — their bodies, minds, and spirits. At the same time, we invite readers to become explorers, using the guide to discover this legacy for themselves through travels to the many parks profiled in the book. For readers who wish to learn more about the CCC and its work in the parks, we recommend four books that were indispensable to our research: *The Civilian Conservation Corps, 1933–1942: A New Deal Case Study*, by John Salmond (Duke University Press, 1967); *The Civilian Conservation Corps and the National Park Service, 1933–1942: An Administrative History*, by John Paige (National Park Service, 1985); *Nature's New Deal: The Civilian Conservation Corps and the Roots of the American Environmental Movement* by Neil Maher (Oxford University Press, 2007); and *The Tree Army: A Pictorial History of the Civilian Conservation Corps, 1933–1942* by Stan Cohen (Pictorial Histories Publishing Company, 1980). Beyond these, there is an increasing number of books about the work of the Corps in specific states or in individual parks. An internet search or a visit to a local library will reveal a treasure trove of sources that may be explored.

Researching and writing this book would have been impossible without the help, guidance, and enthusiastic support of many people who shared our passion for communicating the story of the CCC in the parks. Beyond those listed in Appendix VI, several deserve special mention. These include Donna Broome and Harry Dallas of the National Association of Civilian Conservation Corps Alumni (NACCCA, now a part of the CCC Legacy Foundation) in Saint Louis, Missouri; Eugene Morris at the National Archives and Records Administration (NARA) in College Park, Maryland; Tom Durant (now retired), curator of the National Park Service's Historic Images Collection in Charlestown, West Virginia; National Park Service historian John Paige, who read the manuscript and provided invaluable insights; retired Director of the National Park Service Robert Stanton, who took time from his busy schedule to pen the Foreword; and Jamil Zainaldin, Ph.D., Executive Director of the Georgia Humanities Council, who read the manuscript and offered his guidance. Each was exceptionally generous with his or her time and resources and their contributions were indispensable to the completion of this project. We also wish to thank Jerry McDonald, Trish Newcomb, and the staff at McDonald & Woodward Publishing Company for their support in bringing this book to reality.

Finally, we wish to dedicate this book to the late David Osier, our friend and publisher of *Georgia Journal Magazine.* In 1997, he gave us an assignment to write an article about the legacy of the CCC in Georgia for the magazine. That project started us on this unforgettable journey.

# SECTION I

## A Brief History of
## the Civilian Conservation Corps

*It is my belief that what is being accomplished will con-
serve our natural resources, create future national
wealth, and prove of moral and spiritual value not only
to those of you taking part, but to the rest of the country
as well.*[1]

— President Franklin D. Roosevelt
Message to CCC enrollees, July 8, 1933

# Out of Chaos

*By bringing to Washington a government determined to govern, Roosevelt unlocked new energies in people who had lost faith, not just in government's ability to meet the economic crisis, but in the ability of anyone to do anything.*[2]

— Arthur Schlesinger, Jr.
*The Coming of the New Deal*

From the shuttered factories of the industrial Northeast to the wind-blown dust bowl of the Great Plains, the Depression of the 1930s rocked our nation's foundations like nothing since the Civil War. Few Americans survived unaffected, but it was the common people, factory workers and farmers, who suffered most. Many were devastated by economic forces they neither understood nor could control.

The decade of the 1920s had been one of boundless optimism. Worker productivity increased more than forty percent from 1919 to 1929, and the presidential administrations of Warren Harding and Calvin Coolidge had been decidedly pro-growth, with Coolidge once remarking that, "the chief business of the American people is business."[3] This apparently endless economic boom was, in reality, a mirage. In the immediate aftermath of World War I, much of Europe was in shambles and Russia roiled in the midst of revolution. The United States, untouched by battle, rapidly rose to become the world's foremost manufacturing center. American industry worked overtime to produce goods for domestic use and for those rebuilding their lives abroad. But signs of unrest and discontent lingered below the surface. Employers demanded greater productivity from workers while refusing to pay higher wages. Like their industrial counterparts, farmers found an almost boundless market for their produce. Exports to

3

Europe and expanding markets at home created pressure to put more acreage into production. The long-term health of agricultural lands was ignored in favor of higher crop yields and even marginal land was plowed and planted.

Through the first half of the decade, industrial and agricultural production exploded, profits soared and most Americans were optimistic about their future. Many believed that the nation had found a formula for perpetual growth. As if to lend credence to this belief, presidential candidate Herbert Hoover, in an October 1928 speech, remarked that Americans "have come nearer to the abolition of poverty, to the abolition of fear and want, than humanity has ever reached before."[4] A few weeks later, in his final State of the Union address, outgoing President Calvin Coolidge told Congress that "the country can regard the present with satisfaction and anticipate the future with optimism."[5]

But there were subtle warning signs of trouble. European countries, struggling to pay off enormous debts or reparations, were increasingly less able to purchase American-made goods; yet, production continued unabated. Ironically, prices rose in an attempt to maintain profits despite declining demand. Before long, American products became too expensive for even its own citizens to buy. Another sign of danger was the increasing number of bank failures. The optimism of the post-war boom had fostered a belief that America's economy was on an unending upward spiral. Banks took on a greater number of unsecured loans, investing the funds in speculative enterprises. These poor management practices heightened instability in the banking system. By the late 1920s, a growing number of banks were declaring insolvency. In 1930, the trickle became a flood as over 1,300 banks shuttered their doors. That number nearly doubled when 2,294 banks failed in 1931.

Millions of these dollars had been borrowed by individuals who invested in the stock market. As Wall Street prospered, money poured in as even the middle class sought to cash in. Increasingly, investors were buying "on margin" — putting down a portion of the stock price and borrowing the rest from a broker who earned interest on the loan. Both investor and broker profited if the price of the stock rose. By the late 1920s, the nation was gripped in what was described as a buying "frenzy." The success of buying on margin depended on rising stock prices, and financiers fed the hysteria with optimistic predictions that stocks would gain value indefinitely. Despite such optimism, the imbalanced economy was rapidly eroding the foundations for this "paper" wealth. Inevitably, with diminishing demand and shrinking markets, stock prices began a steady decline.

Efforts to bolster the market were unsuccessful and after months of steady devaluation, the bottom fell out on "Black Tuesday," October 29, 1929. During that day of panicked selling, the exchange lost more than $8 billion in value. Within a month, losses topped $30 billion and brokers urged investors to increase their margins or risk losing their stocks. Bank accounts were emptied and loans called, in a vain attempt to shore up the hemorrhaging system. Soon, the nation found itself in the midst of an unprecedented financial panic. From Wall Street to Main Street, people faced financial ruin. The statistics would grow to staggering levels.

From 1929 to 1932, the nation's gross national product lost over fifty percent of its value. Industrial production slowed or ceased altogether, throwing thousands out of work. Banks failed and mortgages were foreclosed, leaving many both penniless and homeless. In 1929, approximately 1.5 million workers were unemployed. Within three years, the number of jobless grew ten-fold (Figure 1). The downward cycle of pessimism and despair seemed as endless as the upward climb of optimism that had prevailed only five years before.

During the emerging crisis, President Herbert Hoover maintained that the federal government should not take a proactive role in dealing with what he believed were locally solvable problems. He remained convinced that free enterprise and private charity could support those citizens hurt by the economic setbacks, even stating that "the nation's greatness is the path of self reliance."[6] In his book, *The Great Depression — America in the 1930s*, T. H. Watkins called Hoover's belief that the individual could work through this economic catastrophe a "cruel impossibility."[7]

As shops and factories closed, farmers already in the midst of an agricultural recession were increasingly unable to purchase supplies

**Figure 1.** The Depression had many men looking for work — as was the case shown here in Townsend, Tennessee, in the 1930s.

or pay their taxes. Farm foreclosures reached the tens of thousands. For those able to stay on the land, the reprieve was short as climate changes conspired to ruin them. Beginning in 1930 and continuing for more than five years, America's Midwest heartland experienced rainfall amounts so diminished that millions of acres of crops withered on the stalk and rich topsoil dried up and blew away in choking dust storms. To many, the droughts combined with the economic calamity gave the crisis an almost biblical quality — shaking their very faith in the nation's ability to survive. By the mid-1930s, thousands of farm families from the Midwest's "Dust Bowl" had migrated west to California, Oregon, Washington, and elsewhere in search of work and a new life.

While President Hoover had proven a capable administrator in organizing food relief for starving Belgians following World War I and coordinating the response to devastating floods in the Mississippi River Valley in 1927, he never fully grasped the depth of the crisis confronting the nation. Despite efforts to initiate public works and provide some level of relief, his administration proved ill-equipped to bring government's resources and powers to bear against the deepening crisis. To many, Hoover seemed distant from the problems they faced; he appeared unable to see any way to help them without compromising his belief that government should not interfere in people's private lives.

Frustrations reached a breaking point in the summer of 1932 when unemployed World War I veterans marched on Washington to ask Congress for early payment of promised bonuses for their wartime service, scheduled to be paid in 1945. Assembling by the thousands in abandoned buildings and makeshift shanty-towns dubbed "Hoovervilles," this "Bonus Army" spent weeks marching throughout the city. As summer wore on there were inevitable confrontations with police. Fearful of violence and with the president's reluctant approval, Secretary of War Patrick Hurley ordered Army Chief of Staff General Douglas MacArthur to force the veterans out of Washington. Images of old warriors, with wives and children beside them, being confronted by soldiers helped seal the fate of Hoover's presidency. While the veterans camped in Washington, the Democratic Party met in Chicago to choose a candidate to run against Hoover — who had been re-nominated at the Republican Convention. On July 1, the Democrats nominated New York Governor Franklin D. Roosevelt as their candidate.

As a younger man, Franklin Roosevelt, nephew of President Theodore Roosevelt, had been an up-and-coming political figure in New York and Washington, serving first in the state legislature then as Assistant Secretary of the Navy under President Woodrow Wilson. Roosevelt's political future seemed bright until he was stricken with polio in 1921. With his legs paralyzed, family and friends urged Roosevelt to retire to the family's estate in Hyde Park, New York. Roosevelt would have none of it. Longtime friend and advisor Colonel Louis Howe recognized that illness instilled in the future president, a determination he had never seen before. Richard Harrity and Ralph G. Martin recorded the future president's thoughts in *The Human Side of FDR*:

> There are times, when I think that Franklin might never
> have been president if he had not been stricken . . . He
> had a thousand interests . . . You couldn't pin him down
> . . . Then suddenly there he was flat on his back with

nothing to do but think. He began to read, he began to think, he talked, he gathered people around him — his thoughts expanded, his horizon widened. He began to see the other fellow's point of view. He thought of others who were ill and afflicted and in want. He dwelt on many things that had not bothered him much before. Lying there, he grew bigger, day by day.[8]

Roosevelt doggedly sought a cure for his illness, eventually finding some relief in the soothing waters of Georgia's Warm Springs. After a few years behind the scenes, he ran for and won the governorship of New York in 1928, then presided over the state when the Great Depression struck the next year.

As if in a dress-rehearsal for his next role, Roosevelt marshaled the resources of the government to soften the effects of the crisis, providing relief to thousands of New Yorkers devastated by the economic reversals. Among these actions was a program to put unemployed men to work in reforestation, erosion control, and recreational facilities improvement. His proactive deeds and encouraging words stood in contrast to Washington's inaction. When the Democratic Party met to choose its candidate for the 1932 presidential campaign, few delegates doubted that Roosevelt was their man. In his acceptance speech at the Democratic Convention, the ebullient Roosevelt confidently promised "a new deal for the American people."[9]

While the charismatic Roosevelt drew large and enthusiastic crowds wherever he spoke, President Hoover appeared to gloomily trudge toward November. In an effort to paint the Democrat as a radical, the president remarked during a campaign speech that "this election is not a mere shift from the ins to the outs. It means deciding the direction our nation will take over a century to come."[10] On November 8, 1932, the American people chose that new direction, electing Roosevelt in a landslide. Four months later, on March 4, 1933, he stood at a podium beneath the Capitol dome, his paralyzed legs held rigidly in place by heavy braces, to take the oath as President of the United States. In his book, *FDR — A Biography*, Ted Morgan captured what Roosevelt symbolized by writing:

**Figure 2.** At Franklin Roosevelt's Presidential Inauguration in 1933, he assured Americans that "the only thing we have to fear is fear itself."

> If this man had the courage to lift himself by the sheer power of his spirit from the bed of invalidism, had the determination and patience to make himself walk, then he must have within him the qualities to lead a nation to recovery.[11]

These qualities were embodied in the prophetic words of his inaugural address (Figure 2). Witnessed by thousands standing in frigid cold and heard by anxious millions tuning in by radio, he assured his fellow citizens that:

> The only thing we have to fear is fear itself — nameless, unreasoning, unjustified terror . . . We are stricken by no plague of locusts. Plenty is at our doorstep, but a generous use of it languishes in the very sight of supply.[12]

Franklin Roosevelt had won the presidency largely because he believed that the battle to right the nation's economy was a struggle in which the federal government must play an active part. Hinting at what was to come; Roosevelt continued his remarks by noting that:

> Our greatest primary task is to put people to work. This is no unsolvable problem if we face it wisely and courageously . . . It can be accomplished in part by direct recruiting by the government itself, treating the task as we would treat the emergency of war, but at the same time, through this employment, accomplishing greatly needed projects to stimulate and reorganize the use of our natural resources.[13]

The active involvement by the government in rebuilding the lives of the people was the essence of Roosevelt's "New Deal." During those first weeks, the president and his senior advisors worked tirelessly to put the bureaucratic wheels in motion, determined to help solve the nation's problems. Within days of his inauguration, Roosevelt returned to Congress, called back into special session, with the first of many proposals to create a host of government agencies and programs intended to stabilize the nation's economy. From mid-March through June, 1933, Congress passed an "alphabet soup" of legislation, such as the Agricultural Adjustment Act (AAA), the National Industrial Recovery Act (NIRA), the Public Works Administration (PWA), the National Recovery Act (NRA), and the Emergency Conservation Work Act (ECW) — the legislation creating the Civilian Conservation Corps (CCC). Through these initiatives the administration took the first strides toward restoring Americans' confidence in their system of government.

On the morning of March 9, 1933, Roosevelt called a meeting with the secretaries of Agriculture (Henry Wallace), Interior (Harold Ickes), and War (George Dern), the Director of the Budget (Lewis Douglas), the US Army Judge Advocate General (Colonel Kyle Rucker), and the Solicitor of the Department of the Interior Department (Edward Finney) to outline a program that could conserve both the nation's natural and human resources. The president asked Rucker and Finney to draft a bill for his review by that evening. Working without a break, the two men presented their plan to Roosevelt at 9 P.M. On March 14, after discussions and revisions, the president sent the following memorandum to the secretaries of War, Interior,

Agriculture, and Labor: "I am asking you to constitute yourselves an informed committee of the cabinet to co-ordinate plans for the proposed Civilian Conservation Corps."[14]

# A Miracle of Cooperation

*The CCC program brought together many subdivisions of government in such a way as to help them realize that the protection of natural resources was a problem common to all.* [15]

— Conrad Wirth
Report to Interior Secretary Harold Ickes, 1943

On March 21, 1933, President Roosevelt presented to Congress his proposal for Emergency Conservation Work (ECW), described as "an Act for the Relief of Unemployment through the Performance of Useful Public Works and Other Purposes." He urged passage, noting:

> It is essential to our recovery program that measures immediately be enacted aimed at employment relief . . . I propose to create a civilian conservation corps to be used in simple work, not interfering with normal employment, and confining itself to forestry, the prevention of soil erosion, flood control, and similar projects. I call your attention to the fact that this type of work is of definite practical value, not only through the prevention of great financial loss but also as a means of creating future national wealth. [16]

FDR concluded with a vision for the historical significance of this endeavor:

> This enterprise . . . will conserve our precious natural resources. It will pay dividends to the present and future generations. It will make improvements in National and State domains which have been largely forgotten in the past few years of industrial development . . . More

important, however, than the material gains will be the moral and spiritual value of such work . . . We can take a vast army of these unemployed out into healthful surroundings. We can eliminate to some extent at least the threat that enforced idleness brings to spiritual and moral stability. It is not a panacea for all the unemployment, but it is an essential step in this emergency.[17]

As Roosevelt noted, the "civilian conservation corps" was intended to "build men, (and) to accomplish constructive results in our vast federal, state, private forest and other resource properties."[18] Ambitiously, the president called for the employment of more than a quarter million young men in restoring the nation's forests and depleted farmlands by that summer — an enormous undertaking requiring an almost unheard of degree of cooperation among governmental agencies.

With only token opposition, the ECW Act passed and was sent to Roosevelt with this response:

> The President is authorized . . . to provide for employing citizens of the United States who are unemployed in the construction, maintenance, and carrying out of works of a public nature in connection with forestation of lands belonging to the United States or to the several states which are suitable for timber production; the prevention of forest fires, floods, and soil erosion; plant, pest, and disease control; the construction, maintenance, or repair of paths, trails, and fire-lanes in the national parks and national forests; and such work on the public domain, national and state government reservations incidental to or necessary in connection with any projects.[19]

On March 31, Roosevelt signed the bill into law, moving quickly to put in place an organization to coordinate the massive effort of recruiting, training, and putting to work hundreds of thousands of men. In a significant historical footnote, Illinois Representative Oscar de Priest, an African American, introduced an amendment to the bill prohibiting discrimination in enrollee selection based on race, color, or creed. It was adopted, but consistent enforcement across the country, and especially in the South, proved troublesome throughout the life of the program.

At an April 3rd meeting with the participating departments, Roosevelt outlined each agency's responsibilities, as described by John Salmond in *The Civilian Conservation Corps, 1933–1942: A New Deal Case Study:*

> The Department of Labor was directed to select the men for enrollment; the War Department was to enroll the men, feed, clothe, house, and condition them, and transport them to the camps; the Departments of Agriculture and Interior, through their various bureaus, were to select the work projects, to supervise the work, and to administer the camps.[20]

Choosing the appropriate person to oversee this complex task became one of the president's priorities. The individual would need exceptional skills in fostering collaboration among governmental agencies, the ability to create and manage a rapidly expanding public works program that would reach every corner of the nation, and have credibility with organized labor. On April 5, 1933, after much discussion with advisors, Roosevelt appointed Robert Fechner as Executive Director of the ECW program and the CCC (Figure 3). The Tennessee-born Fechner was a lifelong union man, then serving as vice-president of both the International Association of Machinists and the American Federation of Labor. He proved to be an ideal person for the job. A scrupulously honest, hard-working, able administrator and an experienced labor negotiator, Fechner doggedly molded the diverse agencies charged with creating and managing the CCC into a cohesive unit that successfully carried out what would be the largest peacetime mobilization in the nation's history (Figure 4). To meet FDR's deadline, Fechner wasted no time in forming his Advisory Council and identifying the tasks and responsibilities each agency must accept to meet the president's goals. So consuming was Fechner's commitment to the CCC that the stress may have led to the heart attack that took his life in December, 1939.

**Figure 3.** Robert Fechner was the director of the CCC from 1933 to 1939.

**Figure 4.** The CCC displayed this exhibit at the Texas Centennial Celebration in 1936. Exhibits of this type were one method used by the CCC to reach the many potential enrollees so widely distributed across the country.

The decision also was made that initial enrollment in the CCC would be limited to single men, ages 18 to 25, primarily but not exclusively from families on public relief rolls; this would become a requirement in 1936. Their pay would be $30 per month, with $22 to $25 allotted to their families. Recognizing the over-arching importance of putting people to work, the president stipulated that the majority of program funds would go into labor costs, not in equipment. The president also insisted on six-month enrollment periods and that each camp house 200 men.

On April 5, 1933, President Roosevelt signed Executive Order 6101 implementing the ECW program, appointing Fechner as director, and establishing the Advisory Council composed of representatives from the participating agencies. Four cabinet-level departments would have initial responsibility for CCC work, and each designated a council representative: Army Colonel Duncan Major, Jr. (War), National Park Service (NPS) Director Horace Albright (Interior), Forest Service Chief Forester R. Y. Stuart (Agriculture), and Frank Persons (Labor). Anticipating what needed to be done, several of the agencies had begun planning even before the legislation had been passed by Congress.

## Labor Department

Under the guidance of Secretary Frances Perkins, the first female cabinet secretary in US history, the Labor Department was charged with establishing criteria for enrollee selection, setting state quotas, and recruiting. Perkins had served as Roosevelt's Labor Department director in New York and had worked closely with the future president in recruiting men for the New York labor program in 1930. This experience prepared her well for the enormous task her department faced.

In addition to the unemployed young men, three other groups were soon added to the enrollment pool. On April 14, Native Americans were approved for work on reservation lands — where the men could return to their homes each day. On May 11, employment was opened to "local experienced men" (LEMs) living near CCC camps who possessed critically needed technical skills to train enrollees and assist in supervising the work. And, finally, on May 22, unemployed military veterans were offered enrollment and assignment to designated camps where work was adjusted to meet their age and physical limitations.

Secretary Perkins, recognizing that there was not enough time to build a nationwide organization to carry out these critical tasks, sought support from local relief agencies already at work. To direct this effort, she employed W. Frank Persons, a senior advisor to the American Red Cross, as director of the newly established United States Employment Service responsible for selection of CCC enrollees, and as Labor's representative to the Advisory Council. Persons proved exceptionally capable and remained in this role for the life of the Corps.

On the same day that Roosevelt signed the Executive Order, Persons met in Washington with relief agency representatives from the nation's seventeen largest cities to develop guidelines for enrollee selection. He also appointed a director of selection in each state who was charged with coordinating recruitment. In addition, Persons calculated numerical selection quotas based on population to assure enrollment equity across the country (Figure 5). Remarkably, on April

**Figure 5.** CCC recruits shown here in Carrollton, Georgia, in 1933 are awaiting transport to a conditioning camp prior to receiving their work assignment.

7, 1933, only four days after Persons arrived, the CCC enrolled its first worker, Henry Rich from Alexandria, Virginia.

# War Department

The Army General Staff, charged with outfitting, conditioning, and housing enrollees, developed a military style organization for the CCC. They divided the nation into nine Corps Areas, each under the command of a general officer. Selected military bases in each area served as headquarters and conditioning camps. After physical examinations and conditioning, enrollees traveled by train and/or Army transports to camp sites close to the designated work areas. The first workers on site would be charged with erecting temporary tent housing and initiating assigned project work. Tents would eventually be replaced with prefabricated structures that could be assembled on site. At the outset, the Army placed regular officers in charge of the CCC camps; however, in the effort to employ more people, they were replaced by reserve officers beginning in 1934.

In the original ECW plan, the Army's role did not extend beyond conditioning enrollees and setting up camps; operations were under the direction of the technical agencies that included the Agriculture and Interior departments, the Soil Conservation Service, the Bureau of Reclamation, the Tennessee Valley Authority, and the Bureau of Indian Affairs. Despite assurances from forester Stuart that his agency could manage the hundreds of camps to be established by July 1, 1933, it quickly became apparent that the department did not possess the staff, equipment, or experience to manage projects on such a scale. Salmond recounts the details of an April 8, 1933, letter to presidential secretary Louis Howe in which:

> Stuart urgently insisted that a division of authority between the Army and the technical agencies was the only practical arrangement by which the camps could run. He was now convinced that the Army alone had the resources to build and operate the camps, transport, feed, and discipline the men. The technical agencies would be responsible only for the work project and for the men during working hours.[21]

The Army accepted this expanded role, recognizing that it was the only agency capable of accomplishing this enormous task.

# Agriculture Department

Agriculture Secretary Henry A. Wallace assigned Chief Forester Stuart, his representative on the Advisory Council, the task of coordinating Corps work in national, and later, state forests. Anticipating Agriculture's role in the program, the department commissioned a survey, with an emphasis on forest areas where work was critically needed. This report became the basis for the Forest Service's initial work plan. Also, on April 6, 1933, Secretary Wallace held a conference with state forest authorities to discuss the possible extension of the ECW program to state-owned lands.

As noted, the Forest Service recognized that it lacked the resources to manage both the camps and the work program. There was also increasing concern for the safety of the thousands of young men, many from urban areas, who would be unfamiliar with the type of work to be performed. The agency responded to these problems through the division of camp and work responsibilities with the Army, and through the hiring of 8–12 LEMs per camp who could teach enrollees the necessary skills and supervise the work. Camps under the supervision of other agencies also relied heavily on LEMs. Through the life of the Corps, the Department of Agriculture oversaw more than half of the work performed by the CCC.

# Interior Department

Harold L. Ickes, Secretary of the Interior, was a consummate "New Dealer" who was determined to remake his department from an agency whose mission was to dispose of federal lands, to one responsible for stewardship of the nation's natural resources. From the outset, Ickes was a strong advocate for the ECW program, seeing it as an extraordinary chance to reclaim abused public lands, improve and expand parks, and create new opportunities for recreation for all Americans.

NPS Director Horace Albright, the department's representative to the advisory council, had begun his career with the Park Service in

1917 as an assistant to Director Stephen Mather. He went on to serve as superintendent of Yellowstone National Park before succeeding Mather as NPS Director in 1929. In this capacity, he urged expansion of the national parks, at the time located primarily in the west, into eastern areas so that more Americans could visit and enjoy the outdoors, and he introduced historic preservation into the mission of the park service. In 1933, Albright also proposed to the president that NPS assume responsibility for national monuments from the Department of Agriculture and for national military parks from the War Department. Roosevelt agreed and authorized a reorganization that dramatically expanded both the scale and scope of the national parks. Later that year, Albright resigned and was replaced by Arno Cammerer, also a strong advocate for CCC, who would guide the Corps' work in the parks for the duration of the program (Figure 6).

In the weeks following authorization of the ECW program, National Parks' staff mobilized parks to initiate CCC work projects. Like the Forest Service, the agency was overwhelmed by the sheer numbers of enrollees to be assigned, the slow process of securing project approvals, and the lack of technical expertise and manpower to oversee the work. Despite the challenges, the first Park Service CCC camps opened on May 11, 1933, with one in the proposed Shenandoah National Park and two near Yorktown as part of the Colonial National Monument (now Colonial National Historical Park). By the end of the month, there were 63 CCC camps in national parks and monuments and the first enrollees were on their way from conditioning

**Figure 6.** Arno Cammerer was the director of the National Park Service from 1933 to 1940.

20

camps at Fort Monroe, Virginia, and Fort Meade, Maryland, to parks in the Rocky Mountain states.

Facing President Roosevelt's July 1, 1933, deadline, the staffs of ECW and the technical agencies wrestled with complex logistics and unwieldy bureaucracies. By early May, there were 52,000 men enrolled and at work in 42 camps. This was far short of the president's goal and Advisory Council members despaired, believing that reaching Roosevelt's target was impossible. A key issue, slowing the process, remained disagreement between the War Department and the technical agencies over supervision in the camps. Fechner asked Colonel Major to examine the problem and offer a solution.

At the council's May 12, 1933, meeting, Major presented the following recommendations to the group: take immediate action; waive peacetime restrictions covering bids, contracts, deliveries, and open-market purchases, and authorize the fullest possible freedom of purchase; delegate wide authority over transportation to the War Department; maintain a flow of 8,540 CCC enrollees per day; give the Army wider disciplinary powers over recruits; and approve 290 more work projects by June 1, 1933.

Major's recommendations were unanimously adopted and presented by Fechner to the president who accepted them. Almost immediately, the obstacles began to dissolve. In a June 30, 1933, report to Fechner, Major wrote:

> The task assumed by the War Department was awesome . . . (and) men received, processed, and equipped per day was greater than the average for the United States during the World War for both the Army and the Navy combined.[22]

In a concerted effort that still defies belief, Fechner and his team exceeded Roosevelt's goal. On July 1, 1933, there were 274,375 men enrolled in more than 1,300 CCC camps across the nation. In summing up this extraordinary accomplishment, Salmond wrote:

> In the short span of three months, the CCC had developed from a statutory authorization to the largest peacetime government labor force the United States had ever

known. Col. Major, more than anyone else, deserves the praise for the CCC's successful mobilization . . . Gruff, obdurate, relentless in argument, Major became devoted to the CCC and served the agency admirably. Unlike some of his fellow officers, he was wholehearted in his belief that it was "a most beneficial source of training for those lucky enough to have any part of it."[23]

# Building Men

Woodrow Grant, a member of Company 431 SP-2 based at Vogel State Park in Georgia, wrote:

I'd been in the CCC only a few days when a fellow tried to talk me into going over the hill. He said, "I can't take it anymore, they're working us like slaves!" I said, "Work? I feel like I'm on vacation."[24]

By July, 1933, the first CCC recruit was joined by a quarter-million others, all anxious to begin work in America's forests and parks. For many, the CCC simply represented an opportunity for a paying job, with little thought beyond helping themselves and their families. For Roosevelt, Ickes, and Fechner, the CCC offered much more. Salmond summed it up:

The Civilian Conservation Corps was . . . in one sense, a catalyst. Through it, a new and vital precedent, Franklin D. Roosevelt, brought together two wasted resources, the young men and the land, in an attempt to save both.[25]

During a CCC veterans' reunion, Ed Stearman, once an enrollee stationed at Georgia's Little Ocmulgee State Park, offered his personal reflection, "The CCC was a blessing. I had five brothers and sisters and the $25 that was sent home every month helped them survive. Because of the CCC, I never felt I was a burden to my family."[26]

For the agencies responsible for the program, the first six-month enrollment period, April to September, 1933, was a time of planning, coordination, and experimentation. After enrollment, the men had to be outfitted and prepared for work. Thousands of surplus military

**Figure 7.** In 1933, President Roosevelt, shown here with advisors, made his first visit to a CCC camp at Shenandoah National Park, Virginia. During the visit, the party enjoyed a picnic with CCC men.

uniforms and tents were distributed, millions of tools and pieces of equipment were purchased, and hundreds of trucks and trains were committed to transport recruits to project sites from coast to coast. The first CCC camp, dubbed "Camp Roosevelt," opened on April 11, 1933, in the George Washington National Forest near Luray, Virginia. By July 1, 1933, men were at work in 1,331 camps nationwide, nearly 250 of them located in state or national parks. President Roosevelt made his first visit to a CCC camp on August 12, 1933, spending time with men at Camp Roosevelt before enjoying a picnic lunch with enrollees at Shenandoah National Park's Big Meadows (Figure 7).

For many of the young men, this was their first time away from home and a grand adventure. Schlesinger captured the moment in *The Coming of the New Deal*:

> They came from large cities and small towns, from slum street corners and hobo jungles . . . Some had never seen

a mountain before, had never waded in a running brook or slept in open air. Boys from the East side of New York found themselves in Glacier Park, boys from New Jersey at Mount Hood, Oregon.[27]

To turn the recruits into a productive workforce, the CCC established a tight organizational structure headquartered in Washington. Each of the nine Corps Areas (Figure 8) oversaw several districts, usually within a state or geographic region. Senior military officers served as District Commanders, supervising lower-ranking officers who commanded individual camps. Each camp was established to carry out projects undertaken by the Park Service, Forest Service, Soil Conservation Service, Tennessee Valley Authority, Grazing Service (now the Bureau of Land Management), and other agencies. Each enrollee was a member of a work group assigned tasks ranging from trail-building and debris-removal to fire-suppression and building construction (Figure 9).

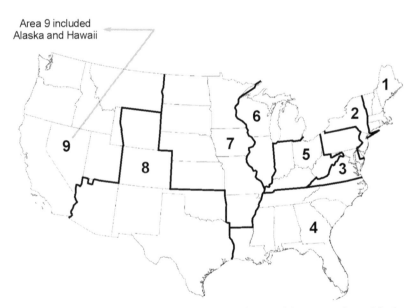

**Figure 8.** The forty-eight United States, along with possessions Alaska and Hawaii, were divided into nine regions for purposes of administering and managing the efforts of the CCC.

**Figure 9.** CCC men shown here are fighting a fire in a wooded area in West Virginia.

At the outset, project foremen did not believe the unskilled recruits could master complex building projects, so the men were assigned simple work. When given the opportunity, though, CCC men proved exceptionally skilled in managing more complicated tasks from the construction of lakes, dams, lodges, and cabins to laying water lines, stringing telephone wires, and even assisting in archaeological excavations (Figure 10). Enrollees were also a ready resource in case of emergencies. Thousands were trained as fire-lookouts, fire-fighters, and, in remote parks, members of search-and-rescue teams. During blizzards, snowstorms, floods, and other disasters, enrollees often joined with local authorities in preparations or clean-up efforts.

Camp life was regimented in a quasi-military fashion. Men typically lived in 50-person barracks, surrounding a mess hall, recreation building, officers' quarters, latrines, and maintenance shops. When work was required in remote areas, tented side- or "spike-" camps would often be set up for 25–50 workers who would travel to the project site on Monday and return to the main camp on Friday. Days started early with reveille at 6:00 A.M., followed by calisthenics and breakfast. Project work began at 8:00 A.M. and concluded at 4:30 P.M. After supper, enrollees were free to relax, play cards or pool, enjoy

**Figure 10.** CCC men are at work clearing brush in Glacier National Park, Montana.

music, read in the camp library, or take classes. Following a directive from the president, all camps provided educational advisors who arranged academic or technical classes for students to learn skills or earn a high school diploma. It is estimated that more than 100,000 men learned to read and write during their CCC enlistments.

Saturdays were usually spent on camp chores (policing camp, doing laundry, splitting firewood), in recreation (nearly every camp had sports teams and rivalries grew between camps or with local squads), or in trips to nearby towns for 5¢ movies and 10¢ dances (figures 11–15). Watkins described the many aspects of camp life as a combination of "a military operation with those of an urban construction gang, a YMCA summer camp, and a Chautauqua session."[28]

Many enrollees felt that, for the first time, they belonged to something bigger than themselves. Despite the mixing of men from different areas and backgrounds, camp morale was usually high and desertion rates low (Figure 16). The men gained strength, weight, and a healthy dose of self confidence, and lifelong friendships were forged through team-work and common experience. Enrollees adopted the

**Figure 11.** CCC men, stationed at a side camp in Glacier National Park, take time to do their laundry.

**Figure 12.** During his time off, a CCC worker in Glacier National Park gets a haircut from a fellow enrollee.

**Figure 13.** Each CCC barracks, like this one at Giant City State Park, Illinois, was designed to house fifty enrollees.

**Figure 14.** The CCC basketball team at Jefferson Barracks, Missouri, poses here with its 1936 championship award.

**Figure 15.** The CCC baseball team at Yellowstone National Park poses at the park's north entrance on its way to a tournament.

**Figure 16.** CCC enrollees enjoy a winter break in Minnesota's Itasca State Park.

motto "We Can Take It!" while proclaiming their willingness and determination to tackle any task. New recruits were sometimes homesick, but most adapted quickly to camp life and were often reluctant to leave when their enlistments were up. During a reunion, enrollee C. W. Pulley recalled his days in the CCC, "I was an orphan . . . CCC camp was the first home I ever had. It was a wonderful life. I saw grown men cry when their enlistments were up and they had to leave." [29]

President Roosevelt visited camps whenever he could, spending time chatting with enrollees and learning about their work. None were closer to the president than the crews assigned to Georgia's new Pine Mountain (now Franklin Roosevelt) State Park (Plate 1, top). During his visits to the Little White House in nearby Warm Springs, the president spent hours with the Pine Mountain enrollees, offering suggestions on projects and even supervising work (the park's bell-shaped pool is reputedly FDR's design). On his arrival and departure from the local railroad depot, CCC men lined the road, serving as his honor guard (Figure 17).

**Figure 17.** At Pine Mountain State Park, Georgia, near Warm Springs, the CCC enrollees surround a young polio victim with braces.

# African Americans in the CCC

Emblematic of the times, nearly all camps were racially segregated although a few, mostly in the Midwest and far West, were integrated (Figure 18). The all-black camps and integrated camps were supervised by white military officers and foremen. An all-black CCC company established at Gettysburg NMP in 1935 was the first to be led by black military officers and work supervisors.

Despite a commitment to non-discrimination in the CCC, Fechner directed that African-American enrollment in the Corps should never exceed ten percent which, while reflective of the racial mix of the nation, did not adequately meet the desperate needs of the much higher ratio of black Americans left destitute by the Depression (ultimately, 300,000 African Americans, including 30,000 military veterans, served in the Corps). Fechner also stipulated that new black companies would be recruited only to replace black camps scheduled for closure. Issues also arose as many communities opposed the establishment of an African-American camp in their vicinity, leading to placement of most black camps in remote locations or on federal property. As a consequence, NPS supervised a proportionally larger share of African-American camps than did other agencies (Figure 19).

Beginning in 1934, The National Association for the Advancement of Colored People (NAACP) and other African-American support organizations and media urged President Roosevelt to give qualified blacks an opportunity to serve in ECW supervisory positions. The following year, the president issued an Executive Order instructing Fechner to employ blacks in "official" positions. Despite some opposition from the Advisory Council, agencies moved ahead in complying with the president's directive. The NPS selected Gettysburg National Military Park as the site for establishment of the first camp composed of black military officers, work supervisors, technicians, and enrollees. One group of black veterans, assigned to Colonial National Historic Park, proved so skilled at reproducing Colonial era furnishings and military equipment that the men provided items to numerous other national and state parks. Despite these positive gains, Salmond noted that, "The Negro never gained the measure of relief

**Figure 18.** This integrated baseball team was from the camp at Giant City State Park, Illinois. Many camps hosted teams, but few were integrated.

**Figure 19.** The African-American CCC enrollees, along with enrollees from other area camps, took turns working underground in Mammoth Cave National Park, Kentucky.

from the Agency's activities to which his economic privations entitled him."[30]

～

Corps enrollment peaked in early 1936 with nearly 600,000 men at work in 2,514 camps in forty-eight states and territories. As pressures to balance the federal budget increased, funds appropriated to CCC projects began to shrink. Enrollments slowed and, consequently, camp numbers spiraled downward. The following year, Congress passed legislation establishing the Civilian Conservation Corps as an independent agency but declined Roosevelt's request that it be made a permanent organization. Instead, the agency was reauthorized for two more years.

When Congress passed the Reorganization Act of 1939, the CCC was placed under the newly created Federal Relief Agency. In early 1940, as military mobilization expanded, many reserve officers were withdrawn from the CCC and assigned to active duty. Following the fall of France to the Germans in June, 1940, President Roosevelt ordered a limited national emergency and many CCC companies were transferred to military bases and assigned to defense projects including constructing buildings (often relocated CCC camp buildings), airfields, obstacle courses, and firing ranges. In 1941, despite efforts by the Administration and many in Congress to again make the CCC permanent, it was evident that the program could not be sustained as the nation prepared for war. Congress refused to reauthorize funding, and the CCC ceased operations on July 1, 1942, ending a remarkable and unsurpassed era of resource conservation, forest restoration, and parks development.

Watkins recorded the remarks of a district forester who wrote:

> The history of these nine years is a saga of service in which the largest body of men in the country, working as a single unit, have labored with tractor, pick, shovel and planting tools in rebuilding the resources of a nation.[31]

Summing up the inherent value of the CCC experience as the nation entered World War II, Salmond wrote:

It had provided the sinews of a military force. It had given young officers valuable training in command techniques, and the nearly three million young men who had passed through the camps had received experience of military life upon which the Army was able to build.[32]

Soon, the young CCC enrollees would become the men of Guadalcanal, Normandy, and Iwo Jima.

# Love of the Land

*For those of us who lived through the era of the New Deal, Franklin D. Roosevelt was the hero of the conservation movement.*[33]

— William Leuchtenberg
*FDR and the Environment*

## Forester-in-Chief

Franklin Roosevelt always considered himself an outdoorsman. As a child growing up on the family estate in Hyde Park, New York, he had had access to thousands of acres of woodlands and meadows for recreation, and he spent countless hours exploring the land and learning all he could about the trees and plants that grew there. In 1910, he took over management of the property, working diligently to restore worn out agricultural fields and renewing surrounding forests. That same year, he was elected to the New York state senate where he chaired the committee overseeing forests, fish, and game. In that role, he was able to apply his principles of land stewardship to the woodlands and rivers beyond the boundaries of his home. Nonetheless, Hyde Park remained his laboratory and, over the years, he would plant nearly a quarter-million trees on the grounds. Morgan wrote:

> Planting trees made him feel good. It was a positive act, you could see the results, and it was something you could pass on to your children down the generations so that you were, like nature, a part of a continuing process rather than an isolated individual.[34]

Roosevelt did more than simply plant trees. Working closely with his friend and consultant, Dr. Nelson Brown, professor at the New

York College of Forestry at Syracuse University, he applied the latest scientific knowledge to his botanical endeavors. In many ways, his enduring love for the fields and forests at Hyde Park transformed him. As a young man, the forests were a retreat from the rigors of public life. Following his affliction with polio, they were an essential source of renewal and reflection on his life's direction. In many ways, Franklin Roosevelt was heir to the conservation ethic espoused by his uncle, President Theodore Roosevelt. Each was passionate about preserving the best in nature, with one significant difference. For Theodore, parks and monuments were to be preserved as a realm apart with little modification by man, while Franklin's vision was less romantic. For him, land was to be carefully used and sustained, to benefit the people for both economic reward and healthful recreation. Environmental historian Brian Black noted that, "FDR's environmental ethic grew from a Jeffersonian ideal that a connection to the land and hard work helped to make better people."[35]

However, not all labor was productive or beneficial, as Roosevelt observed in 1924 when he first visited Warm Springs, Georgia, seeking relief from his polio. While the waters proved soothing, he found the valleys and Appalachian foothills surrounding nearby Pine Mountain devastated from years of poor agricultural practices and slash forestry of the native pine trees. The local people were warm and welcoming, yet apparently unaware of the scientific principles he employed in managing the woodlands at Hyde Park.

In the midst of the struggles against his disability, Roosevelt purchased land on Pine Mountain with plans to develop a model farm to demonstrate his techniques. He built a small white cottage and, over the remainder of his life, visited as often as he could to soak in the springs, picnic at a favorite promontory called Dowdells Knob, and tour the countryside in his specially-adapted automobile. He also spent time with the farmers that were his Pine Mountain neighbors, discussing everything from crop yields to the latest political news. It has been said that it was through these encounters that this scion of northeastern aristocracy became a true friend of, and staunch advocate for, America's common people. When Roosevelt died at his "Little White House" on April 12, 1945, the nation mourned a champion of democracy while the people of Pine Mountain mourned a friend and neighbor. Today, FDR's Little White House, a Georgia State Historic Site, is preserved as it was the day he died.

In 1924, Roosevelt returned to limited public life, serving as manager for New York Governor Alfred E. Smith's unsuccessful presidential campaign. Four years later, he reclaimed the spotlight by winning the governorship of New York. As Roosevelt considered a campaign to challenge Hoover for the presidency in 1932, his years of experience in conservation, combined with the success of his reforestation efforts in New York, crystallized in his mind plans to send men into the nation's forests to restore both the natural resources and themselves. During his acceptance speech at the Democratic Convention in Chicago that July, he offered the first hints about his vision for what would become the Civilian Conservation Corps, noting that:

> Every European Nation has a definite land policy . . . We have none. Having none, we face a future of soil erosion and timber famine. It is clear that economic foresight and immediate employment march hand in hand in the call for reforestation of these vast areas . . . In so doing, employment can be given to a million men. This is the kind of work that is self sustaining.[36]

Following his election and inauguration, Roosevelt set out immediately to bring his vision to reality. He believed that the same stewardship he applied at Hyde Park could be utilized in the over-cut forests and over-farmed agricultural lands across the country, and could restore a national landscape that had been poorly used for more than a century. In *The Roosevelt I Knew,* Labor Secretary Frances Perkins recalled the president's concerns:

> In March 1933, he brought up the idea that became the Civilian Conservation Corps. Roosevelt loved trees and hated to see them cut and not replaced. It was natural for him to wish to put large numbers of the unemployed to repairing such devastation.[37]

During his briefings with the press, FDR sometimes remarked that his occupation, outside of politics, was as a "farmer." In his Foreword to the 1937 book *The New America: The Spirit of the Civilian Conservation Corps*, Roosevelt wrote:

> Our forests with their manifold resources and products, with the abundant opportunities they provide for recreation and inspiration, have long been and continue to be a part of the basic pattern woven into our national fabric. Their well being is essential to the well being of our people.[38]

Given this connection between the land and the people, it came as no surprise when FDR, in describing his role in bringing to reality the plans for the ECW program and the CCC, often referred to himself as the "forester-in-chief."[39]

## The Parks Movement

In 1945, Conrad Wirth expressed the opinion:

> It is believed that the work accomplished in the parks conservation field in the ten years of the CCC was equal to what might have been expected in 50 years without assistance.[40]

While parks are not an American invention, the setting aside of public preserves or "commons" have punctuated our history. Possibly the nation's oldest park, Boston Common, was established in 1634 as a public pasture and militia parade ground. Nearly two centuries later, natural springs in Georgia (1825) and Arkansas (1832) were set aside for all people in perpetuity. Today Georgia's Indian Springs claims to be the nation's oldest state park and features several CCC-built structures. In 1857, New York City commissioned Frederick Law Olmsted to turn a boulder-strewn swamp into Central Park. During the Civil War, President Abraham Lincoln deeded Yosemite's Mariposa Grove of giant sequoias to California as a preserve. Finally, on the strength of the reports and images from the Hayden Expedition to Yellowstone, the federal government set aside the area as the world's first "national park" in 1872.

The creation of this national park was unprecedented and not without opposition from grazing, mining, and timber interests.

Nonetheless, in the four succeeding decades, fourteen national parks would be established in the United States. Among them icons such as Yosemite (1890), Mount Rainier (1899), Crater Lake (1902), Glacier (1910), and Rocky Mountain (1915). During those same years, states began designating lands as "forest preserves" or "parks." In *The State Park Movement in America: A Critical Review*, Ney C. Landrum noted that these early efforts reflected "the people's new found interest in nature and the timely awakening of the post-pioneer generation to the pressing need to preserve some of the country's magnificent scenic wonders."[41]

The individual states took several different approaches to parks development. In the east, lands were acquired for restoration following years of intensive and often destructive use; while western conservationists sought to preserve vestiges of wilderness before they were lost. In nearly every instance, initiatives were local with no plans or funding for a system of parks. As a consequence, development remained fragmented until well into the 20th century. Nonetheless, many sites that remain at the heart of state parks systems owe their origins to these early conservation efforts. Among these are Texas's San Jacinto Battlefield State Park (1883), Minnesota's Itasca State Park and New Hampshire's Miller State Park (both in 1891), Massachusetts' Mount Greylock State Reservation (1898), Wisconsin's St. Croix State Park (1900), California's Big Basin Redwoods State Park (1902), and New York's Letchworth State Park (1907). A number of these early projects were promoted as potential "national parks." One congressional representative even introduced a bill to establish at least one "national park" in every state. These efforts raised questions regarding how such lands should be designated, and the need for criteria for creation of national parks.

Significant steps in land acquisition for parks and forests came during the administration of President Theodore Roosevelt, a pioneer in America's conservation movement. During his tenure, Roosevelt created several new national parks including the previously mentioned Crater Lake (1902), Wind Cave (1903), Mesa Verde (1906), and Platt (1906, re-designated Chickasaw National Recreation Area in 1976). He also set aside thousands of acres for national forests, designated the first national wildlife refuges, and signed the Antiquities Act, granting the president authority to preserve lands of "historic or scientific interest" as national monuments. From 1907 to 1909, Roosevelt established several monuments that would later become national parks, among them California's Lassen Peak, Arizona's Grand Canyon, and Washington's Mount Olympus.

As the number of national parks increased, there was concern as to how they should be managed for public use. At the time, many remote parks were patrolled by the military. There was little control over commercial enterprises, few campgrounds, poor roads, and no plans for interpretation of the scenic and historic resources. Several groups, including the American Society of Landscape Architects and the newly established Sierra Club, called for a creation of a government agency to manage the parks.

In 1914, Interior Secretary Franklin Lane received a letter from a Chicago business leader critical of the department's failure to stop the exploitation of parks. Impressed with the correspondent's knowledge, Lane traveled to Chicago to meet him. That was the secretary's introduction to Stephen T. Mather. A year later, he appointed Mather as his assistant charged with oversight of the parks. Mather was named the Park Service's first director following passage of the Organic Act of 1916 which created the National Park Service with the mission

> to conserve the scenery and the natural and historic objects and the wild life therein and . . . provide for the enjoyment of the same in such manner and by such means as will leave them unimpaired for the enjoyment of future generations.[42]

Within two years, Mather added several new parks including Alaska's Mount McKinley in 1917 and Grand Canyon and Zion in 1919. That same year, Lafayette National Park (renamed Acadia in 1929) was established in Maine, becoming the first NPS unit east of the Mississippi River. This was an important step in Mather's plan to establish parks closer to the nation's population centers. He also moved aggressively to establish standards for park facilities, place tighter controls on concessionaires, and develop clear criteria for parks selection.

At the same time, he wrestled with how to address the increasing number of parks proposals. Mather believed that promotion of state-supported parks was critical and convened a group of advisors to discuss the issues. At this meeting, held in Chicago in 1920, Landrum noted that while there was

> consensus that the integrity of the national park system had to be protected, there was also general agreement that many of the park properties found lacking for national park status still had substantial merit and deserved protection through some other appropriate means.[43]

Mather organized a meeting of representatives from NPS and the states to address these ideas. This First Conference on Parks convened in Des Moines, Iowa, in January, 1921, with 200 delegates representing 24 states discussing future directions for both national and state parks. An important outcome of the meeting was establishment of the National Conference on State Parks, organized to provide a framework for parks development. In *Presenting Nature: The Historic Landscape Design of the National Park Service, 1916 to 1942,* Linda F. McClelland noted that:

> The organization's purpose was to urge governments . . . to acquire additional land and water areas for the study of natural history and its scenic aspects, for the preservation of wildlife, and for recreation. Its goal was to put public parks, forests, and preserves within reach of all citizens.[44]

While the conference's emphasis was on state parks, it represented the first steps in forming a partnership between NPS and the fledgling state park agencies that would reach full blossom during the New Deal.

Through the 1920s, parks development moved rapidly ahead. The Park Service proposed three new eastern parks: Great Smoky Mountains along the Tennessee and North Carolina border, Mammoth Cave in Kentucky, and Shenandoah in Virginia. Unlike western parks located on federal land, creation of these parks required acquisition of thousands of acres of private property, efforts that would lead to an unprecedented level of state and federal cooperation.

Though only a consultative body, the National Conference on State Parks provided guidelines and principles for park development across the country. By 1928, park projects were under consideration or in development in all forty-eight states. That same year, Stephen Mather suffered a stroke, forcing his retirement. His successor as NPS director, Horace Albright, would lead the parks movement through the dark days of the early Depression to the threshold of a new "golden age."

# A New Deal for Parks

With the onset of the Depression, parks work virtually ceased. Few could contemplate funding parks when businesses were going bankrupt, banks were failing, farms were being foreclosed, and millions were out of work. In the national parks, some previously funded projects proceeded, but most were cancelled as parks faced austerity budgets. While many saw little hope for further parks development, Franklin Roosevelt saw an unprecedented opportunity to combine critically needed conservation efforts with men eager for work.

For projects in national parks, Roosevelt had an enthusiastic partner in Horace Albright. Albright had joined the Park Service as Mather's assistant in 1917, and, from 1919 to 1929, he had combined field supervision with the management of Yellowstone National Park. This experience provided him with critical insights into both the details of individual park management and oversight of the entire system. Like Mather, Albright was a proponent of parks development in the east. He also introduced historic preservation as an element of the NPS mission. An early example of this was the creation of Colonial National Monument in southeastern Virginia which preserved early American history at Jamestown and the nearby Revolutionary War battlefield at Yorktown (Figure 20).

During the dark, early days of the Depression, Albright instructed park superintendents to review their master plans for projects that could be implemented if funds became available. When money and manpower from the ECW program were appropriated, these plans were used to put CCC enrollees to work almost immediately. Albright

**Figure 20.** At Yorktown in what is now Colonial National Historical Park, Virginia, CCC men reproduced fortifications of the Revolutionary War era.

assigned NPS Chief Forester John D. Coffman responsibility for overseeing projects in national parks and Assistant Director Conrad Wirth with oversight of work in state parks. To meet the higher degree of coordination required for management of the state parks program, Herbert Evison, Director of the National Conference on State Parks, was appointed to serve as Wirth's assistant.

On April 5, 1933, director Fechner sent a telegram to the governors of all forty-eight states describing the ECW program and outlining how each state might benefit from participation. He urged states with existing or planned parks to request CCC camps to support development, at the same time encouraging those without programs to move ahead with the preparation of plans or face being left out. Eager to put people to work, the states responded by proposing hundreds of projects. By the end of 1933, eleven states initiated development of their first state parks and many more were aggressively planning projects.

ECW in national parks would be coordinated from Washington, with specific project responsibilities assigned to each park superintendent.

The state parks program, under the new ECW Branch of Planning and State Cooperation, would be coordinated through four district offices, located in Washington (East), Indianapolis (Midwest), Denver (Rocky Mountains), and San Francisco (West). The four district directors — John Hoffman, Paul Brown, Herbert Maier, and Lawrence Merriam, respectively — working closely with the evolving state parks agencies, would plan, supervise, and inspect parks work in the states within their districts. In some instances, ECW staff assisted states in drafting legislation needed for parks planning and construction. While the mission of both national and state parks focused on conservation and restoration of natural and cultural resources, state parks projects added greater emphasis on recreational facilities development as a new and significant third component.

At the same time, Albright proposed to the president a reorganization of the National Park Service that would dramatically expand its responsibilities. On June 10, 1933, Roosevelt signed Executive Order 6166 transferring to NPS the national monuments that were then under the supervision of the US Forest Service; the national battlefields, military parks, and national cemeteries overseen by the War Department; and the numerous federally owned parks and monuments within the nation's capital. With a stroke of his pen, Roosevelt more than doubled the acreage under Park Service control. Shortly afterward, Albright resigned and was succeeded by his longtime assistant, Arno Cammerer. Much of the success of the partnership of NPS and the CCC was attributable to Cammerer and his team who, under enormous pressure, achieved successes in parks development that continue to reap benefits three-quarters of a century later.

In 1935, Conrad Wirth's program of regionalization within the Branch of Planning further expanded with the opening of four new district offices to provide closer supervision of the hundreds of state park projects. A year later, Cammerer decided to reduce duplication through a consolidation of all CCC parks work under the Branch of Planning. On June 1, 1936, based on Wirth's recommendation, Cammerer's endorsement, and Ickes' approval, management of the NPS was decentralized through creation of district offices, similar to those administering the CCC parks program.

A short time later, Congress passed the Park, Parkway, and Recreational Area Study Act that codified the relationship between NPS and state parks that had evolved through the ECW program. The Act also broadened the Park Service's scope to incorporate new types of parks such as national recreation areas and national seashores and lakeshores. In addition, funds were appropriated to conduct studies of parks and recreation issues, an effort that culminated in the 1941 publication of *A Study of the Park and Recreation Problem in the United States*, a guide that would serve, to some degree, as a blueprint for park development following World War II.

Despite the challenges and occasional setbacks, the growth of parks during the 1930s was unparalleled in the nation's history and contributed to the achievement of President Roosevelt's twin goals of restoring America's natural and human resources (Figure 21). Decades later, McClelland summarized this effort by writing:

> Wirth and the other park service officials saw their work as a social-humanitarian effort. They were laying the foundation of a federal and state partnership in recreation that would significantly contribute to the human wealth of the nation.[45]

Similarly, James Lyons observed that "The investments he [FDR] made in parks and forests created the roads, trails, and campgrounds we enjoy today."[46]

## Parks for All

In his youth and early adulthood, Franklin Roosevelt had been a frequent visitor to New York's Adirondack Mountains where America's wealthiest families maintained rustically elegant "camps" and retreats. Despite his wealth and privilege, he grew to understand that access to the outdoors for healthful recreation was essential for all Americans, and especially for those living in crowded cities.

In 1934, as president, Roosevelt signed two executive orders granting the federal government authority to buy marginal or abandoned lands for reforestation and restoration as recreation areas. This marked an important shift in parks development as previous ECW

**Figure 21.** Using mostly manual labor, CCC enrollees carried out many road-building projects.

projects required that states purchase the land. Working through several agencies, most notably the Resettlement Administration, $25 million was appropriated for this project.

These new parks, called Recreation Demonstration Areas (RDAs), would be unlike any others. By 1936, four hundred properties were under consideration as RDAs. Eventually, 46 sites in 24 states were selected. Conrad Wirth, head of the Branch of Planning and State Cooperation, reported that "studies indicated an urgent need for natural areas relatively close to population centers and available to large numbers of people for weekend and even day use."[47] Oversight of CCC work in the RDAs was assigned to Wirth's agency. During the next five years, CCC enrollees, often working alongside WPA workers in parks around the country, excavated for lakes and ponds, carved trails, and built rustic group camps featuring bunkhouses, dining halls, recreation buildings, infirmaries, and other structures (Plate 1, bottom).

In most instances, the federal government entered into arrangements with local organizations like the YMCA, Boys and Girls clubs, and Boy and Girl scouts to operate the camps. Two parks near Washington, DC, served as models for RDAs nationwide. With only a few exceptions, such as Catoctin Mountain in Maryland and Chopawamsic in Virginia, RDAs were turned over to the states following completion. In addition, funds were allocated from this program for development of recreation sites along the Skyline Drive and the Blue Ridge Parkway, then under development. Today, many of the RDA parks, from Georgia's Hard Labor Creek State Park and South Dakota's Custer State Park to California's Mendocino Woodlands State Park, remain important components of state park systems.

# An Enduring Legacy

*In less than 10 years the CCC left a lasting legacy for America and the National Park Service. The extensive development and park expansion made possible by the CCC was in large part responsible for the modern national and state park systems.*[48]

— John C. Paige
*The Civilian Conservation Corps and the National Park Service, 1933–1942: An Administrative History*

The legacy of the CCC lives on in hundreds of parks across the country. From Tanglewood group camp in Maine's Camden Hills, underground trails in Florida Caverns, and reconstructed buildings of Lincoln's New Salem Village in Illinois to rough stone cottages in Texas's Bastrop State Park, trails to the depths of the Grand Canyon, and a rustic group lodge at Oregon's Silver Falls State Park, the Corps left treasured footprints on the land for the recreation and renewal of generations to come.

In the broadest sense, the New Deal era, building on the foundations laid by President Theodore Roosevelt, represented a "second golden age" of conservation. Under FDR's leadership, the national forests expanded, adding more than 20 million acres in the Midwest and East, the number of national wildlife refuges more than doubled, and NPS became, for the first time, a truly *national* parks agency. Historian Richard N. L. Andrews wrote:

> No other era in American history produced such an extraordinary record of both restoring and enhancing the environment and of creating an improved sense of harmony between human communities and their environmental surroundings.[49]

These efforts also fostered greater appreciation for preserving or restoring the nation's natural heritage. The expansion of the Park Service and the development of hundreds of municipal, regional, and state parks created unprecedented opportunities for Americans to experience the wild outdoors — often for the first time. It still seems improbable that a devastating economic crisis proved to be the impetus for an unequaled era of parks development and improvement. Yet, the statistics reveal a remarkable story of achievement. From 1933 to 1942, the CCC and other agencies worked in 71 national parks, 405 state parks, and 46 RDAs. Enrollees built hundreds of bathhouses and thousands of cabins and shelters, developed nearly 17,000 acres of campgrounds and 6,000 acres of picnic areas, spent more than 1.5 million man-days fighting fires in or near parks, and, when parks and forests are combined, planted more than 3 billion trees (Figure 22). Indeed, a 1960s study noted that half the trees *ever* planted in the United States, up to that time, were planted by the CCC).

While only twenty percent of CCC camps were located in parks (3,348 of 16,953), the projects these men completed remain among the most tangible and accessible evidence of their contributions to our nation's natural and structural heritage. Beyond the leadership of

**Figure 22.** Millions of trees were planted by CCC crews in efforts to reforest extensive tracts of disturbed land.

**Figure 23.** Elkmont Bridge in Great Smoky Mountains National Park, Tennessee, is shown here under construction by CCC crews.

the Roosevelt Administration, the work carried out in the parks benefited immeasurably from the vision of a remarkable cadre of architects, engineers, landscape designers, park planners, and others who worked tirelessly to create models for parks nationwide. Individuals like Thomas Vint, Herbert Maier, Dr. Emilio Meinecke, and to a lesser extent, Albert H. Good, Dorothy Waugh, and George Grant built a foundation for parks of enduring quality and accessibility for all (Figure 23).

Thomas Vint joined the NPS in 1922 as a draftsman, thereafter rising to become the Service's Chief Landscape Architect. He believed in minimizing human influence on the land by integrating roads, trails, campgrounds, and other structures so that they seemed a part of their surroundings. In 1929, his NPS Landscape Division took on responsibility for all facets of park development by introducing a program of mandatory master planning. These plans were the blueprint for many of the ECW projects carried out by the CCC. In the mid-1920s, Vint began working with architect Herbert Maier on projects at Yosemite and Yellowstone. This relationship would have lasting effects on parks planning and building design for decades to come.

Herbert Maier came to Washington in the early 1920s as architect for the American Association of Museums, a role that brought him into frequent collaboration with Vint. Maier was influenced by the rustic architectural styles of the Adirondack Great Camps and brought these concepts to NPS when he was named Director of District III (Southwest) of the ECW program in 1933. Maier soon became the Park Service's expert on park structures, and to aid planners and designers, he developed the first "plan-book" filled with drawings and photographs of example structures in 1934. With the assistance of Ohio architect Albert H. Good, this booklet was expanded and published, in 1935, in a portfolio called *Park Structures and Facilities* (Figure 24). As CCC projects were completed, the guide grew to three volumes of detailed drawings and images and re-released in 1938 as *Park and Recreation Structures.* The book remains an eloquent statement of the design philosophy and genius of Maier, Vint, and countless others who carried out the hundreds of listed projects. McClelland noted that Maier's influence on park designs possessed an

> amazing ability to clearly express the qualities of naturalistic architectural and landscape design [and] developed an effective process for translating NPS principles and practices to the CCC camps responsible for developing state and local parks.[50]

Both Vint and Maier believed in designs that focused on site planning, structural scale, and use of native materials so that man-made features did not overwhelm their surroundings. Their synergistic vision yielded building styles that have become associated with the New Deal era. These structures, often hand-constructed of native, rough-hewn materials such as logs, stones, masonry, or adobe bricks, were noted for their quality of construction, scale, and durability.

Writing in his "Apologia" to *Park and Recreation Structures,* Good described what has become known as the National Park or Government "Rustic" style.

> When successfully handled, it is a style which, through the use of native materials in proper scale, and through

51

the avoidance of severely straight lines and over-sophistication, gives the feeling of having been executed by pioneer craftsmen with limited hand tools. It thus achieves sympathy with natural surroundings and with the past.[51]

For a weary nation yearning for the romance of a simpler past, the parks with their rustic cabins, lodges, and shelters offered ideal respite from the difficulties of the times.

Dr. Emilio P. Meinecke was a plant pathologist who spent much of his career studying the effects of human intrusion on the natural landscape. Working with the Forest Service and the Park Service, he developed what became known as the "Meinecke Plan" for campgrounds and picnic areas. Prior to his work, parks often allowed visitors to camp and picnic wherever they wished, a practice that caused widespread damage to soil and vegetation. Meinecke developed a design for camping and picnicking areas notable for its use of narrow one-way lanes, pull-outs for automobiles (and later pull-through lanes for trailers), and well defined campsites with tent spaces, camp stove,

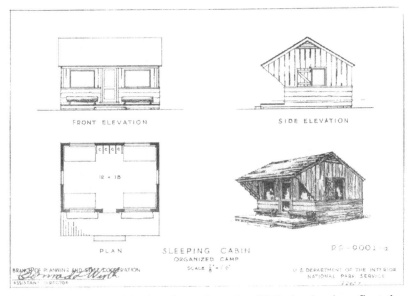

**Figure 24.** These cabin drawings, from the CCC plan book, reflect the rustic design model.

and picnic table, often surrounded by natural vegetation for privacy. This design allowed parks to concentrate camping in defined areas and reduce damage elsewhere. Nearly every park and forest campground developed since the 1930s has been designed around Dr. Meinecke's principles.

Dorothy Waugh and George Grant, each a gifted artist, used their talents to portray park projects and scenes to the public. Waugh, art production supervisor for the Park Service, illustrated numerous guidebooks, posters, architectural planning books, and other publications, capturing with pen and ink the limitless recreational opportunities parks had to offer. At the same time, George Grant, the first Chief Photographer for the Park Service, traveled the country eloquently capturing on film the natural beauty of the parks and the contributions of CCC enrollees working within them (Figure 25). Many of his images were used to illustrate NPS publications from brochures to annual reports. Today, Grant is recognized as one of the nation's preeminent early nature photographers, taking his place among such notables as William Henry Jackson and Ansel Adams.

While praise for the work of the CCC in the parks has been widespread and enduring, it has not been without criticism — both at the time and in retrospect. During the 1930s, several respected environmentalists expressed concerns that CCC work, especially road- and trail-building projects, would expose remote wilderness areas to overuse, resulting in damage to fragile ecosystems. Among those expressing critical views were three founding members of the Wilderness Society — Wisconsin naturalist Aldo Leopold, author of *A Sand County Almanac*; forester Bob Marshall, for whom the Bob Marshall Wilderness in Montana is named; and Benton MacKaye, visionary creator of the Appalachian National Scenic Trail. Despite their concerns, all three expressed overall support for the New Deal's conservation efforts. Both Bob Marshall and MacKaye worked for the federal government during the Depression, Marshall as first director of the US Forest Service's Division of Recreation and Lands and MacKaye as a planner for the Tennessee Valley Authority (TVA).

As scientists came to better understand the role of fire in forests, the CCC's philosophy of aggressive fire prevention and suppression

**Figure 25.** CCC workers pose for a photograph taken by George Grant in 1933 near their "Camp Many Glacier" in Glacier National Park. The man in the center, Dominick Laulette, was reputed to have been the shortest enrollee in the Corps.

was criticized as having led to overgrown and unhealthy woodlands susceptible to devastating fires. It has been suggested that the fires that blazed through Yellowstone National Park in 1988 were an outcome of obsolete forest management practices left over from the 1930s.

While there may be facets of the CCC program that warrant critical scrutiny, from racial segregation practices to the now outdated understanding of certain dimensions of ecosystem management, there is substantial evidence to confirm that the CCC had the positive and lasting effect of giving Americans from all walks of life a greater opportunity to enjoy the outdoors.

Many of the children of the 1940s and 1950s — who first experienced the natural world during family vacations to the country's national parks and monuments, on weekends camping and hiking in CCC-developed state parks, or during youth outings to RDA group camps — became active in the environmental movement during the

1960s and 1970s. This second "tree army," honoring the labors of their forebears, led a new environmental movement to preserve, restore, and safeguard America's, and the world's, wild places and endangered creatures. This love of the land, more than any single structure, road, or trail, may be the most enduring legacy given to us all by the "veterans" of the Civilian Conservation Corps.

---

# Endnotes for Section I

### Section I Title Page

[1] Franklin D. Roosevelt, "Greetings to the Civilian Conservation Corps." Originally published in the CCC newspaper, *Happy Days*, July 8, 1933. Reprinted in *The Public Papers and Addresses of Franklin D. Roosevelt*, Volume 2, 1933. New York: Random House, 1938, 271.

### "Out of Chaos"

[2] Arthur M. Schlesinger, Jr., *The Coming of the New Deal*. Boston: Houghton Mifflin, 1958, 22.

[3] Calvin Coolidge, address to American Society of Newspaper Editors, Washington, DC, January 17, 1925.

[4] Herbert Hoover, Republican presidential nomination acceptance speech, June 22, 1928.

[5] Calvin Coolidge, State of the Union Address, December 4, 1928.

[6] Herbert Hoover, Memorial Day Address, Valley Forge, Pennsylvania, May 31, 1931.

[7] T. H. Watkins, *The Great Depression: America in the 1930s*. New York: Little, Brown and Co., 1993, 50.

[8] Richard Harrity and Ralph G. Martin, *The Human Side of FDR*. New York: Duell, Sloan and Pearce, 1960, 13.

[9] Franklin D. Roosevelt, acceptance speech at Democratic Party Convention, July 2, 1932.

[10] Herbert Hoover, campaign speech, Madison Square Garden, New York City, October 31, 1932.

[11] Ted Morgan, *FDR — A Biography*. New York: Simon and Schuster, 1985, 374–375.

[12] Franklin D. Roosevelt, inaugural address, March 4, 1933.

[13] Ibid.

[14] Franklin D. Roosevelt, Memorandum to Cabinet Secretaries, March 14, 1933.

**"A Miracle of Cooperation"**

[15] Conrad L. Wirth, *Civilian Conservation Corps Program of the United States Department of the Interior, March 1933 to June 30, 1943, Report to Interior Secretary Harold L. Ickes*. Washington, DC: Government Printing Office, 1945, 3.

[16] Franklin D. Roosevelt, *Message from the President of the United States on Unemployment Relief*, (Document 6, 73rd Congress, 1st Session, March 21, 1933), 2.

[17] Ibid.

[18] Ibid.

[19] Emergency Conservation Work Act, 73rd Congress, 1st Session, March 31, 1933.

[20] John A. Salmond, *The Civilian Conservation Corps, 1933–1942: A New Deal Case Study*. Durham: Duke University Press, 1967, 2.

[21] Ibid, 32.

[22] Col. Duncan Major, *Report to Robert Fechner*, June 30, 1933, from Salmond, 41.

[23] Salmond, 45.

[24] Woodrow Grant, interview with authors, 1997.

[25] Salmond, 4.

[26] Ed Stearman, interview with authors, 1997.

[27] Schlesinger, 338.

[28] T. H. Watkins, *The Hungry Years: A Narrative History of the Great Depression in America*. New York: Henry Holt and Co., 1999, 163.

[29] C. W. Pulley, interview with authors, 1997.

[30] Salmond, 99.

[31] Watkins, *The Hungry Years*, 165.

[32] Salmond, 221.

**"Love of the Land"**

[33] William Leuchtenberg, *Foreword* to Henry L. Henderson and David B. Woolner, eds., *FDR and the Environment*, New York: Palgrave MacMillan, 2005, ix.

[34] Morgan, 37.

[35] Brian Black, "The Complex Environmentalist: FDR and the Ethos of New Deal Conservation." In Henderson and Woolner, eds., *FDR and the Environment*, 20.

[36] Franklin D. Roosevelt, acceptance speech at the Democratic Party Convention, July 2, 1932.

[37] Frances Perkins, *The Roosevelt I Knew*. New York: Viking Press, 1946, 177.

[38] Franklin D. Roosevelt, *Foreword* to A. C. Oliver and Harold M. Dudley, *The New America: The Spirit of the Civilian Conservation Corps*. New York: Longmans, Green and Co., 1937, xix.

[39] Black, 35.

[40] Wirth, 1945, 30.

[41] Ney C. Landrum, *The State Park Movement in America: A Cultural Review*. Columbia: University of Missouri Press, 2004, 8.

[42] The National Park Service Organic Act (16, U.S.C. 1), August 15, 1916.

[43] Landrum, 2.

[44] Linda F. McClelland, *Presenting Nature: The Historic Landscape Design of the National Park Service, 1916–1942.*Washington: National Park Service, 1993, 32.

[45] McClelland, 253.

[46] James Lyons, "FDR and Environmental Leadership." In Henderson and Woolner, eds., *FDR and the Environment*. 214.

[47] Conrad L. Wirth, *Parks, Politics, and the People*. Norman: University of Oklahoma Press, 1980, 177.
*http://www.nps.gov/history/historyonline_books/wirth2/*

### "An Enduring Legacy"

[48] John C. Paige, *The Civilian Conservation Corps and the National Park Service, 1933–1942: An Administrative History.* Washington: National Park Service, 1985, 132.
*http://nps.gov/history/history/online_books/ccc/index.htm*

[49] Richard N. L. Andrews, from Leuchtenberg, x.

[50] McClelland, 234.

[51] Albert H. Good, *Park and Recreation Structures, Part I: Administrative and Basic Service Facilities.* Washington: National Park Service, 1938, 5.

# Section II

## A Guide to the Legacy
## of the CCC

*Future visitors to the parks and monuments will get an
added degree of enjoyment of the natural beauties they
behold as a result of the loyal efforts of the CCC.*[1]

— Isabelle Story
*The National Park Service and
Emergency Conservation Work,* 1936

# Introduction to Section II

The CCC worked in more than 700 local, state, and national parks. From the outset, we recognized that this was a number of parks too large to effectively profile individually in a book of reasonable length. Our decision was to focus this guide on a selection of state, regional, and national parks that best represented the breadth of work by the Corps in all parks. From there, we subdivided the parks into two categories — destination parks and other CCC-related parks.

**Destination Parks** have significant links to the CCC and feature substantial and outstanding evidence of the program's work in architectural structures and landscape features. We have identified at least one such destination park for most of the states, and those destinations collectively include many of our nation's best known and most popular state and national parks. For each destination site we have provided a detailed description of the Corps' work in the park as well as contact information for planning a visit to that park. We also have provided a map showing the location of each destination park, primary roads near and leading to the park, and public lands that include — and sometimes abut or surround — the destination park itself.

**Other CCC-Related Parks** include 260 additional parks, each with a tangible and enduring link to the CCC. Each entry for these other parks provides the reader with a brief overview of the park's history and amenities, notes on its CCC features, and essential contact information.

The use of global positioning system (GPS) devices is becoming increasingly popular and we have provided GPS coordinates for each park. However, given the size of many of the parks, the GPS coordinates should be used primarily as a general way-finding reference, and readers should review current park-specific information for detailed directions. Website information is included for all of the parks identified in this section. In each instance, we have made every effort to provide correct locational information and we accept responsibility for any inaccuracies.

We have chosen to organize and present information about the CCC parks by geographic region and, accordingly, have recognized seven regions for that purpose (Figure 26). We have provided a simple map at the beginning of each regional section as a reminder of the states that are included in that region. And, a simple state map is located at the beginning of each state account to show the location of the CCC-related parks within the state. On the state map, the destination park or parks are identified with the letter D and an Arabic numeral corresponding to the sequence in which the parks are described in the text. D1, for example, would identify the location of the first destination park described for the state. Other CCC-related parks are identified by Arabic numerals alone, also according to the sequence in which the parks are described in the text. The numeral 1, for example, would identify the location of the first Other-CCC-Related park described for the state.

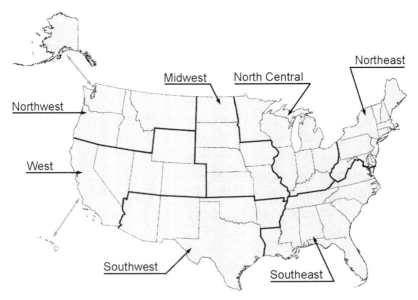

**Figure 26.** The seven regions by which CCC-related parks are identified and described in this book.

When planning a visit to one or more of the described parks, we recommend checking in advance to confirm the days and hours of operation and to obtain current accessibility information since any number of environmental or administrative circumstances may potentially bring about changes. In addition, some parks are only open seasonally, and this has been noted when appropriate in park profiles.

## CRACKING THE CCC CODE

Civilian Conservation Corps camps were identified by a company number and a designation indicating the type and location of the camp.

**COMPANY:** Identified by state and Corps area. For three-digit company numbers, the first digit identified the Corps area (1–9) while the next two digits identified the order of establishment within a state. For four digit CCC companies, the first digit denoted the state in which the company was formed, the second digit the Corps area in which the company was formed, and the last two digits the order of establishment within the state (e.g., Company 2413V SP-2 was the thirteenth CCC company established in South Carolina which was part of Corps Area Four. It was a World-War-I-veterans company assigned to South Carolina's second state park at Givhans Ferry). Companies composed of African-American enrollees would often have a "C" (for "colored") suffix (e.g., Company 1464C) and veterans' companies would have a "V" suffix following the company number (e.g., Company 1785V). A company composed of black veterans would have the combined suffix "VC."

**CAMP:** Often identified by state, project type, and number based on the chronological order of project assignments within a state or Corps area (e.g., GA MP-1 would identify the first camp established at Chickamauga and Chattanooga National Military Park).

SELECTED PROJECT TYPES:

**D** = Drainage and Erosion Control
**F** = Forestry (on state or federal land)
**P** = Forestry (on private land)
**SCS** = Soil Conservation Service
**SP** = State Park
**NP** = National Park
**NM** = National Monument
**MP** = Military Park or National Battlefield
**TVA** = Tennessee Valley Authority
**BS/BF** = Federal Game Refuge
**BR** = Bureau of Reclamation
**AF** = Armed Forces installation

In addition to the official designations, some companies gave their camps nicknames in recognition of individuals or camp locations. For example, Company 1464C MP-1, an African-American company assigned to Georgia's Chickamauga battlefield in Chickamauga and Chattanooga National Military Park, nicknamed its camp "Camp Booker T. Washington." A comprehensive listing of CCC camps by state is available from the CCC Legacy Foundation (*www.ccclegacy.org*).

# *Southeast Region*

## ALABAMA

## Destination Parks

### D1. CHEAHA STATE PARK

*Views seventy-five miles across are worth seeing every-where. The vivid colors of autumn blend well with the heavy blue haze that is found in so many southern mountains.*[2]

— O. R. Head, Acting Superintendent
C.C.C. Camp SP-7, 1934

Rugged promontories and forests of oak and hickory mark the slopes of Cheaha Mountain ("Cheaha" is Creek for "high up"). At 2,407 feet above sea level, it is the highest point in Alabama and the most prominent peak in the Talladega Range, southern terminus of the Appalachian Mountains. Noted for its exceptional beauty, Cheaha Mountain was one of the first sites selected for an

Alabama state park. Shortly after President Franklin Roosevelt's inauguration, the Alabama Department of Conservation began planning a system of state parks to be developed with assistance from the ECW program and the NPS.

Work at Cheaha began in the fall of 1933 with the arrival of CCC Company 468 SP-2. The men built a road to the summit, excavated for a lake with campground, comfort station and bathhouse; erected eleven rustic cabins; carved hiking and horse trails; and began work on the stone Cheaha Lodge (renovated in 2005 and renamed the Bald Rock Group Conference Center and Lodge), built with support from the Anniston and Talladega Chambers of Commerce. They also started work on the 75-foot-high Bunker Tower (Plate 2), built of native stone, located atop Cheaha's summit, and offering views of the surrounding Talladega National Forest. The tower, Bald Rock Lodge, and a small stone-lined pond and walkway remain among the most prominent CCC structures in the park.

The men of Company 468 worked at Cheaha until 1936. They were replaced by Company 2420C SP-7 composed of African-American veterans of WW I. These men continued work at the park by completing the dam and filling Cheaha Lake, putting final touches on the lodge, topping out Bunker Tower, and landscaping the 2,799 acres with thousands of trees and shrubs. Today, Cheaha State Park is a major destination along the Talladega National Scenic Byway (*www.alabamabyways.org*).

While the park now features a modern motel, restaurant, swimming pool and contemporary chalets, it has sustained the legacy of the CCC men through the preservation and modernization of the rustic cabins, the old lodge, and ongoing renovations to Bunker Tower. Future plans call for setting aside a portion of the building for a CCC museum.

*Additional Information:* 19644 Highway 281, Delta, AL 36258 (Figure 27); 256-488-5111; *www.alapark.com.* **GPS:** N33.28.83/ W85.48.62. Facilities include RV/tent sites, motel and restaurant, cabins and chalets, group lodge, picnic areas and shelters, lake, beach with bathhouse, boating facilities, observation tower, ADA accessible boardwalk, trails.

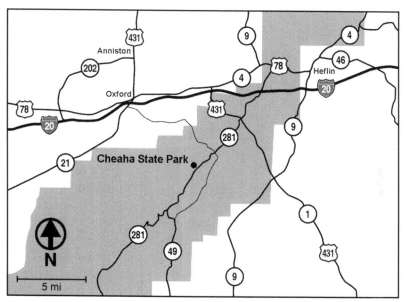

**Figure 27.** The location of Cheaha State Park.

# Other CCC-Related Parks

## State Parks

**1.** CHEWACLA STATE PARK, 124 Shell Toomer Parkway, Auburn, AL 36830; 334-887-5621; *www.alapark.com.* **GPS:** N32.33.27/ W85.28.88. **Background:** Developed by the CCC, this park is located in Piedmont woodlands near Auburn University. **Facilities:** Tent/ RV sites, cabins, lake, beach, bathhouse, picnic shelters, trails. **CCC Company:** 4448 SP-12. **CCC Features:** Cabins, picnic shelters, lake and dam, bathhouse, trails.

**2.** DESOTO STATE PARK, 13883 County Road 89, Fort Payne, AL 35967; 256-845-005; *www.alapark.com.* **GPS:** N34.29.74/W85.37.13. **Background:** This landscape of streams, forests, and dramatic DeSoto Falls is a popular destination on Lookout Mountain. Park development was carried out by the CCC. **Facilities:** Visitor center, RV/tent sites, cabins, lodge and restaurant, picnic shelters, trails. **CCC Companies:** 472 and 1425 SP-5. **CCC Features:** Park roads, stonework, lodge, cabins (Figure 28), trails, quarry site, unfinished bridge.

**3. GULF STATE PARK,** 20115 State Highway 135, Gulf Shores, AL 36542; 251-948-7275; *www.alapark.com*. **GPS:** N30.15.82/ W87.40.66. **Background:** Located near Gulf Shores, this beachfront park was developed by CCC enrollees who built roads, cottages, piers, and picnic areas. Workers also dug canals connecting several freshwater lakes. **Facilities:** Tent/RV sites, cabins, hotel and conference center, picnic shelters, trails, marina, pier, golf course. **CCC Companies:** 259 and 2436 SP-6. **CCC Features:** Picnic areas, cabins.

**4. MONTE SANO STATE PARK,** 5105 Nolen Avenue, Huntsville, AL 35801; 256-534-3757; *www.alapark.com*. **GPS:** N34.44.64/ W86.30.61. **Background:** Initial development of this park near Huntsville was carried out by the CCC as part of a TVA project. Monte Sano Lodge burned in 1947 and was reconstructed, based on the original design, in 2004. **Facilities:** Tent/RV sites, cabins, trails, picnic areas and shelters, amphitheater, lodge. **CCC Companies:** 5402 TVA-12 and 3486 TVA-13. **CCC Features**: Old entrance and check-in station, overlook, cottages (Figure 29), Monte Sano Lodge, amphitheatre, picnic shelters, trails.

**5. OAK MOUNTAIN STATE PARK,** 200 Terrace Avenue, Pelham, AL 35124; 205-620-2520; *www.alapark.com*. **GPS:** N33.19.36/ W86.45.09. **Background:** Located near Birmingham, this 9,940-acre

**Figure 28.** The CCC used local stone and lumber milled on site to build this cottage at DeSoto State Park.

**Figure 29.** This CCC fieldstone cottage at Monte Sano State Park shows the lasting construction of these hand-built structures finished more than 75 years ago.

park is Alabama's largest. The site was initially developed as an RDA. **Facilities:** RV/tent sites, cabins, lakes, trails, wildlife center, demonstration farm, golf course, amphitheater. **CCC Company:** 487 NP-1/ SP-8. **CCC Features:** Lakes and beach, trails, picnic shelters.

## Other Park

**6.** MOUNDVILLE ARCHAEOLOGICAL PARK, 634 Mound Parkway, Moundville, AL 35474; 205-371-2234; *www.moundville.ua.edu.* **GPS:** N33.0.18/W87.37.70. **Background:** This site, managed by the University of Alabama, preserves one of the largest Mississippian Indian sites in the nation (Figure 30). CCC enrollees assisted in archeological work on the many mounds located in this park and constructed the Jones Archaeological Museum. **Facilities:** Museum, nature trails, recreated Indian structures, crafts pavilion. **CCC Companies:** 444 SP-10 and SP-15. **CCC Features:** Stabilized prehistoric Indian mounds, museum.

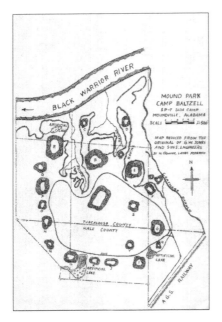

**Figure 30.** This site map of Moundville Archaeological Park, from the National Archives, shows the design of the mounds complex.

# FLORIDA

## Destination Parks

### D1. HIGHLANDS HAMMOCK STATE PARK

*It was soon apparent that through the Civilian Conservation Corps the dreams and objectives of the founders of these conservation areas were now to be realized.[3]*

— C. Ray Vinten, Superintendent
Company 453 SP-3

Hammocks, forest lands uplifted from surrounding marshes, provide habitat for flowering plants, trees, and wildlife. Few places in the nation better preserve this landscape than Highlands Hammock. In the 1930s, the lush forest was saved from destruction when local citizens joined together to preserve what was then called "Hooker Hammock."

Much of the early preservation work was generously funded by the Margaret Shippen Roebling family. After Highlands Hammock Park opened in 1931, it was suggested that a botanical garden and arboretum be developed on the site. The park's trustees argued that the hammock should remain undisturbed. However, Harry L. Baker, state forester and first park executive, believed the idea had merit.

In 1933, Baker proposed that two sections of the hammock (sections 4 and 33) be set aside for establishment of the garden and arboretum. With support from Highlands Hammock, Inc., plans for the Florida Botanical Garden and Arboretum were developed and a CCC camp was authorized to provide the labor. Interestingly the secretary for the garden and arboretum, Clara Thomas, became a CCC camp supervisor — one of the few women to hold such a position.

The first CCC enrollees from Company 262 SP-3 arrived in June 1934, setting up camp in Sebring. They later moved into quarters near Section 33, west of Lake Jackson. After three years of work, the crew was replaced by Company 453 SP-10. During their time in the park the CCC felled dead trees, removed stumps, carved roads and trails, and created water catchment areas along Tiger Branch Creek to provide reliable water for the nursery test beds and demonstration forests. This work was followed by construction of a herbarium building, a greenhouse, and garden plots for palms, conifers, bamboo, and other plants. The men also built a saw mill to produce lumber for park structures, including staff residences, an auditorium, a refreshment building, picnic shelters, a visitor center, and maintenance facilities.

Florida's state park system was formally established in 1935 and Highlands Hammock became one of the four original units. Today, the park is home to the Florida Civilian Conservation Corps Museum (Figure 31) and a *Spirit of the CCC* statue (Plate 3).

***Additional Information:*** 5931 Hammock Road, Sebring, FL 33872 (Figure 32); 863-386-6094; *www.floridastateparks.org.* **GPS:** N27.26.99/W81.31.14. Facilities include a visitor center and CCC

**Figure 31.** The CCC Museum at Highlands Hammock State Park has several displays about the life of the men in the CCC.

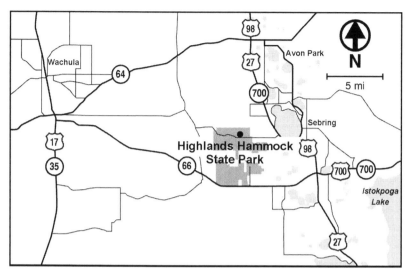

**Figure 32.** The location of Highlands Hammock State Park.

museum, Hammock Inn Restaurant, trails including swamp board-walks, and guided tram tours.

# Other CCC-Related Parks

### State Parks

**1. FLORIDA CAVERNS STATE PARK,** 3345 Caverns Road, Marianna, FL 32446; 850-482-9598; *www.floridastateparks.org.* **GPS:** N30.48.58/ W85.13.47. **Background:** Created from dissolving Ocala Limestone laid down millions of years ago, dry Florida Cavern is a geological rarity. The CCC made the caverns accessible to the public. **Facilities:** Visitor center, RV/tent sites, picnic areas and shelters, trails and cave passages, youth camp, boat ramps on Chipola River. **CCC Company:** 2415V SP-12. **CCC Features:** Visitor center with CCC exhibits, cave passages, lighting system, trails, picnic pavilions, park entrance.

**2. FORT CLINCH STATE PARK,** 2601 Atlantic Avenue, Fernandina Beach, FL 32034; 904-277-7274; *www.floridastateparks.org.* **GPS:** N30.41.83/W81.26.49. **Background:** Work began in the in the mid-19th century on this fort as part of the coastal defense system, but was never completed. It was occupied by both Federal and Confederate troops during the Civil War. In 1935, the state acquired the abandoned fort and CCC enrollees carried out restoration and development projects. **Facilities:** Visitor center, RV/tent sites, picnic areas, trails, youth camp. **CCC Company:** 1420 SP-8. **CCC Features:** Restored fort, historic features, trails, picnic area.

**3. MYAKKA RIVER STATE PARK,** 13207 SR 72, Sarasota, FL 34241; 941-361-6511; *www.floridastateparks.org.* **GPS:** N27.13.79/ W82.17.81. **Background:** Once a cattle ranch, the park preserves rare Florida dry prairie along the Myakka River. **Facilities:** RV/tent sites, cabins, lakes, river, restaurant, picnic areas and shelters, trails, amphitheater, historic Potter Palmer Ranch house. **CCC Companies:** 5430C and 2444 SP-4. **CCC Features:** Park roads, trails, picnic areas and shelters, palm-log cabins (Figure 33).

**4. TORREYA STATE PARK,** 2576 NW Torreya Park Road, Bristol, FL 32321; 850-643-2674; *www.floridastateparks.org.* **GPS:** N30.34.13/ W84.56.79. **Background:** Located on bluffs overlooking the Apalachicola River, the park is home to the rare Torreya tree, an evergreen often called "stinking cedar" for its pungent resin. During the Civil War, a Confederate artillery battery was located on the bluffs. The CCC developed the park and relocated the antebellum Gregory

**Figure 33.** This CCC cabin was built using local palm logs at Myakka River State Park.

family house from Ocheesee Point on the opposite bank of the Apalachicola River to what is now Torreya State Park. **Facilities:** RV/tent sites, youth camp, trails, picnic areas. **CCC Company:** 4453C SP-6. **CCC Features:** Campground, trails, picnic areas, Gregory house.

# GEORGIA

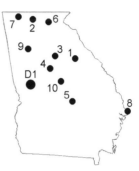

## Destination Parks

### D1. FRANKLIN D. ROOSEVELT STATE PARK

*Of the first nine state parks constructed in Georgia during the CCC years (1933–1942), FDR State Park received the most attention because of its proximity to Roosevelt's Little White House.*[4]

— Lucy Ann Lawless
Master of Landscape Architecture Thesis
University of Georgia, 1992

In 1924, Franklin Roosevelt came to Warm Springs, Georgia, seeking relief from the debilitating effects of polio in the soothing waters. Few knew then what a profound effect this scion of a wealthy New York family would have on the people of this impoverished region of Georgia — and the nation. Roosevelt fell in love with the Piedmont hills and the hard-working people who lived there. He purchased land for a model farm and built a small cottage, later dubbed "the Little White House." The president died there on April 12, 1945, and the house and grounds are now a state historic site. After Roosevelt won the presidency, his experiences among the people of Pine Mountain

75

formed an integral part of his vision for the New Deal programs that would restore the land there and across the country.

The state of Georgia purchased property along Pine Mountain for a park and in the spring of 1934, CCC workers arrived to begin work at the site. Company 1429 P-56/SP-7, "Camp Meriwether" (Figure 34), was established near Warm Springs and Company 4463 SP-13, "Camp Kimbrough," was located on Pine Mountain. Working with PWA employees and WPA workers, the CCC built park roads, bridges, Pine Mountain Inn (now the visitor center); cabins, campgrounds, group camps, picnic areas and shelters, trails, pool and bathhouse, Lakes Delano and Roosevelt, and other structures. During his frequent visits to Warm Springs for both polio therapy and brief vacations, President Roosevelt frequently met with the CCC workers who often served as honor guards when the president's train arrived at the depot. He enjoyed watching the work and occasionally offered suggestions. Historians believe he may have participated in the design of the Pine Mountain Inn and patio and in the plan for the large, Liberty-Bell-shaped swimming pool.

**Figure 34.** The CCC's "Camp Meriwether" on Pine Mountain was near FDR's Little White House in Warm Springs, Georgia.

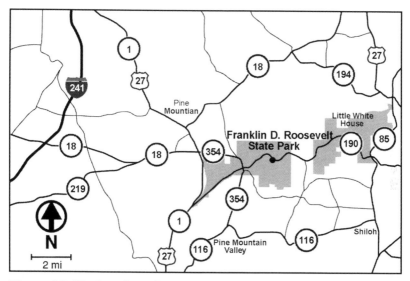

**Figure 35.** The location of Franklin D. Roosevelt State Park.

Originally known as "Pine Mountain State Park," the 9,000-acre property was rededicated to Roosevelt's memory late in the 1940s. It is now a National Historic Landmark. Of the hundreds of parks developed by the CCC, none has a more tangible link to President Franklin D. Roosevelt than this oasis in the hills of western Georgia. *Additional Information:* 2970 GA 190, Pine Mountain, GA 31822 (Figure 35); 706-663-4858; *www.gastateparks.org*. **GPS:** N32.50.31/ W84.48.93. **Facilities**: Visitor center, RV/tent sites, primitive sites, cabins, group camps, lakes, pool and bathhouse, Dowdells Knob (FDR's favorite picnic site), stables, Pine Mountain Trail.

## Other CCC-Related Parks

## State Parks

**1. ALEXANDER H. STEPHENS STATE PARK,** 456 Alexander Street North, Crawfordville, GA 30631; 706-456-2602; *www.gastateparks.org*. **GPS:** N33.34.04/W82.53.79. **Background:** This park was developed around Liberty Hall, the plantation owned by Alexander Stephens, US Congressman, Confederate Vice President, and Georgia Governor. The park was originally developed as an RDA. **Facilities:** Park office and bathhouse, Tent/RV sites, cabins, picnic areas and shelters, ponds, pool, group camp, trails. **CCC Company:** 478 SP-5. **CCC Features:** Park office and bathhouse, group camp, restored historic structures, Lake Liberty, trails, picnic areas and shelters, wooden fire lookout tower.

**2. FORT MOUNTAIN STATE PARK,** 181 Fort Mountain Road, Chatsworth, GA 30705; 706-422-1932; *www.gastateparks.org*. **GPS:** N34.45.66/ W84.42.01. **Background:** Set in the Cohutta Mountains and adjacent to the rugged Cohutta Wilderness, the park preserves an ancient stone wall believed to have been constructed by Indians more than 1,000 years ago. The CCC developed many facilities in this park, including a stone observation tower near the summit (Figure 36). This tower features a rock carved in the shape of a heart by a CCC foreman in honor of his fiancée (Plate 4, top). **Facilities:** Tent/RV sites, cabins, lake, beach, picnic shelters, trails. **CCC Company:** 447 SP-15. **CCC Features:** Restored archeological area; lake and dam, shelters, trails, stone steps, landscaping, lookout tower.

**3. HARD LABOR CREEK STATE PARK,** 5 Hard Labor Creek Road, Rutledge, GA 30663; 706-557-3001; *www.gastateparks.org*. **GPS:** N33.39.34/W83.36.29. **Background:** The park's unusual name may come from slave stories of back-breaking work on the area's cotton plantations. The site was originally developed as an RDA. **Facilities:** RV/tent/equestrian sites, cabins, lakes, beach, bathhouse, picnic areas and shelters, group camps, trails, 18-hole golf course. **CCC Companies:** 459 NP-6/SP-8 and 3442 SP-11. **CCC Features:** Blacksmith shop (now an exhibit featuring the CCC), group camp with restored CCC barracks, picnic areas, lake and dam, CCC camp ruins.

**4. INDIAN SPRINGS STATE PARK,** 678 Lake Clark Road, Flovilla, GA 30216; 770-504-2277; *www.gastateparks.org*. **GPS:** N33.14.88/ W83.55.49. **Background:** As one of the nation's oldest public recreation areas, this park preserves natural springs set aside in the 1825 Treaty of Indian Springs. The CCC built many park structures including an entrance bridge dubbed the "24 Hour Bridge" because it was built in one day so that camp supplies could be delivered to the park. **Facilities:** Tent/RV sites, cabins, picnic shelters, group camp, lake, trails, museum. **CCC Company:** 459 SP-1. **CCC Features:** Park roads, bridge, spring house, picnic pavilion, museum with CCC exhibits.

**5. LITTLE OCMULGEE STATE PARK,** 80 Live Oak Trail, Helena, GA 31037; 229-868-7474; *www.gastateparks.org*. **GPS:** N32.05.61/

**Figure 36.** Visitors still enjoy the view from the Observation Tower built by the CCC at Fort Mountain State Park.

W82.53.76. **Background:** This CCC park in Georgia's pine hills was developed near the hometown of Depression-era Governor Eugene Talmadge. **Facilities:** Tent/RV sites, cabins, restaurant, lodge/conference center, lake and beach, pool, tennis courts, amphitheater, picnic shelters, trails, 18-hole golf course. **CCC Company:** 2419 P-63/SP-14. **CCC Features:** Group shelter, trails, picnic shelters, lake and dam.

**6. VOGEL STATE PARK,** 7485 Vogel State Park Road, Blairsville, GA 30512; 706-745-2628; *www.gastateparks.org.* **GPS:** N34.45.94/ W83.55.42. **Background:** Nestled in the Appalachian Mountains, this park is surrounded by the Chattahoochee National Forest. The site was Georgia's second state park and the original facilities were developed by the CCC. **Facilities:** Tent/RV sites, cabins, lake with pavilion and beach, picnic areas and shelters, trails, miniature golf course, CCC Museum. **CCC Company:** 431 SP-2. **CCC Features:** Park entrance roads, bridges and stone-work, Lake Trahlyta and dam, rustic cottages, visitor center, trails, picnic areas. A few CCC camp buildings remain in the nearby Goose Creek Resort.

# National Parks

**7. CHICKAMAUGA-CHATTANOOGA NATIONAL MILITARY PARK,** 3370 LaFayette Road, Fort Oglethorpe, GA 30742; 706-866-9241; *www.nps.gov/chch.* **GPS:** N34.56.42/W85.15.60. **Background:** Set aside in 1890 to preserve two major Civil War battlefields from 1863, the park includes sites in northwestern Georgia along Missionary Ridge and atop Lookout Mountain in Tennessee. Chickamauga became the country's first National Military Park in 1895. CCC enrollees carried out landscaping, road and trail work, building stabilization, and other projects. **Facilities:** Chickamauga and Point Park visitor centers and museums, scenic roads, trails, historical structures, picnic areas, interpretive programs. **CCC Companies:** Chickamauga Battlefield: 1464C MP-1/NP-1 and 2402C MP-2/NP-2; Lookout Mountain: 4497C MP-5/NP-4, 5426 and 1290 MP-6/NP-5, and 420 NP-8. **CCC Features:** Trails, stabilized structures, picnic areas, Ochs Museum (at Point Park), Camp ruins (at Lookout Mountain).

**8. FORT PULASKI NATIONAL MONUMENT,** PO Box 30757, Highway 80 East, Savannah, GA 31410-0757; 912-786-5787; *www.nps.gov/fopu.* **GPS:** N32.01.38/W80.53.25. **Background:** Established in the 1820s as part of the coastal defense system, Robert E. Lee worked on the fort's construction as an army engineer. Occupied by Rebels in 1861,

**Figure 37.** CCC enrollees constructed drainage canals around Fort Pulaski National Monument as part of the restoration process.

the fort was nearly destroyed by Union rifled artillery in April, 1862. It was designated a National Monument in 1924. The CCC carried out repair and stabilization projects (Figure 37). **Facilities:** Visitor center, trails, picnic areas. **CCC Company:** 460 NM-1/NP-3. **CCC Features:** Restored fort, dikes, drainage canals, trails, mainland bridge.

**9. Kennesaw Mountain National Battlefield Park,** 900 Kennesaw Mountain Drive, Kennesaw, GA 30152; 770-427-4686; *www.nps.gov/kemo.* **GPS:** N33.58.95/W84.34.69. **Background:** Initially created from 60 acres around Cheatham Hill in 1926, the remaining land, including the mountain, was acquired in 1937. The site was designated a National Battlefield Park two years later. **Facilities:** Visitor center and museum, trails, historical sites and structures, picnic areas. **CCC Company:** 431 NM-3/NP-4. **CCC Features:** Cheatham Hill Road, stabilized earthworks, trails, CCC camp ruins.

**10. Ocmulgee National Monument,** 1207 Emery Highway, Macon, GA 31217; 478-752-8257; *www.nps.gov/ocmu.* **GPS:** N32.50.62/W83.36.24. **Background:** Notable for its large ceremonial mounds, earth lodge, and other evidence of habitation over thousands of years, the site on the Ocmulgee River was set aside as a National Monument in 1936. CCC and WPA workers collaborated in park development projects and archeological excavations (Figure 38). **Facilities:** Visitor

**Figure 38.** The archeological excavations supported by the CCC men at Ocmulgee National Monument produced many of the artifacts now on display at the visitors center museum.

center (Plate 4, bottom), preserved mounds, reconstructed earth lodge, trails, picnic areas. **CCC Companies:** 1426 and 2417V NM-4/NP-5. **CCC Features:** Visitor center, stabilized historic structures, earth lodge, trails.

# LOUISIANA

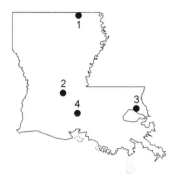

## Other CCC-Related Parks

## State Parks

**1. CHEMIN-A-HAUT STATE PARK,** 14656 State Park Road, Bastrop, LA 71220; 888-677-2436; *www.crt.state.la.us/parks*. **GPS:** N32.54.60/ W91.50.70. **Background:** When CCC enrollees arrived at this proposed park site, they found a landscape that was a "mass of pine logs and tree tops, nothing left of commercial value." Over time, the men turned the site into a wooded park overlooking Bayou Bartholomew. **Facilities:** RV/tent sites, cabins, group camp, lodge, picnic areas and shelters, boating facilities, trails. **CCC Company** 478 SP-4. **CCC Features:** Park roads, cabin, lodge with CCC exhibit.

**2. CHICOT STATE PARK,** 3469 Chicot Park Road, Ville Platte, LA 70586; 888-677-2442; *www.crt.state.la.us/parks*. **GPS:** N30.48.02/ W92.16.78. **Background:** Chicot is the largest of Louisiana's four original parks. The park preserves bottomland hardwood forests along the shores of Lake Chicot. The Louisiana State Arboretum is adjacent to the park. **Facilities:** Visitor center, RV/tent sites, cabins, group lodges and camp facilities, picnic areas and shelters, Lake Chicot, pools, trails. **CCC Company:** 1427 SP-6. **CCC Features:** Park roads, dam and spillway, picnic areas and shelters, group camp dining hall.

**3. FONTAINEBLEAU STATE PARK,** 67825 Hwy 190, Mandeville, LA 70448; 888-677-3668; *www.crt.state.la.us/parks*. **GPS:** N30.34.52/ W90.02.27. **Background:** Originally called Tchefuncte State Park, this area of pine forests and marshes along Lake Pontchartrain preserves the ruins of an early 19th century sugar mill and plantation that owner Bernard de Marigny de Mandeville named "Fontainbleau." Land for the park was acquired in 1936 and developed by the CCC.

**Facilities:** Visitor center, historic sites, RV/tent sites, picnic areas and shelters, group camp, water sports facilities, trails. **CCC Companies:** 1495 and 478 SP-5. **CCC Features:** Park entrances, roads, office, picnic areas, comfort stations, East and West pavilions, group camp, bathhouse with brick walkway and beach.

**4.** Longfellow-Evangeline State Historic Site, 1200 North Main Street, Saint Martinville, LA 70582-3516; 888-677-2900; *www.crt.state.la.us/parks.* **GPS:** N30.08.03/W91.49.60. **Background:** One of Louisiana's first state parks, this site was set aside in 1934 to preserve the legacy of the 1755 expulsion of French Canadians from Nova Scotia and their emigration to Louisiana as retold in Henry Wadsworth Longfellow's poem *Evangeline.* CCC enrollees assisted in restorations and in developing park facilities. **Facilities:** Visitor center, historic and reconstructed structures, picnic areas, trails. **CCC Company:** 277 SP-1. **CCC Features:** Park roads, picnic areas, trails, historic structures.

# MISSISSIPPI

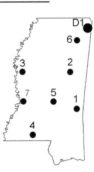

## Destination Parks

### D1. Tishomingo State Park

*The famous swinging bridge, the CCC pond and dam, and the rustic Loochapola Lodge and cabin buildings that define the park were all constructed by the CCC in the 1930s and 1940s.*[5]

— Pamela McRae
*Tishomingo County News*

Nestled in Mississippi's Appalachian foothills, Tishomingo State Park is known for its diverse flora, abundant wildlife, and unique geology. The area is also rich in human history, sitting only a short distance from the historic Natchez Trace. Today, the Natchez Trace Parkway bisects the park. At the onset of the Depression, Mississippi was mired in a lengthy agricultural recession; thousands were unemployed, and farms had been and were being foreclosed or abandoned. With the creation of the CCC and its promise of employment, the state purchased several parcels of land for parks. Tishomingo was established through the acquisition of 1,500 acres around Bear Creek and, in May, 1935, CCC Company 3497 SP-5 arrived to begin work. The men set up a quarry to carve the area's abundant Highland Church Sandstone; constructed a mill for the lumber used in park buildings; and laid out roads, picnic areas, and other facilities.

In 1936, the men began work on the log-and-stone Loochapola Lodge and six tourist cabins; followed by the excavation of a pond, construction of a dam and spillway; erection of a 200-foot-long swinging bridge across Bear Creek (Figure 39); and building of a pool,

**Figure 39.** This amazing suspension bridge was built by the CCC at Tishomingo State Park.

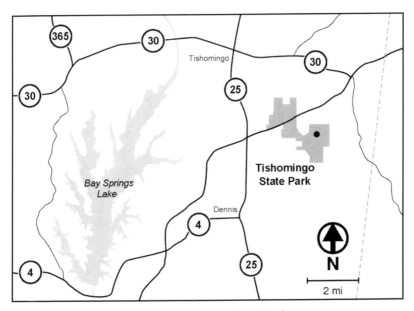

**Figure 40.** The location of Tishomingo State Park.

bathhouse, group camp, and administrative, maintenance, and residential structures. The men also laid out trails through woodlands, among sandstone outcrops, and along the banks of Bear Creek. Additionally, the enrollees were taught woodworking and metal-crafting skills. One of the park's most significant CCC artifacts is an original information sign, crafted by CCC blacksmith Ernest Clausel, with a silhouetted image of Chickasaw Chief Tishomingo (Plate 5). The Nature Center (open by request) houses exhibits about the Corps' work at Tishomingo and in Mississippi's other parks.

More recent additions to the park include 45-acre Haynes Lake, a relocated pioneer cabin, and a disc golf course. *Outside Magazine* listed Tishomingo as one of the "top 50" hiking destinations in the nation. The park remains a legacy to the lasting quality and craftsmanship of the CCC and is listed on the National Register of Historic Places.

***Additional Information:*** 105 State Park Road, Tishomingo, MS 38873 (Figure 40); 662-438-6914; *www.mdwfp.com.* **GPS:** N34.36.85/ W88.11.55. **Facilities**: Visitor center, historic cabin, RV/tent sites, group camps, cabins, picnic areas and shelters, Loochpoola Lodge, nature center, pool and bathhouse, recreation fields, disc golf courses, lake, trails.

# Other CCC-Related Parks
## State Parks

**1. CLARKCO STATE PARK,** 386 Clarkco Road, Quitman, MS 39355; 601-776-6651; *www.mdwfp.com*. **GPS:** N32.05.95/W88.41.57. **Background:** Established in 1938, the park preserves hills and woods surrounding Clarkco Lake. **Facilities:** Visitor center/activity buildings, RV/tent sites, picnic areas and shelters, trails, lake, recreation field, tennis courts, disc golf course. **CCC Companies:** 4424 P-75 and 1437 SP-3. **CCC Features:** Park roads, cabins, picnic shelters, manager's residence.

**2. LEGION STATE PARK,** 635 Legion State Park Road, Louisville, MS 39339-8803; 662-773-8323; *www.mdwfp.com*. **GPS:** N33.09.14/ W89.02.67. **Background:** Located in the "Red Hills" of northeastern Mississippi near the Tombigbee National Forest, Legion was the state's fourth park. Much of the site retains the integrity of the park service's design and rustic architecture. Especially notable is the Legion Lodge built in 1937. Virtually unaltered since its construction, it is the oldest permanent facility in the state parks system and is a designated Mississippi Landmark. **Facilities:** Visitor center/lodge, RV/tent sites, primitive campground, picnic areas and shelters, trails, archery range, lakes. **CCC Company** 480 SP-4. **CCC Features:** Park roads, Legion Lodge, cabins, lakes Toppasha and Palila.

**3. LEROY PERCY STATE PARK,** 1400-A, Mississippi Highway 12, Hollandale, MS 38748; 662-827-5436; *www.mdwfp.com*. **GPS:** N33.09.65/W90.56.17. **Background:** Mississippi's oldest park preserves a landscape of artesian springs, cypress forests, live oaks, marshes, and a small lake. **Facilities:** RV/tent sites, group camp, cabins, restaurant, picnic area and shelters, trails, recreation field, Alligator Lake. **CCC Companies:** 2422 and 5467 SP-1. **CCC Features:** Park roads, cabins.

**4. PERCY QUINN STATE PARK,** 2036 Percy Quinn Drive, McComb, MS 39648; 601-684-3938; *www.mdwfp.com*. **GPS:** N31.09.65/W90.30.67. **Background:** Percy Quinn was one of the state's first parks and remains among the most popular. Notable features include Lake

Tangipahoa, Quail Hollow Golf Course, and CCC-built brick cabins. **Facilities:** Visitor center, RV/tent sites, tent-only campground, cabins, motel, group camp, picnic areas and shelters, marina, beach and bathhouse, pool, tennis courts, trails, recreation fields, golf course, Wayside Chapel. **CCC Company:** 2442V SP-9. **CCC Features:** Park roads, group pavilion, lodge, cabins, manager's residence, pump house.

**5. ROOSEVELT STATE PARK,** 2149 Highway 13 South, Morton, MS 39117; 601-732-6316; *www.mdwfp.com.* **GPS:** N32.19.18/W89.40.05. **Background:** Developed by the CCC, this park is named to honor the president that gave them meaningful work in a beautiful setting. The park is designated a Mississippi Landmark. **Facilities:** Visitor center/activity building, RV/tent sites, cabins, lodge, group camp, picnic areas and shelters, Shadow Lake, trails, tennis courts, pool, recreation field. **CCC Company:** 4444 SP-7. **CCC Features:** Park roads, cabins, group picnic pavilion, picnic shelters, utility buildings.

**6. TOMBIGBEE STATE PARK,** 264 Cabin Drive, Tupelo, MS 38804; 662-842-7669; *www.mdwfp.com.* **GPS:** N34.13.97/W88.37.80. **Background:** Nestled amid pines and hardwoods near the historic Natchez Trace, the park is a designated Mississippi Landmark. **Facilities:** Visitor center, RV/tent sites, primitive campground, group camp, picnic area and shelters, trails, recreation fields, tennis court, Lake Lee. **CCC Companies:** 402 and 482 SP-2. **CCC Features:** Park roads, cabins, lodge, manager's residence.

# National Parks

**7. VICKSBURG NATIONAL MILITARY PARK,** 3201 Clay Street, Vicksburg, MS 39183-3495; 601-636-0583; *www.nps.gov/vick.* **GPS:** N32.20.67/W90.51.17. **Background:** Established in 1899, the park commemorates and preserves the site of the battle and siege of Vicksburg by Union forces commanded by General Ulysses S. Grant. The city's surrender on July 4, 1863, gave control of the Mississippi River to Union forces. CCC enrollees assisted in archeological work, restored fortifications and monuments, preserved the site of Fort Nogales (Fort Hill), and carried out erosion control projects to preserve the park's terrain and topography. **Facilities:** Visitor center, *USS Cairo* Museum, General Pemberton's Headquarters, trails, scenic drives, historic sites and monuments. **CCC Companies:** 469 MP-1, 293 MP-2, 474 MP-3, 1430 & 2419V MP-4. **CCC Features:** Restored fortifications, drains and culverts, tree plantings for erosion control.

# North Carolina

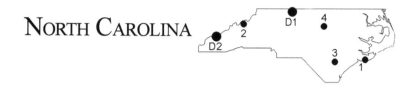

# Destination Parks

### D1. Hanging Rock State Park

*The lake constructed by the CCC has been enjoyed by many tens of thousands of visitors since the park opened. . . The CCC facilities, such as the bathhouse, have served as models for future construction projects in the park.*[6]

— Eric Nygard, Superintendent
Hanging Rock State Park

The Sauratown Mountains, named for the native Saura people who once lived here, are among the most easterly in North Carolina. With elevations between 1,700 and 2,500 feet above sea level, they rest in the shadow of the massive Blue Ridge range. The Sauratowns are known for unusual quartzite outcrops along high ridges and summits. Among the most notable high points are Moores Knob, Moores Wall, Cooks Wall, Devils Chimney, Wolf Rock, and Hanging Rock.

This is also a land of rich human history. During the American Revolution, there were skirmishes among patriots and Tories (British sympathizers), and a cave at Hanging Rock State Park is called "Torys Den" for its role as the hiding place of a kidnapped patriot leader's daughter. More recently, the area was the setting for fictional "Mayberry" in a 1960s television show starring North Carolina native Andy Griffith.

With creation of the ECW program, there was strong support for a state park in the mountains. Beginning in 1936, more than 3,000 acres of land around Hanging Rock Mountain were donated. A short time later, CCC Company 3422 SP-5 arrived to begin development. Enrollees graded and paved a road half-way up Hanging Rock Mountain

89

**Figure 41.** This CCC bathhouse building at Hanging Rock State Park is still in use.

to provide access for other projects. Over a six-year period, the workers constructed roads and bridges, picnic areas, shelters, and comfort stations. They blazed more than a dozen miles of hiking trails including a summit path, trails to Upper and Lower Cascade Falls and another to Torys Den; and dammed Cascade Creek for 12-acre Hanging Rock Lake. They went on to construct a stone bathhouse (Figure 41), beach, and diving tower, and dug the foundation for a recreation building before the camp closed in 1942. Today, much of the park retains the rustic integrity of the CCC era. The park visitor center, designed in a rustic style reminiscent of the CCC and completed in 1996, features exhibits about the work of the CCC at Hanging Rock.

***Additional Information:*** 2015 Hanging Rock Park Road, Danbury, NC 27016 (Figure 42); 336-593-8480; *www.ncparks.gov*. **GPS:** N36.41.19/W80.25.41. Facilities include visitor center, RV/tent sites, cabins, group camp, picnic areas and shelters, lake with beach and bathhouse, observation tower, trails.

**D2. GREAT SMOKY MOUNTAINS NATIONAL PARK** (see Tennessee Destination Park D1, pages 100–103 below)

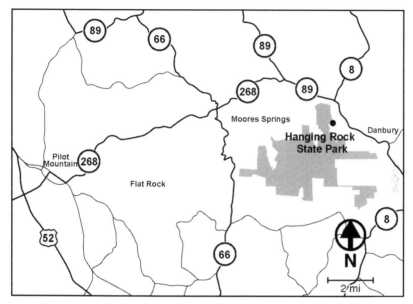

**Figure 42.** The location of Hanging Rock State Park.

# Other CCC-Related Parks

## State Parks

**1. FORT MACON STATE PARK,** 2300 East Fort Macon Road, Atlantic Beach, NC 28512; 252-726-3775; *www.ncparks.gov*. **GPS:** N34.69.80/ W76.67.83. **Background:** Work began on this coastal defense fort at the entrance to Beaufort Inlet in 1826. The fort was captured by Confederate troops in 1861 and later recaptured by Union forces. It closed in 1903 and became a state park in 1923. CCC enrollees restored the fort and built day-use facilities. The fort was reactivated during WW II and returned to use as a park in 1946. **Facilities:** Visitor center, fort, picnic areas, beach, bathhouse. **CCC Company:** 432 SP-1. **CCC Features:** Park road, restored fort, picnic area, park warden's residence.

**2. MOUNT MITCHELL STATE PARK,** 2388 State Highway 128, Burnsville, NC 28714; 828-675-4611; *www.ncparks.gov*. **GPS:** N35.75.28/ W82.27.37. **Background:** In 1835, Dr. Elisha Mitchell, a professor at the University of North Carolina, determined that this 6684-foot peak was the highest in the Black Mountains, and possibly the highest

**Figure 43.** The Maple Hill Shelter is at William B. Umstead State Park.

in the eastern United States. Dr. Mitchell fell to his death during an expedition in 1857, and the mountain was named in his memory. In 1915, it became North Carolina's first state park. **Facilities:** Visitor center and summit tower, RV/tent sites, picnic areas and shelters, trails. **CCC Companies:** 401 F-4 and F-27, 5437 and 2410 SP-2. **CCC Features:** Park road, landscaping, trails, ranger residence, CCC barracks.

**3. SINGLETARY LAKE STATE PARK,** 6707 NC 53 Highway East, Kelly, NC 28448; 910-669-2928; *www.ncparks.gov.* **GPS:** N34.58.31/ W78.44.96. **Background:** Named for Richard Singletary who received this land in a 1729 grant, the park opened as an RDA in 1939. **Facilities:** Loblolly Bay and Carolina Ipecac group camps, Singletary Lake, bathhouse, trails. **CCC Company:** 4482 P-68. **CCC Features:** Group camps, staff housing, trails.

**4. WILLIAM B. UMSTEAD STATE PARK,** 8801 Glenwood Avenue, Raleigh, NC 27612; 919-571-4170; *www.ncparks.gov.* **GPS:** N35.89.05/ W78.75.02. **Background:** In 1934, marginal land near Raleigh was purchased for the planned Crabtree Meadows RDA. CCC and WPA developed day-use areas and cabin camps at this place. Segregated until 1966, the Reedy Creek area served African-American visitors. One group camp became a rest area for British sailors during WW II.

The park was renamed for Governor William B. Umstead. **Facilities:** Visitor center and auditorium, RV/tent sites, group campground, three group cabin camps, picnic areas and shelters, trails, Big Lake. **CCC Company:** 447 NP-24. **CCC Features:** Park roads, bridges, dams and culverts, picnic areas, Maple Hill Shelter (Figure 43).

# SOUTH CAROLINA

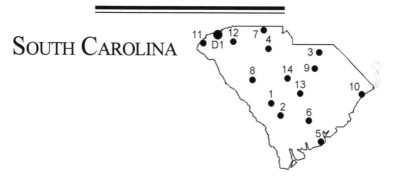

## Destination Parks

### D1. TABLE ROCK STATE PARK

*In design and craftsmanship, the lodge (at Table Rock State Park) may be one of the highpoints of achievement by the CCC in South Carolina.*[7]

— Tommy Sims
South Carolina Department of Archives and History

High in South Carolina's "Upcountry," where the Blue Ridge Escarpment rises from the Piedmont, one mountain stands out from the rest. Table Rock Mountain, with its bare granite face, rises nearly 2,000 feet above its surroundings. To the Cherokee, these rugged mountains were the "great blue hills of God," and Table Rock was his throne. At the onset of the Depression, this was a land of worn out farmlands and deep poverty surrounded by scenic beauty. Conservationists recognized that the new ECW program offered a chance to provide both economic benefits to the people and protection for natural resources.

South Carolina heartily embraced the CCC and its promise to assist states interested in developing parks. By 1934, South Carolina had identified 16 potential park sites, and local communities were eager to donate land for parks and RDAs. CCC camps were established and the state's first park, Myrtle Beach, opened in July, 1936. Several parks were under development at this time, including Table Rock State Park, a 3,083-acre preserve surrounding the imposing mountain. Two CCC crews, Companies 5465 SP-5 and 5466 SP-6, arrived in early 1936 to begin construction. Company 5466 stayed two years, while Company 5465 remained until 1941. During their time at Table Rock, the men laid out roads, excavated Pinnacle Lake, erected seven rustic cabins (three other CCC structures were later remodeled for use as cabins), built picnic shelters and a lakeside bathhouse, and constructed the log and stone Table Rock Lodge (Figure 44). They also blazed portions of the 4.1-mile-long Pinnacle Rock Trail and the 3.4-mile-long Table Rock Trail that climbs nearly 2000 feet to the summit. The latter features a CCC-built shelter and is designated a National Recreation Trail.

Today, Table Rock State Park preserves both the beauty of the Blue Ridge Mountains and the integrity of the park buildings, trails, and other features built by the CCC three-quarters of a century ago.

**Figure 44.** The restored CCC Lodge at Table Rock State Park provides a commanding view of Table Rock Mountain with an upstairs dining room and catering kitchen on the lower level.

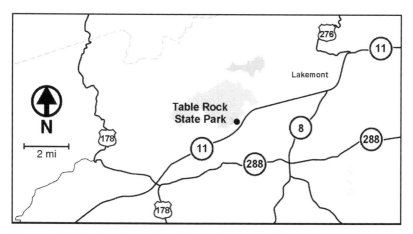

**Figure 45.** The location of Table Rock State Park.

In recognition of the lasting legacy of their work at Table Rock, the state park is listed on the National Register and is a designated South Carolina Heritage Trust Site.

***Additional Information:*** 158 E. Ellison Lane, Pickens, SC 29671 (Figure 45); 864-878-9813; *www.southcarolinaparks.com*. **GPS:** N35.01.62/W82.41.80. Facilities include Blue Ridge Mountains Visitor Center, RV/tent sites, cabins, picnic areas and shelters, Table Rock Lodge, Pinnacle Pavilion, chapel, nature center, Pinnacle Lake and Oolenoy Lake, boat ramp, pier, trails (including sections of the Foothills Trail).

# Other CCC-Related Parks

## State Parks

**1. AIKEN STATE NATURAL AREA,** 1145 State Park Road, Windsor, SC 29856; 803-649-2857; *www.southcarolinaparks.com*. **GPS:** N33.33.03/W81.28.93. **Background:** In 1934, Aiken County donated land on the South Edisto River to the State Forestry Commission for a park. Aiken preserves a landscape of swamps, bottomland hardwood forest, and sandhill pine forest. Facilities were developed by the CCC working for the Forest Service. **Facilities:** RV/tent sites, cabin, picnic areas and shelters, 4 lakes. **CCC Companies:** 1438 P-55 and 4470C S-74. **CCC Features:** Park roads, bathhouse, lakes and dams, picnic shelters, cabin, staff residence.

**2. BARNWELL STATE PARK,** 223 State Park Road, Blackville, SC 29817; 803-284-2212; *www.southcarolinaparks.com.* **GPS:** N33.19.77/ W81.18.20. **Background:** Located in the coastal plain, land for the park was acquired in 1937 and developed by Forest Service CCC enrollees. **Facilities:** RV/tent sites, cabins, group shelter, picnic areas and shelters, lake with bathhouse, trails. **CCC Company:** 4468 P-70. **CCC Features:** Picnic shelters, lake, bathhouse, roads, residence, pumphouse.

**3. CHERAW STATE PARK,** 100 State Park Road, Cheraw, SC 29520; 843-537-9656; *www.southcarolinaparks.com.* **GPS:** N34.38.48/ W79.54.26. **Background:** Cheraw State Park was created as an RDA through a 1934 land gift; the first property set aside for South Carolina's new parks system. The park's Hudsonia Flats Heritage Trust protects rare native plants. Development was carried out by CCC and WPA. **Facilities:** RV/tent sites, equestrian camp, boat-in camp, cabins, picnic areas and shelters, Forest and Juniper group camps, community building, trails, Lake Juniper, golf course. **CCC Company:** 445 NP-3/SP-1. **CCC Features:** Park roads, picnic areas and shelters, cabins, trails, staff residences, administrative buildings, stonework and spillways, Forest and Juniper group camps.

**4. CHESTER STATE PARK,** 759 State Park Drive, Chester, SC 29706; 803-385-2680; *www.southcarolinaparks.com.* **GPS:** N34.41.01/ W81.14.71. **Background:** Tucked into Piedmont hills, this park, established in 1935, features a lake and trails. **Facilities:** RV/tent sites, group camping area, picnic areas and shelters, community building, lake, trails. **CCC Company:** 4475C SP-9, some work by SP-7 from Kings Mountain. **CCC Features:** Park roads, picnic areas and shelters, community building, lake, staff residence.

**5. EDISTO BEACH STATE PARK,** 8377 State Cabin Road, Edisto Island, SC 29438; 843-869-2756; *www.southcarolinaparks.com.* **GPS:** N32.30.70/W80.18.15. **Background:** Located on Edisto Island near Charleston, the park preserves 1.5 miles of beach and acres of maritime forest. **Facilities:** RV/tent sites, picnic areas and shelters, trails, interpretive center, boat access to Big Bay Creek. **CCC Company:** 4480 SP-8. **CCC Features:** Park roads, cabins, contact station, picnic areas and shelters.

**6. GIVHANS FERRY STATE PARK,** 746 Givhans Ferry Road, Ridgeville, SC 29472; 843-873-0692; *www.southcarolinaparks.com.* **GPS:** N33.01.85/W80.23.36. **Background:** Located along the Edisto River, the park draws its name from Philip Givhan who acquired the property in

1777. Situated amid limestone bluffs, the park, originally called "Edisto State Park," was established in 1934. **Facilities:** RV/tent sites, cabins, picnic areas and shelters, trails, administration building and bathhouse, community building, section of the Edisto River Canoe and Kayak Trail. **CCC Companies:** 2413V SP-2 and 4480 SP-8. **CCC Features:** Park roads, cabins, picnic areas and shelters, administration building and bathhouse, staff residence.

**7. KINGS MOUNTAIN STATE PARK,** 1277 Park Road, Blacksburg, SC 29702; 803-222-3209; *www.southcarolinaparks.com.* **GPS:** N35.08.94/W81.20.04. **Background:** Developed as an RDA from land donated in 1934, the site is adjacent to Kings Mountain National Military Park, established in 1931 to preserve the site of a 1780 patriot victory during the Revolution (*www.nps.gov/kimo*). CCC enrollees and WPA laborers worked in both the RDA and the adjacent military park. **Facilities:** RV/tent sites, equestrian campsites, picnic areas and shelters, trails, 19th century historical farm, Camp Cherokee (YMCA) and Camp York group camps, Lake York, Lake Crawford, beach, bath house. **CCC Companies:** State Park: 4479 NP-2/SP-7; National Military Park: 4466 MP-1. **CCC Features:** Park roads, bridges, lakes York and Crawford, dams and spillways, beach, trails, Camp Cherokee and Camp York group camps.

**8. LAKE GREENWOOD STATE RECREATION AREA,** 302 State Park Road, Ninety Six, SC 29666; 864-543-3535; *www.southcarolinaparks.com.* **GPS:** N34.11.82/W81.56.96. **Background:** Created from land donated by Greenwood County in 1938, the park was developed along Lake Greenwood, then under construction. Park features include the John and Sally Self Drummond Conservation Education Conference Center with exhibits about the CCC in South Carolina's parks. **Facilities:** RV/tent sites, group camping area, picnic areas and shelters, trails, lake with boating facilities, museum and conference center. **CCC Company:** 2413 SP-11. **CCC Features:** Picnic shelters, lake retaining wall, boat house, park entrance, residence, gates to the once-segregated African-American section (now on private property).

**9. LEE STATE PARK,** 487 Loop Road, Bishopville, SC 29010; 803-428-5307; *www.southcarolinaparks.com.* **GPS:** N34.11.78/ W80.11.14. **Background:** Located in the Sandhills region, the park preserves artesian springs, hardwood forests, and a mill pond as a state natural area. The land was acquired in 1935 and developed by the Forest Service CCC workers. **Facilities:** RV/tent sites, equestrian camp and stable, cabin, picnic areas and shelters, Artesian Lake, trails. **CCC Company:** 4471 P-88. **CCC Features:** Park entrance pillars, roads, stonework, lake, cabin, picnic shelters, staff residence.

**10. MYRTLE BEACH STATE PARK,** 4401 South Kings Highway, Myrtle Beach, SC 29575; 843-238-5325; *www.southcarolinaparks.com.* **GPS:** N33.39.12/W78.55.91. **Background:** Near Myrtle Beach attractions, the park preserves a vestige of South Carolina's natural heritage. The mile-long beach is among the most popular along the Atlantic coast. Established from a land gift in 1934, this was the first South Carolina State Park opened to the public. **Facilities:** Visitor center, RV/tent sites, cabins, picnic areas and shelters, pier, beach, trails, nature center, outdoor exhibit area. **CCC Company:** 1408 SP-4. **CCC Features:** Park roads, cabins, picnic areas and shelters.

**11. OCONEE STATE PARK,** 624 State Park Road, Mountain Rest, SC 29664; 864-638-5353; *www.southcarolinaparks.com.* **GPS:** N34.51.97/W83.06.29. **Background:** Located amid a landscape of forests and ponds nestled between Station and Stump House mountains, park land was donated in 1935. Oconee was a Sumter National Forest recreation area until it was transferred to the state in 1967. **Facilities:** Visitor center/office, RV/tent sites, picnic areas and shelters, lake with beach and bathhouse, cabins, trails. **CCC Companies:** 3449 S-75 and 439 F-1. **CCC Features:** Park entrance and roads, visitor center with CCC exhibits, cabins, picnic shelters, lake, dam, stone spillway, beach, boating facilities, bathhouse, CCC pump house and waterwheel (Figure 46).

**12. PARIS MOUNTAIN STATE PARK,** 2401 State Park Road, Greenville, SC 29609; 864-244-5565; *www.southcarolinaparks.com.* **GPS:** N34.55.57/W82.21.95. **Background:** Established in 1935, the park was developed from a land gift by the City of Greenville and local businesses. **Facilities:** RV/tent sites, group camp, picnic areas and shelters, lake with beach and bathhouse, trails. **CCC Company:** 440 P-51/S-90. **CCC Features:** Park entrance, roads, bathhouse, office, staff residences, picnic shelters, gazebo, trails, Buckhorn group camp, amphitheater, stone footbridge, comfort stations.

**13. POINSETT STATE PARK,** 6660 Poinsett Park Road, Wedgefield, SC 29168; 803-494-8177; *www.southcarolinaparks.com.* **GPS:** N33.48.27/W80.32.78. **Background:** Land for the park, located between the Sandhills and coastal plain, was donated by Sumter County

**Figure 46.** This working water wheel and pumphouse, built by the CCC at Oconee State Park, is still in use.

in 1934. **Facilities:** RV/tent sites, group camping area, equestrian camp, picnic areas/shelters, trails, Old Levi Mill Lake. **CCC Companies:** 421, 2413V and 4475C SP-3. **CCC Features:** Park roads, bathhouse, picnic areas and shelters, cabins, trails, contact station, residence, restored dam, stone spillways, park entrance, recreation building, campground.

**14.** SESQUICENTENNIAL STATE PARK, 9564 Two Notch Road, Columbia, SC 29223; 803-788-2706; *www.southcarolinaparks.com*. **GPS:** N34.05.22/W80.54.47. **Background:** Land for this park near Columbia was acquired in 1937 and developed by the CCC under the Forest Service. **Facilities:** RV/tent sites, group lodge, picnic areas and shelters, lake, trails. **CCC Company:** 4469 P-71. **CCC Features:** Park entrance and roads, picnic areas and shelters, lake with dam and spillway, bathhouse, staff residences, fire tower.

# TENNESSEE

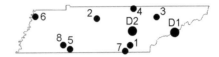

# Destination Parks

### D1. GREAT SMOKY MOUNTAINS NATIONAL PARK

*Perhaps no works of the CCC have gotten more public use than those of the Great Smoky Mountains National Park.*[8]

— James P. Jackson, Historian
Quoted in *The CCC in the Smokies*

Great Smoky Mountains National Park preserves more than a half-million acres of valleys, streams, forests, and peaks, including 6,643-foot Clingmans Dome. Spared glacial ice, the ancient range was a refuge for an astounding variety of plants and animals, including more species of trees than are found in Europe. To the Cherokee this upland area was "Shaconage" — mountains of the blue smoke. Here, the Cherokee fought removal to the west upon the Trail of Tears, allowing some of their people, and later descendants, to remain on the land. Later, Scots-Irish pioneers settled in isolated valleys of the region, such as Cades Cove.

By the 20th century, the forests were being lost to logging and naturalist Horace Kephart campaigned for their preservation, writing "Here today is the last stand of primeval American forest at its best. If saved . . . it will be a joy and a wonder to our people for all time." In 1926, through the efforts of the Great Smoky Mountains Conservation Association, President Calvin Coolidge signed legislation creating the park — if land could be purchased. After seven years, and with a $5 million gift from the Rockefeller Foundation, funds were raised and land was acquired. From 1933 to 1942, the park hosted 26 CCC companies (NP-1-3, NP-6, NP-8, NP-10-13 in Tennessee; NP-4-5, NP-7, NP-9, NP-14, NP-15-20, NP-22-23 in North Carolina).

At times, nearly 4,000 CCC men were at work in the Smokies and the Corps' accomplishments here are unsurpassed. Among the most significant are the Oconaluftee Visitor Center; Rockefeller Plaza at Newfound Gap, walls, tunnels, and overlooks on Newfound Gap and Little River roads; miles of trails including Alum Cave, Bull Head, Sweat Heifer, Sugarland, and Appalachian; original Chimneys and Smokemont picnic areas; an arched stone bridge over the Little River at Elkmont (Figure 23); restored Cable and Mingus mills (Figure 47); Mount Cammerer's White Rock tower (Figure 48); and numerous

**Figure 47.** The CCC restored historic Mingus Mill in Great Smoky Mountains National Park, North Carolina.

**Figure 48.** Mount Cammerer Fire Lookout Tower in Great Smoky Mountains National Park, Tennessee, as it appeared soon after construction. The restored tower can be viewed at the end of a two-mile side-trail off the Appalachian Trail.

administrative structures. CCC camp traces may still be seen along Kephart Prong and at Tremont. Speaking at the September 2, 1940, park dedication, President Franklin D. Roosevelt remarked "that one hundred years from now the Great Smoky National Park will still belong . . . to the people of a free nation."

***Additional Information:*** 107 Park Headquarters Road, Gatlinburg, TN 37738 (Figure 49); 865-436-1200; *www.nps.gov/grsm*. **GPS:** N35.41.14/W83.32.21. Facilities include Oconaluftee, Sugarlands, and Cades Cove visitor centers; historic sites and structures; geological features; RV/tent sites; backcountry campsites; lodging; trails and shelters; lookout towers; trails, including the Appalachian Trail; scenic byways; Fontana Lake; interpretive programs.

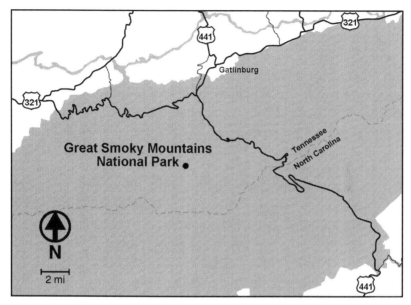

**Figure 49.** The location of Great Smoky Mountains National Park.

## D2. CUMBERLAND MOUNTAIN STATE PARK

*The outstanding feature of the work is the fact that very few of the enrollees had ever done any concrete or masonry work. In spite of these handicaps, the company feels that their dam will be a permanent and beautiful monument to the Civilian Conservation Corps.*[9]

— Official Annual Report
CCC District "C," Fourth Corps Area, 1937

Set in a wooded valley atop the Cumberland Plateau, Cumberland Mountain State Park preserves a remarkable chapter in America's New Deal history. In 1934, hundreds of bankrupted farmers, unemployed industrial workers, and miners stranded by the shutdown of the Missouri Coal and Land Company's mines, were offered a fresh start in the "Cumberland Homesteads," a 10,000-acre community created through the National Industrial Recovery Act (NIRA) and the

103

Resettlement Administration. Selected families built their own homes of prized Crab Orchard stone from standard designs. Officials saw Cumberland Homesteads as one of many "model communities," built on cooperation and mutual support. The Homesteads' centerpiece was a stone Administration Building topped by a tower filled with 50,000 gallons of water for a nearby elementary school. Today, the tower serves as the Cumberland Homesteads Museum with exhibits tracing the community's history. The museum and restored Crabtree House are open seasonally.

More than 1,700 acres of land were set aside to serve as a recreation area for Homesteads' families. Workers from CCC Company 3464 NP-16/ SP-7 arrived in 1935 to construct 16 cabins, campground, beach and bathhouse, trails and administration building (Figure 50). They also began work on a grist mill but the project was halted due to opposition from local millers. The building was subsequently altered for use as a group lodge. The men also dammed Byrds Creek, creating a 50-acre lake. Holding back the waters was the park's centerpiece — a massive, arched, stone bridge and dam, 319 feet long and

**Figure 50.** CCC lodge and mill house at Cumberland Mountain State Park is used today as a group lodge.

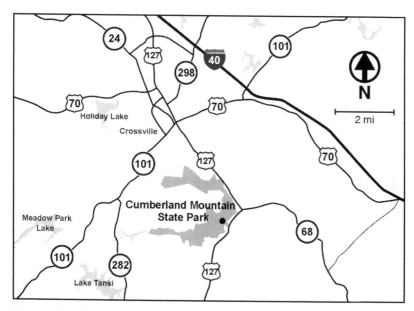

**Figure 51.** The location of Cumberland Mountain State Park.

nearly 30 feet high (Plate 6, top). It remains the single largest masonry project ever undertaken by the CCC. In an historical footnote, one of the project's supervisors was local Cumberland Plateau native Alvin C. York — America's most decorated soldier from WW I. York left Cumberland in 1940 to serve as advisor for the film *Sergeant York*, in which he was portrayed by Gary Cooper.

In 1938, the park was transferred to the Farm Security Administration and opened to the public as a state park in 1940. While Cumberland Mountain State Park has grown to include a Jack Nicklaus-designed golf course that is part of the Bear Trace, the heart of the park remains true to the design of its CCC builders.

***Additional Information:*** Route 8, Box 322, Crossville, TN 38555 (Figure 51); 931-484-6138, 888-867-2757; *www.state.tn.us/environment/parks*. **GPS:** N35.54.01/W84.59.80. Facilities include visitor center, RV/tent sites, cabins, group lodge, picnic areas and shelters, lake, bathhouse, beach, restaurant, trails, golf course. Homesteads Museum: 931-456-9663.

# Other CCC-Related Parks

## State Parks

**1. HARRISON BAY STATE PARK,** 8411 Harrison Bay Road, Harrison, TN 37341; 423-344-6214; *www.state.tn.us/environment/parks*. **GPS:** N35.10.46/W85.07.03. **Background:** Originally developed by TVA, the park is located on Chickamauga Lake. **Facilities:** RV/tent sites, group camp, picnic areas and shelters, trails, lake, marina, pool, meeting facility, restaurant, recreation fields. **CCC Company:** 4495 TVA-15. **CCC Features:** Park entrance pillars, roads, stonework, picnic shelters, boat harbor.

**2. MONTGOMERY BELL STATE PARK,** 1020 Jackson Hill Road, Burns, TN 37029; 615-797-9052; *www.state.tn.us/environment/parks*. **GPS:** N36.06.12/W87.17.01. **Background:** The site of the park was once a rich iron mining area. The park draws its name from Montgomery Bell, an early settler and later a wealthy philanthropist once called "Tennessee's Iron Master." The park was established as an RDA in 1935. **Facilities:** RV/tent sites, cabins, park inn and restaurant, golf course, picnic areas and shelters, group camps, Acorn and Woodhaven lakes, amphitheater, trails. **CCC Companies:** 4497 SP-5 and 3464 NP-15. **CCC Features:** Park roads and entrance stonework, Church Hollow Bridge, lakes Woodhaven and Acorn, Group Camp One, staff residence, office, maintenance buildings (former barracks), water tower.

**3. NORRIS DAM STATE PARK,** 125 Village Green Circle, Lake City, TN 37769; 865-426-7461; *www.state.tn.us/environment/parks*. **GPS:** N36.14.22/W84.06.73. **Background:** The park and reservoir are named for Senator George Norris of Nebraska, considered the "father" of the TVA. Norris Lake Dam was the first TVA project. **Facilities:** RV/tent sites, cabins, picnic areas and shelters, marina, trails, W. G. Lenoir Pioneer Museum (historic farmstead). **CCC Companies:** 4493 TVA-P-1 and 4495 TVA-2. **CCC Features:** Park roads, campground, amphitheater, cabins, conference center, picnic area and shelter, trails, reconstructed gristmill, staff residence, maintenance buildings, CCC camp ruins.

**4. PICKETT STATE PARK,** 4605 Pickett Park Highway, Jamestown, TN 38556; 931-879-5821; *www.state.tn.us/environment/parks*. **GPS:** N36.33.07/W84.47.79. **Background:** Set in the Cumberland Mountains, the park and surrounding forest offer unique botanical and geological features. When combined with the nearby Big South Fork National River and Recreation Area (*www.nps.gov/biso*), there are more than 100,000 acres available for outdoor recreation. The park features a wealth of CCC structures and home to the Pickett CCC Museum. **Facilities:** RV/tent sites, cabins, group camp, picnic areas and shelters, lake with beach and bathhouse, trails, stables. **CCC Companies:** 1471 P-65 and 447 SP-3. **CCC Features:** Original campground, cabins, boathouse, bathhouse, beach, trails, trail shelters, park office, CCC museum.

**5. PICKWICK LANDING STATE PARK,** Park Road, PO Box 15, Pickwick Dam, TN 38365-0015; 731-689-3129; *www.state.tn.us/environment/parks*. **GPS:** N36.03.15/W88.14.42. **Background:** Located south of Pickwick Dam on the Tennessee River, the park grew from a small TVA recreation area built by the CCC. **Facilities:** RV/tent sites, cabins, inn and conference center, picnic areas and shelters, marina, boat ramps, trails, tennis courts, recreation fields. **CCC Company:** 3459C P-11. **CCC Features:** Stone picnic shelters (Figure 52), comfort station.

**6. REELFOOT LAKE STATE PARK,** 3120 State Route 213, Tiptonville, TN 38079; 731-253-8003; *www.state.tn.us/environment/parks*. **GPS:** N36.22.05/W89.26.00. **Background:** Reelfoot Lake is a geologically fascinating landscape created by the flooding of a large cypress forest by the Mississippi River during the New Madrid earthquakes of 1811–1812. Today, stumps still rise from the waters of the lake. Land for the park, acquired in 1934, was landscaped by the CCC. **Facilities:**

**Figure 52.** This picnic shelter at Pickwick Landing State Park is an example of the structures handcrafted of locally quarried stone by CCC enrollees.

Visitor center, RV/tent sites, picnic areas and shelters, trails, water sports facilities. **CCC Company:** 1453 SP-1. **CCC Features:** Park roads, landscaping, old inn building, cabins, Round House picnic shelter.

## National Parks

**7.** CHICKAMAUGA-CHATTANOOGA NATIONAL MILITARY PARK (see Georgia Other CCC-Related Parks, page 80 above)

**8.** SHILOH NATIONAL MILITARY PARK, 1055 Pittsburg Landing Road, Shiloh, TN 38376; 731-689-5696; *www.nps.gov/shil*. **GPS:** N35.09.13/ W88.19.35. **Background:** Situated on the western bank of the Tennessee River near Savannah, this is the site of one of the fiercest battles of the Civil War, fought in April, 1862. The park was established in 1894, shortly after the preservation of sites at Chickamauga, Gettysburg, and Antietam was undertaken. The park was transferred to the NPS in 1933. Two CCC companies of African-American WW I veterans worked in the park and the adjacent National Cemetery. **Facilities:** Visitor center, cemetery, historic sites and structures, restored landscape features, picnic areas, trails, scenic roads, interpretive programs. **CCC Companies:** 2423VC NP-7 and 2425VC NP-9. **CCC Features:** Park roads, comfort stations, administrative buildings (Figure 53).

**Figure 53.** African-American CCC enrollees helped to build this Greek Revival visitor center at Shiloh National Military Park.

# Virginia

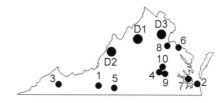

## Destination Parks

### D1. Shenandoah National Park

*My camp built the Skyline Drive, the Appalachian Trail, and laid the first underground telephone lines in Virginia. The CCC was hard work and it changed my life.*[10]

— Waverly Groves
Company NP-2, Shenandoah National Park

Few parks are more closely associated with the CCC than Shenandoah National Park. In 1925, this site in the Appalachians was identified, along with the Great Smoky Mountains and Mammoth Cave, as possible eastern national parks, provided land could be acquired and donated by the individual states. Virginia Governor Harry Byrd worked aggressively to raise funds for Shenandoah and in May, 1926, Congress authorized establishment of the park once the land was secured. The Depression brought further development to a standstill, but President Herbert Hoover authorized funds to begin construction of a "Skyline Drive" through the proposed park. Following his defeat in the 1932 election, Hoover donated land from his "Rapidan Camp" near Big Meadows for the park.

The Roosevelt administration saw Shenandoah as an ideal location near Washington for the first CCC camps. Beginning in May, 1933, enrollees from Company 334 NP-1 of "Camp George Dern," Company 350 NP-2 of "Camp Fechner," and Company 1387 NP-3 of "Camp NIRA" arrived in the park. Over the next nine years, they were joined by additional camps: NP-4, NP-26, NP-5, NP-27, NP-9, NP-10, and NP-12.

While the men did not construct the Skyline Drive, they recreated a natural landscape, from ground that had been heavily farmed and logged, by grading hillsides and planting native trees and shrubs (Figure 54). They set stone and log guard-walls, restored guest cabins at Skyland Resort (Figure 55), built administrative facilities, and constructed campgrounds, picnic areas and comfort stations. They also carved trails, including the relocated Appalachian Trail, and erected back-country shelters. Operating quarries and mills, the men produced the raw materials used in many park projects. On August 12, 1933, President Roosevelt made his first trip to a CCC camp, picnicking at Big Meadows with men from the Shenandoah and George Washington National Forest camps. The park opened in 1936 and remains a testament to President Roosevelt's vision of restoring both the land and its people.

***Additional Information:*** US 211 East, Luray, VA 22835-9036 (Figure 56); 540-999-3500; *www.nps.gov/shen*. **GPS:** N38.31.03/ W78.26.35. Facilities include Byrd Visitor Center with CCC exhibits, Dickey Ridge Visitor Center, Loft Mountain Information Center,

**Figure 54.** This 1930s image shows retaining walls and landscaping that the CCC added to complement the Skyline Drive in Shenandoah National Park.

**Figure 55.** CCC enrollees restored existing cottages at Skyland in Shenandoah National Park.

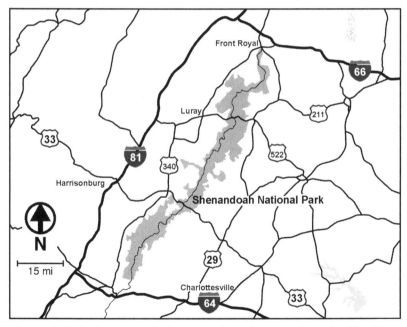

**Figure 56.** The location of Shenandoah National Park, 105 miles long, straddles the Blue Ridge of Virginia from Front Royal to Rockfish Gap.

historic sites and structures, RV/tent sites, Skyland cabins, Big Meadows Lodge, picnic areas, amphitheaters, scenic Skyline Drive, trails (including the Appalachian Trail), interpretive programs.

---

## D2. DOUTHAT STATE PARK

*The integrated site plan is the most notable overall legacy that defines the CCC's contribution to the development of Douthat State Park.*[11]

— Forrest Gladden, District VI Manager
Virginia State Parks

Tucked in the shadow of Virginia's Allegheny Highlands, Douthat State Park is an extraordinary link to the CCC's contribution to Virginia's, and the nation's, state parks. In early 1933, the Douthat Land Company — named for Robert Douthat, an 18th century landowner — donated 1,920 acres of land surrounded by the George Washington National Forest for a park. The Virginia Assembly would later provide funds for an additional 2,500 acres to create the current 4,500-acre park. The site was developed by enrollees from three CCC companies: Company 1374 SP-2 of "Camp Douthat," Company 1386 SP-3 of "Camp Malone," and Company 1373 SP-3 of "Camp Carson." Each company carried out specific tasks under the supervision of a project superintendent. Camp Douthat men constructed roads and erected cabins, Camp Carson crews built the rock spillway and dam (Figure 57) and excavated for Lake Douthat, while Camp Malone enrollees performed forestry work and carved more than forty miles of trails in the park and surrounding mountains.

Douthat is Virginia's oldest state park and served as a test site for NPS planners working on park layouts and structural designs that could be applied elsewhere. This is especially evident in the design of the park's 25 CCC-era cabins. Some were constructed with horizontal logs; while in others the logs were arranged vertically. These cabins also featured a mix of sizes and floor plans. The chosen designs became templates for use in parks across the country. In addition to

**Figure 57.** This beautiful lake and dam built by the CCC are in Douthat State Park.

the cabins, Douthat has a wealth of other CCC-era structures including Creasy and Mountaintop group lodges; Lakeview Restaurant; Lake Douthat with dam, spillway, boat docks, beach, and a two-story bathhouse; picnic areas; comfort stations; staff residences; and Discovery Center located in what was originally a barn.

Three quarters of a century later, many original structures remain as testaments to the quality of work done by the CCC. Douthat has been designated a National Historic Landmark and was recognized by *Outside Family Vacation Guide* as one of America's "ten best" state parks. It was awarded the Centennial Medallion for excellence by the American Society of Landscape Architects in 1999.

***Additional Information:*** 14239 Douthat State Park Road, Millboro, VA 24460 (Figure 58); 540-862-8100; *www.dcr.virginia.gov/ state_parks/dou.* **GPS:** N37.53.70/W79.48.10. **Facilities**: RV/tent sites, cabins, restaurant, group lodge and campground, picnic areas and shelters, lake with beach and bathhouse, Discovery Center, trails.

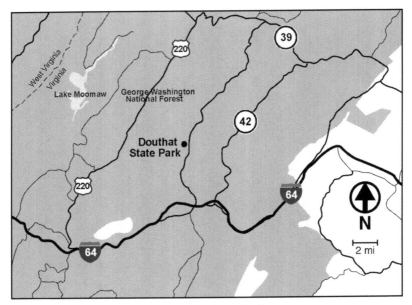

**Figure 58.** The location of Douthat State Park.

---

### D3. PRINCE WILLIAM FOREST PARK

> *A generation of unemployed young men entered the Ci-*
> *vilian Conservation Corps with a dream of adventure,*
> *few skills, little education, and a desire to work and pro-*
> *vide for their families. Prince William Forest Park is a*
> *true testament to the hard work, craftsmanship, and dedi-*
> *cation of these men.[12]*

> — Laura Cohen, Chief of Interpretation
> Prince William Forest Park

From the earliest days of the ECW program, President Roosevelt urged development of parks near urban areas as group camping destinations, primarily for working-class Americans. Through collaboration with the Resettlement Administration, more than forty RDAs were identified for construction by CCC enrollees and WPA workers under

NPS supervision. Sites selected for RDAs were often abandoned farmland or cut-over woodlands, and a location was sought near Washington, DC, to serve as a model for RDA projects nationwide. There was an added sense of urgency as many Washington-area charitable organizations were desperate to find suitable places for group camps.

In 1934, fifteen thousand acres along Chopawamsic Creek, south of the District, were identified as a potential RDA sites. The Resettlement Administration acquired the land and relocated many impoverished families. To Conrad Wirth, NPS director overseeing the RDA program, Chopawamsic was "an ideal experimental station" on which he could model future demonstration areas.

In 1935, CCC enrollees from Companies 1374 SP-22, 2349 SP-25, and 2383 SP-26/NP-16 arrived to turn the eroded landscape into a park. During the next seven years, the men constructed the most extensive group camping facilities to be found in any park (Figure 59). Crews planted thousands of trees and shrubbery, graded miles of roads, blazed trails and built five cabin camps. Each included group cabins, bathhouses, and a dining hall, craft shop, infirmary, and administration

**Figure 59.** These CCC enrollees are constructing a group camp building at Chopawamsic RDA, now called Prince William Forest Park.

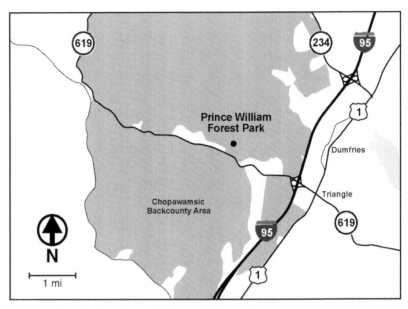

**Figure 60.** The location of Prince William Forest Park.

building. In all, the CCC erected nearly two hundred buildings, most of which remain in active use. Camps 1 through 4 are listed on the National Register of Historic Places. Additionally, workers built dams on the South Fork of Quantico Creek and Quantico Creek to create recreational lakes.

Unlike most RDAs which were later deeded to the states, Chopawamsic remained under the NPS and in 1948 was renamed Prince William Forest Park. At present, a return to the original name is under consideration. Interestingly, during WW II, the park was used by the Office of Strategic Services (OSS), predecessor to the Central Intelligence Agency (CIA), as a training ground for agents who would work behind enemy lines. Today, the park continues to fulfill its historic mission by providing group camps for organizations and cabins and a campground for individuals and families.

***Additional Information:*** 18100 Park Headquarters Road, Triangle, VA 22172 (Figure 60); 703-221-7181; *www.nps.gov/prwi*. **GPS:** N38.33.54/W77.20.96. Facilities include visitor center, RV/tent sites, cabin camps, lakes, trails, scenic drive, interpretive programs.

# Other CCC-Related Parks
## State Parks

**1. FAIRY STONE STATE PARK,** 967 Fairystone Lake Drive, Stuart, VA 24171-9588; 276-930-2424; *www.dcr.virginia.gov/state_parks*. **GPS:** N36.47.18/W80.07.75. **Background:** The largest of Virginia's six original parks, Fairy Stone was created from a gift of land in the hills of south-central Virginia by newspaper publisher Junius Fishburn. The park's name comes from the "fairy stones," small, cross-shaped stones found locally. **Facilities:** Visitor center, RV/tent sites, group camp, cabins, Fairy Stone Lodge, Fayerdale Conference Center, picnic area and shelters, trails, Fairy Stone Lake, beach, bathhouse, boating facilities. **CCC Companies:** 1260 SP-13, 1267 SP-14, and 1279 SP-15. **CCC Features:** Park roads, trails, picnic areas and shelters, cabins (Plate 6, bottom), Fairy Stone Lake and dam, beach, bathhouse, Fayerdale Conference Center, Fairy Stone Lodge.

**2. FIRST LANDING STATE PARK,** 2500 Shore Drive, Virginia Beach, VA 23451-1415; 757-412-2300; *www.dcr.virginia.gov/state_parks*. **GPS:** N36.55.06/W76.03.08. **Background:** Originally called Seashore State Park, the site was dedicated in June, 1936, as one of Virginia's original state parks. In 1997, the name was changed to "First Landing" in recognition of the site's significance in the 1607 founding of Jamestown, the first English settlement in North America. The park is both a National Natural Landmark and a National Historic Landmark. **Facilities:** RV/tent sites, picnic areas and shelter, cabins, Environmental Education Center, trails and Trail Center. **CCC Companies:** 1287 SP-7 and 1375 SP-28. **CCC Features:** Park roads, trails, picnic area, campground, cabins.

**3. HUNGRY MOTHER STATE PARK,** 2854 Park Boulevard, Marion, VA 24354-9323; 276-781-7400; *www.dcr.virginia.gov/state_parks*. **GPS:** N36.52.95/W81.31.54. **Background:** This site along Hungry Mother Creek in the Appalachian Mountains was developed by the CCC as one of Virginia's original parks. **Facilities:** Discovery Center, RV/tent sites, cabins, Hemlock Haven Conference Center, Burson Group Camp, Hungry Mother Lodge, picnic areas and shelters, Hungry Mother Lake, beach, bathhouse, trails, Hungry Mother Restaurant, amphitheater. **CCC Companies:** 1249 and 2388 SP-10, and 1252 SP-11. **CCC Features:** Park roads, picnic area, trails, lake and dam (Figure 61), bathhouse, cabins, lodge, restaurant.

**Figure 61.** This 1930s image of Hungry Mother State Park shows the lake built by the CCC.

**4. POCAHONTAS STATE PARK,** 10301 State Park Road, Chesterfield, VA 23832-6355; 804-796-4255; *www.dcr.virginia.gov/state_parks*. **GPS:** N37.37.40/W77.57.18. **Background:** Located near Richmond, this area was acquired in 1934 for an RDA. Today the park is home to the Virginia CCC Museum (Plate 7, top). **Facilities:** RV/tent sites, group camps, Heritage Center, pool, Swift Creek and Beaver lakes, trails, picnic areas, amphitheater. **CCC Companies:** 1377 NP-35 and 2386 SP-24. **CCC Features:** Park roads, trails, lakes, picnic area, group camps, CCC museum building.

**5. STAUNTON RIVER STATE PARK,** 1170 Staunton Trail, Scottsburg, VA 24589-9636; 434-572-4623; *www.dcr.virginia.gov/state_parks*. **GPS:** N36.69.61/W78.68.53. **Background:** Created in 1933 and opened in 1936, this park preserves woodlands along the Dan and Staunton rivers. **Facilities:** RV/tent sites, cabins, picnic areas and shelters, trails, nearby Kerr Reservoir. **CCC Companies:** 2381 SP-16, 1227 SP-17 and 1220 SP-18. **CCC Features:** Park roads, trails, cabins, picnic areas and shelters.

**6. WESTMORELAND STATE PARK,** 1650 State Park Road, Montross, VA 22520; 804-493-8821; *www.dcr.virginia.gov/state_parks*. **GPS:** N38.16.11/W76.86.50. **Background:** Located in Virginia's historic Northern Neck, Westmoreland State Park is near the birth homes of

George Washington and Robert E. Lee. The park, developed by the CCC and opened in 1936, was one of Virginia's six original parks. **Facilities:** Visitor center, RV/tent sites, cabins, water sports facilities, trails, picnic areas and shelters, conference center. **CCC Company:** 287 SP-19. **CCC Features:** Park roads, campground, picnic area and shelters, trails, conference center.

**National Parks**

**7.** COLONIAL NATIONAL HISTORICAL PARK, 624 Water Street, Yorktown, VA 23690; 757-898-2410; *www.nps.gov/colo.* **GPS:** N37.14.15/ W76.30.34. **Background:** Nestled between the York and James rivers just west of Chesapeake Bay, the units of the park include Jamestown, founded in 1607, and Yorktown, where General George Washington defeated Lord Cornwallis in 1781, ensuring American independence. The sites, along with Historic Williamsburg, are linked by the scenic Colonial Parkway. CCC enrollees carried out landscaping, road and trail construction, archeological excavations, historic site preservation and restoration projects, and furniture manufacturing. **Facilities:** Yorktown and Jamestown visitor centers, historic sites and structures, picnic areas, trails, scenic roads, interpretive programs. **CCC Companies:** 323C NM-1/NP-2; 325C NM-2; 352 NHP-1; 352 and 2305CV NM-4/NHP-2; 246 NHP-3; 247, 354, 1261 and 1351C NM-3/NHP-4; 2303 N-6; and 2303C NM-5/NP-21. **CCC Features:** Yorktown Battlefield: restored fortifications, trails, Wormley Pond dam, tour roads. Jamestown: excavations and restorations of historic sites (Figure 62); Colonial Parkway: landscaping (Figure 63).

**8.** FREDERICKSBURG AND SPOTSYLVANIA NATIONAL MILITARY PARK, 120 Chatham Lane, Fredericksburg, VA 22405; 540-373-6122; *www.nps.gov/frsp.* **GPS:** N38.18.42/W77.27.12. **Background:** Few areas in North America have witnessed bloodshed on the horrific scale as the Civil War battlefields at Fredericksburg, Chancellorsville, and Spotsylvania. CCC enrollees carried out park development, landscaping, and historic site restoration projects. **Facilities:** Visitor centers at Fredericksburg and Chancellorsville, historic sites and structures, picnic areas, scenic roads and trails, interpretive programs. **CCC Companies:** 362 and 1363 MP-1/NP-23; 362 MP-3/NP-11; and 282, 333, and 5434 MP-4/NP-24. **CCC Features:** Fredericksburg Visitor Center, park roads, trails, restored stone wall on Sunken Road, other preserved or restored historic sites and structures, CCC maintenance building in Chancellorsville utility area.

**Figure 62.** Assisting with archeological excavations at Jamestown in Colonial National Historical Park was an important task of the CCC enrollees.

**Figure 63.** CCC enrollees stabilizing a slope alongside Colonial Parkway, a part of Colonial National Historical Park.

**9. PETERSBURG NATIONAL BATTLEFIELD,** 1539 Hickory Hill Road, Petersburg, VA 23803; 804-732-3531; *www.nps.gov/pete.* **GPS:** N37.14.38/W77.21.25. **Background:** The units of this national military park preserve the historic sites associated with the siege of Petersburg from June, 1864, until April, 1865. **Facilities:** Eastern Front (Petersburg), City Point (Grant's headquarters), and Five Forks visitor centers; historic sites and structures; picnic areas; trails, interpretive programs. **CCC Company:** 1364 MP-2/NP(D)-3. **CCC Features:** Park roads, preserved and restored historic fortifications, picnic areas, trails, CCC operations building in park maintenance area.

**10. RICHMOND NATIONAL BATTLEFIELD PARK,** 3215 East Broad Street, Richmond, VA 23223, 804-226-1981; *www.nps.gov/rich.* **GPS:** N37.32.12/W77.26.56. **Background:** Some of the fiercest fighting of the Civil War occurred near the Confederate capital of Richmond. Sites such as Drewrys Bluff, Malvern Hill, Cold Harbor, and Fraysers Farm became symbols of the valor and brutality of war. By the 1930s, most of these sites were nearly forgotten. Establishment of the National Battlefield Park, and the work of the CCC, preserved much of the historic landscape in these areas. **Facilities:** The park unit in Richmond includes Tredegar Iron Works (now a visitor center), Maggie L. Walker National Historic Site, and the Chimborazo Medical Museum. Surrounding units include Cold Harbor visitor center, Garthright House, Gaines Mill and Watt House, Glendale/Fraysers Farm/Malvern Hill visitor center and national cemetery, Fort Harrison visitor center, and Drewrys Bluff (Fort Darling). **CCC Company:** 1375C SP-1, and side camps from Swift Creek RDA. **CCC Features:** Restored fortifications, earthworks, trails, footbridges and picnic areas notably at Fort Harrison, Fort Darling, Gaines Mill and Cold Harbor; landscaping along historic Hoke-Brady Road.

# *Northeast Region*

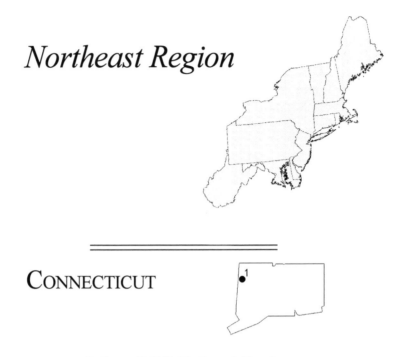

CONNECTICUT

## Other CCC-Related Parks

### State Parks

**1. MACEDONIA BROOK STATE PARK,** 159 Macedonia Brook Road, Kent, CT 06757; 860-927-3238; *www.ct.gov/dep/cwp*. **Background:** Once home to the native Scatacook people, and later a center for mining and milling industries, land for the 2,300-acre park was first donated in 1918. **Facilities:** RV/tent sites, picnic areas and shelters, trails (including the Blue Trail over Cobble Mountain). **CCC Company:** 1191 SP-1. **CCC Features:** Park roads, campground, picnic areas, trails.

# MAINE

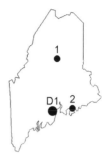

## Destination Parks

### D1. CAMDEN HILLS STATE PARK

*The 1130ᵗʰ Company . . . had successfully carved a 'park'*
*out of land that had been lumbered, burned over, and*
*neglected. It had left its mark on the community and on*
*the hundreds of enrollees that came and went during its*
*existence.*[13]

— Earlyn W. "Stubbie" Wheeler, Foreman
CCC Company 1130 SP-4

The hills overlooking Penobscot Bay have long been renowned for their views of the surrounding land and seascapes. In 1921, a stone tower was erected atop the area's 800-foot Mount Battie as a memorial to local men killed in WW I. Despite the scenic attraction, the area had been heavily logged leaving the hills barren and eroded. With the creation of the ECW program, this situation dramatically changed. In 1935, a state parks commission was established to work with NPS planners in developing a system of Maine parks. Among the properties under consideration was a large tract of marginal land known locally as "Camden Hills." The property was purchased and set aside for development as an RDA featuring picnic shelters, hiking trails, and a large group camp. In June of that year, CCC Company 1130 SP-4 arrived to begin development of the park.

In their work, the enrollees were supervised by Hans Heistad, a Norwegian-born, landscape architect who had immigrated to America in the early 1900s. For many years he worked with John Charles and Frederick Olmsted, sons of Frederick Law Olmsted. From 1935 to 1942, Heistad served as the staff architect for Camden Hills and much of the park's enduring landscape design is a tribute to his exceptional skills in the use of native plants, wood, and stone. Notable CCC features within the park include original, rough-hewn stone entrance portals and contact station (Figure 64), large group pavilion with a hearth featuring a center stone carved in the shape of Maine, and a trail leading down to the Bay. In addition, the Slope Trail on Mount Megunticook follows the course of a CCC-built ski run.

As with other RDAs, a centerpiece of Camden Hills was the group camp. The large complex, known as "Tanglewood," is now operated as a cooperative venture by Maine State Parks, the University of Maine, and the 4-H Tanglewood Camp and Learning Center. Among more than 40 CCC-built structures still in active use are the dining hall, nature center, classroom buildings, cabins and bathhouses. In addition to its summer camps and 4-H activities, Tanglewood offers public programs including courses through Road Scholar.

**Figure 64.** The stone entrance walls, check station and other structures at Camden Hills State Park are the work of the CCC.

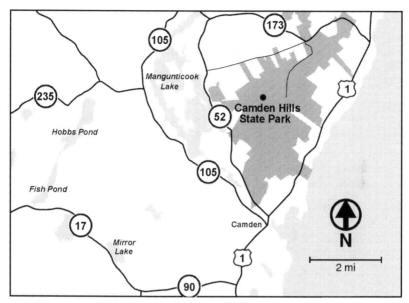

**Figure 65.** The location of Camden Hills State Park.

***Additional Information: Camden Hills State Park:*** 280 Belfast Road, Camden, ME 04843 (Figure 65); 207-236-3109, 207-236-0849 (off-season); *www.maine.gov/doc/parks*. **GPS:** N44.13.85/W69.03.03. Facilities are seasonal and include RV/tent sites, picnic areas and shelters, trails, Mount Battie Auto Road. **Tanglewood 4-H Camp:** 1 Tanglewood Road, Lincolnville, ME 04849-5213; 207-789-5868; *www.umaine.edu/tanglewood*. Facilities include group camps with educational and recreational facilities, school group and Road Scholar (formerly Elderhostel) programs.

# Other CCC-Related Parks

## State Parks

**1. BAXTER STATE PARK,** 64 Balsam Drive, Millinocket, ME 04462, 207-723-5140; *www.baxterstateparkauthority.com*. **GPS:** N45.49.07/ W68.53.13. **Background:** As the glaciers retreated nearly 12,000 years ago, woodlands of spruce and fir began to grow around Mount Katahdin, Maine's highest point. During the early part of the 20th century, conservationists led by Percival Baxter unsuccessfully urged creation of a Katahdin national park. As governor in 1923, Baxter negotiated with timber companies to create the Katahdin Park Game Preserve. After leaving office, he purchased and donated the land to the state. By 1962, Baxter had given more than 200,000 acres of land for the park. Today, Baxter State Park remains remote with only primitive roads and more than 200 miles of trails. Mount Katahdin may be best known as the northern terminus of the Appalachian Trail. **Facilities:** Information center, campgrounds, lean-to shelters, picnic areas, trails. **CCC Companies:** 130 SF-2 and 193 P-41. **CCC Features:** Park roads, trails (including sections of the Appalachian Trail), Katahdin Stream Campground with lean-to shelters.

# National Parks

**2. ACADIA NATIONAL PARK,** 109 Cottage Street, Bar Harbor, ME 04609-0177; 207-288-3338; *www.nps.gov/acad.* **GPS:** N44.23.32/ W68.12.73. **Background:** Acadia preserves more than 35,000 acres of beaches, coves, ponds, and forests surrounding Mount Desert Island's Cadillac Mountain — the highest point on the east coast of the United States. The site was originally set aside in 1913 as Sieur de Monts National Monument. It was re-designated Lafayette National Park in 1919, becoming the first national park east of the Mississippi. The name was changed to Acadia in 1929. The CCC operated three camps within the park, primarily carrying out reforestation, fire prevention, campground construction, and trail-building projects (Figure 66).

**Figure 66.** CCC workers quarrying stone for use in Acadia National Park.

**Facilities:** Visitor centers, historic structures, museums, RV/tent sites, picnic areas, trails and carriage roads (automobiles prohibited), scenic drives, lighthouses, beaches, interpretive programs. **CCC Companies:** 154 NP-1, 158 NP-2, and 193 NP-3. **CCC Features:** Park loop road, Seawall and Blackwoods campgrounds, Pine Hill and Pretty Marsh picnic areas, Great Pond, Perpendicular and other trails.

# MARYLAND AND<br>THE DISTRICT OF COLUMBIA

## Destination Parks

### D1. CHESAPEAKE AND OHIO CANAL NATIONAL HISTORICAL PARK

*We can float boats on the canal because of the C.C.C.*[14]

— Warren Kasper, Park Ranger
Chesapeake and Ohio Canal National Historical Park

As early as 1754, George Washington proposed a system of canals to make the Potomac River navigable from the Ohio River to the coast. Three decades later, the Potowmack Company was organized to build canals around the most difficult sections. In 1823, a Chesapeake and Ohio (C&O) Canal convention was held in Washington, DC, to develop plans for a commercial canal. President John Quincy Adams turned the first spade of dirt at a groundbreaking ceremony held at Little Falls west of Georgetown, in the District of Columbia, on July 4, 1828. Few in attendance understood that the recent invention of the steam locomotive marked the eventual end of the canal-building era. Nonetheless, work continued on the C&O until 1850, at which time the canal stretched 184.5 miles from Georgetown to Cumberland, Maryland. Until it was abandoned in 1924, the canal teemed with barges, most filled with coal from mines in the Appalachians.

In 1938, President Franklin Roosevelt supported the federal government's purchase of the old waterway for restoration as a park. Two CCC Companies, 325C NP-1 and 333C NP-2, were assigned to the project. The African-American enrollees that made up these companies — coming from the inner cities of Philadelphia, Baltimore, and Washington, DC — cleaned debris from the canals and cleared brush from the towpath. They also assisted WPA workers in restoring walls, locks, timber gates, dams, dozens of lock houses, and other structures (Plate 7, bottom). Work was completed on the first 22 miles of the canal, from Georgetown (located in the western part of Washington, DC) to the Great Falls of the Potomac (Figure 67), before America's entry into WW II brought the work to an end.

In 1954, Congress proposed construction of an automobile parkway along the canal route. Supreme Court Justice William O. Douglas vehemently opposed the plan, believing that the canal should be preserved as a national park where visitors might find peace, quiet, and natural beauty only a short distance from the city. To make his point, he invited journalists on a three-day hike along the towpath. Afterwards, public opinion shifted to preservation and Douglas was named president of the C&O Canal Association overseeing plans for the national historical park that opened in 1971. While Douglas is considered the "father" of the park, the men of the CCC and WPA should be remembered for their contributions to its preservation.

*Additional Information:* 1850 Dual Highway, Suite 100, Hagerstown, MD 21740-6620 (Figure 67); 301-739-4200; *www.nps.gov/choh*. **GPS:** N39.0.08/W77.14.77 (Great Falls Visitor Center). **Facilities**: Visitor centers, historic sites and structures, RV/tent sites, campgrounds, picnic areas, trails, water activities, interpretive programs and canal boat tours.

# Other CCC-Related Parks

## State Parks

**1. ELK NECK STATE PARK,** 4395 Turkey Point Road, NE, MD 21901; 410-287-5333; *www.dnr.state.md.us/publiclands*. **GPS:** N39.28.81/ W75.59.10. **Background:** Located along the banks of the Northeast and Elk rivers where they enter Chesapeake Bay, this park is a landscape of marshes, beaches, and bluffs. The historic Turkey Point Lighthouse,

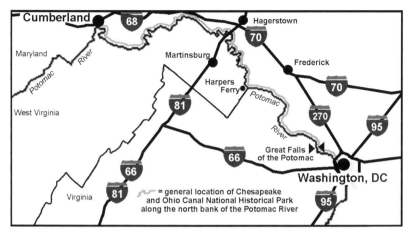

**Figure 67.** The location of the Chesapeake and Ohio Canal National Historical Park. This park includes184.5 miles of parkland in the District of Columbia, Maryland, and West Virginia.

dating from about 1833, is nearby, and the park is a part of the NPS's Chesapeake Bay Gateways Network. **Facilities:** RV/tent sites, cabins, picnic areas and shelters, water sports facilities, concession building. **CCC Company:** 1363 SP-5. **CCC Features:** Cabins.

**2. FORT FREDERICK STATE PARK,** 11100 Fort Frederick Road, Big Pool, MD 21711; 301-842-2155; *www.dnr.state.md.us/publiclands*. **GPS:** N39.37.03/W78.0.16. **Background:** Built along what was then the western frontier of colonial expansion, Fort Frederick was an important fortification during both the French and Indian War and the American Revolution. The site was purchased by the state in 1922 as one of Maryland's first state parks. Under archaeologists' supervision, CCC enrollees restored the fort's stone walls, located building foundations, and took on other projects. They also rebuilt the Washington Monument (ca. 1827) and worked at nearby Greenbrier State Park. **Facilities:** Visitor center, CCC museum (Figure 68), historic ruins, RV/tent sites, picnic areas and shelters, trails, boating facilities. **CCC Company:** 1353 SP-1. **CCC Features:** Fort Frederick: Park roads, fort reconstruction, CCC museum building, picnic area, comfort station, maintenance buildings. Greenbrier: Rebuilt Washington Monument, picnic shelter, administrative structures.

**3. HERRINGTON MANOR AND SWALLOW FALLS STATE PARKS,** 222 Herrington Lane, Oakland, MD 21550; 301-334-9180; *www.dnr.state.md.us/publiclands*. **GPS:** N39.27.28/W79.26.89. **Background:** Located within Garrett State Forest, these parks were originally forest recreation areas. Swallow Falls features the cascade of the Youghiogheny River; while Herrington Manor has a rich CCC legacy. **Facilities:** Herrington Manor: visitor center, RV/tent sites, cabins, picnic area and shelters, Herrington Manor Lake with beach and pier, trails, tennis courts. Swallow Falls: RV/tent sites, picnic areas and shelters, group camping area, amphitheater, Maryland Conservation Corps (MCC) office and nature center, trails. **CCC Companies:** Herrington Manor: 304 S-59; Swallow Falls: 307 S-54. **CCC Features:** Herrington Manor: Cabins, lake and dam, lake pavilion visitor center; Swallow Falls: MCC office building, park office (former barracks), Youghiogheny Canyon Trail.

**4. NEW GERMANY STATE PARK,** 349 Headquarters Lane, Grantsville, MD 21536; 301-895-5453; *www.dnr.state.md.us/publiclands*. **GPS:** N39.37.95/W79.07.26. **Background:** Nestled in the westernmost corner of the state, the park draws its name from a 19th century farming community settled by German immigrants. The park, adjacent to

**Figure 68.** The CCC built the museum at Fort Frederick State Park in the style of a Colonial-era cabin.

Savage River State Forest, features a lake surrounded by mixed stands of hardwoods and evergreens. **Facilities:** RV/tent sites, cabins, picnic areas, trails, New Germany Lake, nature center, recreation building. **CCC Company:** 326 S-52. **CCC Features:** Cabins, lake, and dam.

**5.** PATAPSCO VALLEY STATE PARK, 8020 Baltimore National Pike, Ellicott City, MD 21043; 410-461-5005; *www.dnr.state.md.us/ publiclands*. **GPS:** N39.17.75/W76.47.25. **Background:** Maryland's first state park was established from the donation, in 1907, of 43 acres to the state board of forestry for a "demonstration forest." Proximity to Baltimore made the site a popular destination and, by 1919, the park had grown to 1,000 acres. Today Patapsco features 32 miles of frontage along the Patapsco River. The park centerpiece is the Thomas Viaduct (ca. 1835), the longest multiple-arch stone bridge in the world. **Facilities:** RV/tent sites, picnic areas and shelters, trails, recreation fields, boating facilities. **CCC Companies:** 336 and 356 SP-2. **CCC Features:** Hilton Area shelter #201, Glen Artney Area shelters #s 10 and 66, shelter 1 fireplace (once part of a CCC camp building) and nearby CCC camp ruins, trails (especially Ridge Trail).

# National Parks

**6.** CATOCTIN MOUNTAIN PARK, 66602 Foxville Road, Thurmont, MD 21788-1598; 301-663-9330; *www.nps.gov/cato*. **GPS:** N39.36.92/W77.24.98. **Background:** In 1936, the federal government purchased lands devastated by farming, timbering, and industrial use for an RDA to be used by federal employees from Washington, DC. WPA workers laid out the park and constructed group camp facilities. Beginning in 1939, CCC enrollees carried out reforestation and other projects, including collecting old farm fence rails to be used at Gettysburg National Military Park. At the onset of WW II, one of the group camps was set aside as a retreat for President Roosevelt, who dubbed it "Shangri-la." Later, President Dwight Eisenhower renamed it "Camp David" for his grandson. Today, the camp is the official presidential retreat and is not accessible to the public. After WW II, a portion of the RDA was set aside as Cunningham Falls State Park which is available to the public. **Facilities:** Visitor center, RV/tent sites, group camps, picnic areas, trails, interpretive programs. **CCC Company:** 1374 NP-3. **CCC Features:** Park forests and meadows, landscaping, Appalachian Trail shelters west of the park.

# MASSACHUSETTS

## Destination Parks

### D1. MOUNT GREYLOCK STATE RESERVATION

> *For we'll stick right through, oh we'll stick together,*
> *So it's on to Greylock, on to Greylock*
> *On to Greylock at the break of dawn.*[15]

> — George E. O'Hearn. Superintendent
> CCC Company 107 SP-7

In the rolling Berkshire Mountains, one peak — Mount Greylock — stands above the rest. At 3,500 feet above sea level, Mount Greylock is the highest point in Massachusetts and has long been a tourist destination. On a visit to the summit in 1799, retired Yale University president Timothy Dwight proclaimed the view as "immense and of amazing grandeur."

Within a few years of Dwight's visit to the peak, New England would be the nation's industrial center and the Berkshires were being logged extensively to produce charcoal for iron furnaces, lime kilns, and glass factories. By the 1880s, Mount Greylock's eastern slope was a denuded eyesore. Recognizing that an irreplaceable resource would soon be lost, local citizens formed the Greylock Park Association to purchase 400 acres around the peak. In 1898, the property was donated to the state on the condition that the government would acquire additional land. This "Mount Greylock State Reservation" became Massachusetts' first state park.

By the turn of the 20th century, the park had grown to more than 3,000 acres and drew outdoor enthusiasts from across the Northeast. In 1928, portions of the new Appalachian Trail were blazed beneath the summit. Three years later, work began on a granite monument atop the mountain as a memorial to Massachusetts men killed in WW I. With establishment of the ECW program, development expanded dramatically. In November, 1933, CCC Company 107 SP-7 arrived in the park after six months of work in nearby Savoy State Forest. Over the next six years, enrollees would work at Mount Greylock and in the surrounding Pittsfield State Forest.

At Mount Greylock, the men laid out roads, including improvements to the primitive Summit Road; blazed trails, including sections of the Appalachian Trail; and built shelters. They carved ski trails, among them the popular Thunderbolt Trail, and carried out forest restoration work. The Corps' signature project at Mount Greylock was the construction of Bascom Lodge beneath the summit (Plate 8, top). Completed in 1937, the rustic stone and log inn offered overnight accommodations with panoramic views of the Berkshire Mountains and Hoosic River Valley. The summit road and Bascom Lodge reopened in 2009 following three years of repairs and renovations. The park visitor center, located at the base of the mountain, offers exhibits on the park's CCC legacy. The lodge and memorial are listed on the National Register of Historic Places.

***Additional Information:*** 30 Rockwell Road, Lanesborough, MA 01238 (Figure 69); 413-499-4262; *www.mass.gov/dcr/forparks.htm.* **GPS:** N42.33.13/73.12.90. **Facilities:** Visitor center, RV/tent sites, picnic areas and shelters, back-country shelters, trails (including sections of the Appalachian Trail), historic War Memorial.

# Other CCC-Related Parks

## State Parks

**1. BLUE HILLS RESERVATION,** 695 Hillside Street, Milton, MA 02186; 617-698-1802; *www.mass.gov/dcr/forparks.htm.* **GPS:** N42.72.85/ W71.05.59. **Background:** Located near Boston, Blue Hills was established in 1893. Park features include Great Blue Hill, Trailside Museum, Weather Observatory (ca. 1885), Houghtons Pond, historic Prowse Farm, and 125 miles of trails. **Facilities:** Visitor center, RV/ tent sites, picnic areas, group shelters, trails, museum, observatory and science center, pond, Appalachian Mountain Club cabins, golf

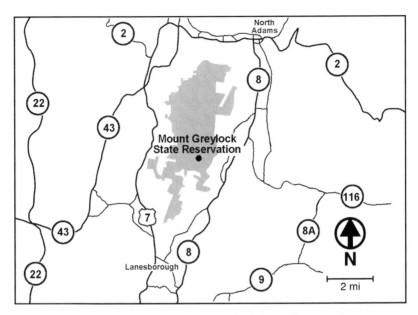

**Figure 69.** The location of Mount Greylock State Reservation.

course, ice-skating facilities, recreation fields, 19th century farm. **CCC Companies:** 394V S-1 and 1170 SP-1. **CCC Features:** Stone observation towers, trails, CCC camp ruins.

**2.** MOHAWK TRAIL and SAVOY MOUNTAIN STATE FORESTS: **Mohawk Trail,** 175 Mohawk Trail/Route 2, Charlemont, MA 01247; 413-339-5504; *www.mass.gov/dcr/forparks.htm.* **GPS:** N42.37.68/W72.52.29. **Savoy Mountain,** 260 Central Shaft Road, Florida, MA 01247; 413-663-8469; *www.mass.gov/dcr/forparks.htm.* **GPS:** N42.39.82/W73.02.72. **Background:** These adjacent forest parks feature woodlands and streams in the Hoosac Mountains. CCC enrollees carried out reforestation and facilities development. **Facilities:** RV/tent sites, group camp, cabins, picnic areas, swimming and fishing facilities. **CCC Companies: Mohawk Trail:** 371V S-51 and 1115V SP-6; **Savoy Mountain:** 111 and 107 S-70, 1171 S-94, 128 SP-12, 143 SP-21. **CCC Features:** Reforested areas; cabins; trails; shelters; dams at Bog, Burnett and Tanney Creeks (Savoy Mountain); administration buildings.

134

**3. PITTSFIELD STATE FOREST,** 1041 Cascade Street, Pittsfield, MA 01201; 413-442-8992; *www.mass.gov/dcr/forparks.htm.* **GPS:** N42.28.87/W73.18.08. **Background:** Following the glacier-carved Taconic Mountains that form part of the Massachusetts-New York border, this park was developed by the CCC in the 1930s upon worn out agricultural lands. Park features include the 165-ton Balance Rock, Taconic Crest Trail, and CCC-built ski lodge. **Facilities:** RV/tent sites, group campground, picnic areas and shelters, Berry Pond, trails, ski lodge and winter sports facilities. **CCC Company:** 127 SP-23. **CCC Features:** Berry Pond Circuit Road, earthen dams, historic ski lodge, restored CCC camp administration building with exhibits and archives.

# NEW HAMPSHIRE

## Destination Parks

### D1. BEAR BROOK STATE PARK

> *Built in 1936 with a life expectancy of a mere decade, the CCC buildings continue to serve the people of New Hampshire. In so doing, they have acquired national significance.*[16]

> — James L. Garvin
> New Hampshire Division of Historical Resources

Early in the 20th century, the villages of Allenstown and Deerfield, New Hampshire, prospered as commercial logging centers. In 1914, disaster struck when a massive forest fire consumed thousands of acres of standing trees, destroyed lumber mills, and damaged other structures. Only the heroic efforts of firefighters spared the historic Allenstown Meeting House (ca.1817). The conflagration drove local loggers out of business, leaving a scarred landscape that sat neglected for nearly two decades.

Following initiation of the ECW program, attention returned to the devastated area around Deerfield and Allenstown. The Resettlement Administration expressed interest in purchasing the land for an RDA which could be developed to offer recreational opportunities for locals and city-dwellers in Manchester and Portsmouth. The state sold nearly 7,000 acres of burned-over land and, in October 1935, CCC Company 1123 SP-2 arrived in what was then called the "Bear Brook Area." The men constructed park roads and bridges, planted thousands of trees to replace those lost, blazed trails, and dammed Bear Brook to create a pond with beach and swimming area. They erected two lakeside group camps, one at Bear Pond and the other at Spruce Pond, each featuring 24 cabins, four lodges, a dining hall, an infirmary, and utility buildings.

In October 1938, Company 1123 was replaced by Company 1107V, a crew of WW I veterans. Over the next four years, they completed unfinished work and carried out projects of their own. Among these were construction of a Day Use Area with bathhouse (Figure 70), picnic facilities, comfort station, a large group pavilion with a stone fireplace, and an adjacent "Nature Lore Building." The men also planted nearly 30,000 Norway pine seedlings in an area adjacent to the Old Allenstown Meeting House. This 50-acre plot, sponsored by the Daughters of the American Revolution, was called the "Golden Jubilee Penny Forest" for the pennies donated to purchase seedlings.

During WW II, the CCC camp and group camps served as rest areas for American and British sailors. For many years, the CCC camp buildings served as storage facilities and, remarkably, have survived as one of the most complete CCC camps still in existence. Today the buildings, listed on the National Register of Historic Places, house a snowshoe museum, family camping museum, nature center, and, fittingly, a CCC museum.

***Additional Information:*** NH Route 28, Allenstown, NH 03275 (Figure 71); 603-485-9874; *www.nhstateparks.org*. **GPS:** N43.09.26/ W71.21.98. Facilities available seasonally include RV/tent sites, group camps, picnic areas and shelters, ponds, beaches and bathhouse, fishing,

**Figure 70.** The CCC-built bathhouse at Bear Brook State Park, New Hampshire's largest state park, is still in use.

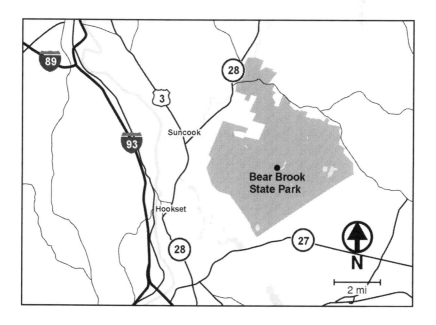

**Figure 71.** The location of Bear Brook State Park.

boat rentals, archery course, hiking/winter sports trails, museums, nature center.

## Other CCC-Related Parks

## State Parks

**1. MOOSE BROOK STATE PARK,** Route 2, Jimtown Road, Gorham, NH 03581; 603-466-3680; *www.nhstateparks.org*. **GPS:** N44.40.44/ W71.23.08. **Background:** Situated in the White Mountains near Mount Washington, the park has long been a vacation destination. The land was acquired in 1934 and the park opened in 1936. **Facilities:** RV/tent sites, picnic areas, trails, swimming area and bathhouse on Moose Brook. **CCC Companies:** 392V and 1116 SP-1. **CCC Features:** Administration building, campground, bathhouse.

# NEW JERSEY

## Destination Parks

### D1. HACKLEBARNEY AND VOORHEES STATE PARKS

*I'm getting a lot of good training. It's fascinating. And when I get out of the C.C.C., watch Me!*[17]

— Tom Davis, Enrollee
Company 1268 SP-*5*

Hacklebarney and Voorhees state parks, located only a few miles apart, owe their existence to the generosity of private citizens and their initial development to the CCC. Located near New York City,

Newark, Trenton, and Philadelphia, the two parks are oases of green amid urban development. They represent the legacy of the work done by the CCC that remains as invaluable today as when the parks were created.

Hacklebarney grew from a gift of 32 acres made by Adolphe Borie in 1924 as a memorial to his mother, Susan Borie, and to his niece Susan Patterson, a heroine of the 1912 *Titanic* disaster. Debate surrounds the park's unusual name. Some claim it is derived from a Native-American term, "hakiboni," meaning "wood fire on the ground." Others believe it comes from the region's iron-mining days when furnace foreman Barney Tracey was the target of harassment — "heckle barney." Nearby, Voorhees was developed from "Hill Acres," a 325-acre farm donated to the state in 1929 by former New Jersey Governor Foster M. Voorhees. Development of the parks began with the arrival of CCC Company 1268 SP-5 of "Camp Voorhees" on October 15, 1933. Interestingly, some of the enrollees in this company were from Idaho.

At Voorhees, the CCC enrollees built Hill Acres and State Park roads and bridges, carved trails (Figure 72), and erected three stone and wood pavilions of which Hoppock Grove shelter survives. They constructed the main entrance and maintenance buildings, including a barn that was previously part of the CCC camp, and carried out tree planting and landscaping work. At nearby Hacklebarney State Park, enrollees blazed miles of trails, constructed the main entrance and park roads, installed six miles of water lines and numerous drinking fountains, and erected an office that now houses a nature center.

Both parks have expanded through the years. Voorhees now includes 640 acres and features an exercise course and the New Jersey Astronomical Association's observatory, housed in the Edwin E. "Buzz" Aldrin Center, named for the New Jersey native and Apollo 11 astronaut. Hacklebarney has grown to include more than 900 acres, much of it preserved as a natural area providing habitat for wildlife amid hardwood forests, glacially scoured rocks, ravines, and the waters of the Black River.

***Additional Information:*** Hacklebarney: 119 Hacklebarney Road, Long Valley, NJ 07853-9525 (Figure 73); 908-638-8572; *www.njparksandforests.org.* **GPS:** N40.45.05/W74.44.10. Facilities include picnic areas, trails, Black River water activities. Voorhees:

**Figure 72.** The CCC built bridge and stone work at Voorhees State Park was constructed of locally quarried stone and milled lumber.

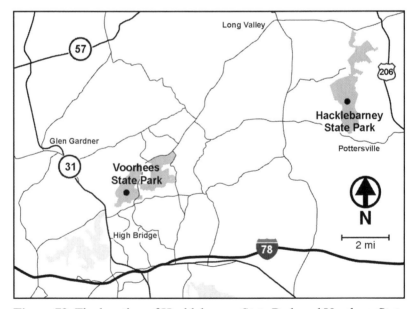

**Figure 73.** The location of Hacklebarney State Park and Voorhees State Park.

251 County Route 513, Glen Garden, NJ 08826; 908-638-8572; *www.njparksandforests.org.* **GPS:** N40.41.46/W74.53.14. Facilities include park office with CCC exhibits, RV/tent sites, picnic areas and shelters, recreation fields, trails, astronomical observatory.

# Other CCC-Related Parks

## State Parks

**1.** HIGH POINT STATE PARK, 1480 Route 23, Sussex, NJ 07461; 973-875-4800; *www.njparksandforests.org.* **GPS:** N41.18.23/W74.40.15. **Background:** This park, created in 1923 through the generosity of Colonel and Mrs. Anthony Kuser, surrounds the state's highest peak. Atop the summit is a monument to the state's war dead. The site offers views of the Pocono and Catskill mountains as well as the Wallkill River Valley. The park was designed by the Olmsted brothers and early development was carried out by the CCC. **Facilities:** RV/tent sites, group camp, cabins, picnic areas and shelters, trails (including a section of the Appalachian Trail), lakes Marcia and Sawkill. **CCC Company:** 1280 SP-8. **CCC Features:** Sawmill Lake and dam, campground, stone fireplaces, bathhouse, Monument Trail, Appalachian Trail.

**2.** PARVIN STATE PARK, 701 Almond Road, Pittsgrove, NJ 08318-3928; 856-358-8616; *www.njparksandforests.org.* **GPS:** N39.30.15/W75.07.50. **Background:** Near the Pine Barrens, the park features mixed forests, swamps, and lakes. In 1943, the closed CCC camp served successively as a summer retreat for children of displaced Japanese-Americans, a German POW camp (1944–1945), and a refugee camp for Russian Mongols (1952). **Facilities:** Visitor center, RV/tent sites, group camp, cabins, lakes, picnic areas, trails, water sports facilities. **CCC Companies:** 1225 and 2229V SP-4. **CCC Features:** Thundergust cabins, Thundergust Lake and dam, roads, trails, CCC Recreation Hall.

## National Parks

**3.** MORRISTOWN NATIONAL HISTORICAL PARK, 30 Washington Place, Morristown, NJ 07960-4299; 973-539-2016; *www.nps.gov/morr.* **GPS:** N40.45.66/W74.32.50. **Background:** Established in 1933, the site preserves four areas that served as winter encampments for the Continental Army in 1777 and 1779–1780. In the park is the Ford Mansion (General George Washington's headquarters), the site of Fort Nonsense, Jockey Hollow with reconstructed soldiers' huts, and the New Jersey

Brigade Area. CCC assisted with archeological excavations and structural stabilization (figures 74 and 75). **Facilities:** Jockey Hollow Visitor Center, Washington's Headquarters and Museum, picnic areas, trails. **CCC Company:** 241 F-1. **CCC Features:** Fort Nonsense, reconstructed soldiers' huts.

**Figure 74.** CCC workers made wood shingles at Morristown National Historical Park.

**Figure 75.** CCC men are restoring the steps outside Washington's headquarters at Morristown National Historical Park.

# NEW YORK

## Destination Parks

### D1. GILBERT LAKE STATE PARK

*Company 212, Laurens, N.Y., has been turning out cab-*
*ins along nearby Gilbert Lake almost like Henry Ford*
*builds motor cars. Plans are afoot to build 28 of them.*
*Under good leaders and foremen, this work has pro-*
*gressed rapidly despite the blizzardly weather the camp*
*has been experiencing.*[18]

— C. Larsen
*Happy Days*, March 24, 1934

Carved by glaciers, Gilbert Lake, named for settler Benjamin Gilbert, a Revolutionary War veteran, has long drawn visitors to its wooded foothills of the Catskill Mountains. For more than a century, area forests were heavily logged and, by the 1920s, local citizens urged preservation of the lake and surrounding woodlands. In 1926, Gilbert Lake State Park was established. An administration building was erected and a campground laid out before the Depression brought further work to a halt.

In 1933, the Central New York State Parks Commission requested a CCC camp for Gilbert Lake to complete the unfinished work. In May, Company 212 SP-11 arrived; their first tasks were to improve roads, plant trees and shrubs, and build dams to impound Twin Fawns and Ice Pond lakes as wildlife refuges. They followed by blazing a dozen miles of trails, laying out a picnic area, erecting stone fireplaces, and constructing maintenance buildings and park manager's residence.

In 1936, enrollees constructed five rustic cottages of hand-hewn, native log and stone. They also built picnic shelters (Figure 76) and fenced in a 12-acre "deer yard" for wildlife. Before the camp closed in 1941, the men added two dozen cottages, expanded parking and picnic facilities, enlarged the beach and built a lake-side shelter called Briggs Pavilion. They also erected a fire lookout tower that was relocated in 1947. In the summer of 1935, crews from Company 212 responded to a flood emergency that threatened the valleys of the Susquehanna and Delaware rivers. The men worked tirelessly in preparing for the flood and, afterward, in aiding the communities of Unadilla and Delhi in cleaning up the flood debris.

Today, Gilbert Lake is one of several New York state parks that preserve the rustic designs of the CCC era. Fittingly, the park is home to the New York State CCC Museum which features exhibits and artifacts chronicling the work of the Corps both in this park and across the Empire State.

***Additional Information:*** 18 CCC Road, Laurens, NY 13796 (Figure 77); 607-432-2114; *http://nysparks.state.ny.us.* GPS: N42.58.72/ W75.13.32. Facilities include visitor center/museum, RV/tent sites, cabins, picnic areas and shelters, lake with bathhouse and water activities, trails.

**Figure 76.** This large stone shelter was built by the CCC at Gilbert Lake State Park.

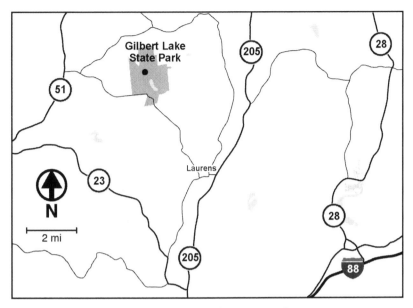

**Figure 77.** The location of Gilbert Lake State Park.

# Other CCC-Related Parks

## State Parks

**1. ALLEGANY STATE PARK,** 2373 ASP, Route 1, Salamanca, NY 14779; 716-354-9121; *www.nysparks.com*. **GPS:** N42.05.47/W78.76.43. **Background:** Covering a terrain of hardwood forests, Allegany is New York's largest state park. In 1921 it was created from a purchase of logged-over forest land and parcels donated by the Jamestown Club. Early development was carried out by CCC companies located in the Red House and Quaker areas of the park. **Facilities:** Red House Administration Building, Old Quaker Store Museum, RV/tent sites, cabins, Pitt Cottage, Fancher Cottages, three group camps, picnic areas and shelters, Quaker and Red House lakes with beaches, multi-use trails, Art Rosco Ski Touring Area. **CCC Companies:** 1288 SP-18, 27 and 56; 249 SP-19, 33 and 51; 1250 SP-50; 2205V SP-39; 2218 SP-39. **CCC Features:** Park roads including Stone Tower loop and the access road to Thunder Rocks, bridges, stone work, Quaker Area administrative building and amphitheater, Twin Springs reservoir, Red

House entrance pillars, Ryan trail cabins, Red House Beach bathhouse, Bee Hunter Trail, Red Jacket Nature Trail, Red House and Quaker area picnic shelters, abandoned Bova ski slopes, Stone Tower observation platform, CCC infirmary and headquarters area maintenance buildings.

**2. CHENANGO VALLEY STATE PARK,** 153 State Park Road, Chenango Forks, NY 13746; 607-648-5251; *www.nysparks.com.* **GPS:** N42.21.61/W75.83.65. **Background:** Stretching for more than two miles along the Chenango River, the park preserves an Ice Age landscape of lakes, bogs, hills, and alluvial till. CCC workers enlarged Chenango Lake. **Facilities:** RV/tent sites, cabins, picnic areas and shelters, nature center with CCC exhibits, trails, winter sports facilities, Lily Lake, Chenango Lake and beach, recreation building, golf course. **CCC Company:** 236C SP-13. **CCC Features:** Park roads, trails, Chenango Lake, Pine Bluff campground, comfort station.

**3. CLARENCE FAHNESTOCK STATE PARK,** 1498 Route 301, Carmel, NY 10512; 845-225-7207; *www.nysparks.com.* **GPS:** N41.44.97/W73.85.97. **Background:** In 1929, Dr. Ernest Fahnestock donated land for a park in memory of his brother, Major Clarence Fahnestock, M.D., who died in France in 1918. Later donations have greatly enlarged the park. **Facilities:** Campground, picnic areas and shelters, Lake Canopus, beach, water sports facilities, trails (including a section of the Appalachian Trail), winter park, Taconic Outdoor Education Center. **CCC Company:** 209 SP-4. **CCC Features:** Campground, comfort station, picnic areas, Lake Canopus, Stillwater Pond.

**4. LAKE TAGHKANIC STATE PARK,** 1528 Route 82, Ancram, NY 12502; 518-851-3631; *www.nysparks.com.* **GPS:** N42.09.28/W73.70.59. **Background:** Developed from land donated to the state in 1929 by Dr. McRa Livingston, the park is nestled on the shores of Lake Taghkanic between the Catskill and Adirondack mountains. **Facilities:** RV/tent sites, cabins, picnic areas and shelters, beaches, bathhouse, boat ramps, trails. **CCC Company:** 202 SP-3. **CCC Features:** East Beach, bathhouse, campground, cabins, water tower.

**5. LETCHWORTH STATE PARK,** 1 Letchworth State Park, Castile, NY 14427; 585-493-3600; *www.nysparks.com.* **GPS:** N42.64.59/W77.97.60. **Background:** In the heart of this park, the Genesee River cascades over dramatic falls in what many call the "Grand Canyon of the East." Land for the park was a bequest of William P. Letchworth who donated his Glen Iris estate in 1907. Much of the park's layout was developed by the CCC (Figure 78). **Facilities:** Visitor center, RV/tent sites, cabins, Glen Iris Inn, picnic areas and shelters, trails, pools, winter sports facilities. **CCC Companies:** 228 SP-5, 213 SP-17, 224 SP-37, and 201 SP-49. **CCC Features:** Park roads, stone walls and steps, Lower Falls stone bridge, picnic areas with tables, benches and fireplaces, shelters, cabins, reflection pond.

**6. MILLS-NORRIE STATE PARK,** Old Post Road, PO Box 893, Staatsburg, NY 12580; 845-889-4646; *www.nysparks.com.* **GPS:** N41.84.21/ W73.94.01. **Background:** Offering views of the Hudson River Valley, land for the park was given by the Norrie family in 1934. The adjacent "Staatsburg" estate, built in 1893 by Ogden and Ruth Livingston Mills, was donated later. The property includes "Dinsmore," one of the nation's oldest golf courses. **Facilities:** RV/ tent sites, cabins, picnic areas and shelters, marina, winter sports facilities, trails, Environmental Education Center. **CCC Company:** 1274 SP-32. **CCC Features:** Park entrance and road system, railroad underpass, bridges, cabins, Norrie Inn (now the Environmental Education Center), campground, comfort station, stone water tower, CCC camp buildings (maintenance facilities).

**7. ROBERT H. TREMAN STATE PARK,** 105 Enfield Falls Road, Ithaca, NY 14850; 607-273-3440; *www.nysparks.com.* **GPS:** N42.40.04/ W76.57.70. **Background:** Located near Cornell University, this park is named for Robert H. Treman, a local businessman, who donated

**Figure 78.** This quarried stone, removed by the CCC men, was used to carry out work at Letchworth State Park.

land for the park in 1920. A park centerpiece is Enfield Gorge lined with cascades including dramatic Lucifer Falls. **Facilities:** RV/tent sites, cabins, trails, picnic areas and shelters, beach. **CCC Company:** 1265 SP-6. **CCC Features:** Park roads, stone walls, steps, and bridges, picnic areas and shelters, dam on Fishkill Creek near historic mill.

**8. Watkins Glen State Park,** PO Box 304, Watkins Glen, NY 14891; 607-535-4511; *www.nysparks.com.* **GPS:** N42.36.73/W76.90.57. **Background:** Purchased by the state in 1906, the park preserves the scenic Watkins Glen Gorge. Fast moving water cascades over 19 falls as it descends more than 400 feet in less than two miles. Following a devastating flood in 1935, the CCC did extensive cleanup work and rebuilt or repaired buildings and stonework along paths in the gorge. The CCC's White Hollow Camp was converted for use as a group camp after WW II. Today, the park's Hidden Valley 4-H Camp contains many original CCC buildings. **Facilities:** RV/tent sites, picnic areas and shelters, pool, trails (including a section of the Finger Lakes Trail). **CCC Company:** 1243 SP-44. **CCC Features:** Gorge trail and stonework; Hidden Valley 4-H Camp infirmary, barracks, dining hall, paths, flag pole.

# National Park

**9. Saratoga National Historical Park,** 648 County Route 32, Stillwater, NY 12170; 518-664-9821; www.nps.gov/sara. **GPS:** N43.0.75/W73.38.89. **Background:** Set aside as a state historic preserve in 1927 and as a national historical park in 1938, the park preserves the site of two pivotal battles of the American Revolution fought in the autumn of 1777. The American victory at Saratoga, the first against a major British army, led to French intervention on the Colonies behalf and is considered one of the most significant battles in American history. One hero of the battle was General Benedict Arnold, who later betrayed the patriot cause. The battlefield was a favorite destination of President Franklin Roosevelt during visits to his family home in nearby Hyde Park, New York. CCC enrollees laid out the original tour road and re-forested areas of the battlefield that had become farm fields (Plate 8, bottom). **Facilities:** Visitor center, original and reconstructed structures, trails, tour road. **CCC Company:** 3283 MP-2. **CCC Features:** Tour road, woodlands

# PENNSYLVANIA

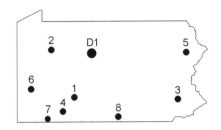

## Destination Parks

### D1. PARKER DAM STATE PARK

*The character of Parker Dam State Park owes the CCC*
*— nothing built today equals the rugged beauty of what*
*the Civilian Conservation Corps was able to do.*[19]

> — Eric Rensel, Environmental Education Specialist
> Parker Dam State Park

By the 1930s, Pennsylvania's once vast forests had been devastated from more than a century of logging to fuel America's industrial growth and expansion. With Franklin Roosevelt's election in 1932, and his commitment to restoring the nation's forest resources, Pennsylvanians prepared to undertake the work needed to reclaim their natural heritage. None was more anxious to get started than Governor Gifford Pinchot. Renowned as a conservationist, friend, and mentor to President Theodore Roosevelt, Pinchot was a trained forester whose work in developing the US Forest Service had earned him the sobriquet of "father of the national forests." Pinchot embraced the ECW program and recognized the benefits Pennsylvania would garner from the work of the CCC. Not surprisingly, Pennsylvania hosted more CCC camps than any other state except California (Figure 79).

The future Parker Dam State Park, located in the Allegheny Mountains, was a barren, eroded landscape in 1930 when the property was purchased from the Central Pennsylvania Lumber Company for $3 an acre. Following establishment of the ECW program, the first CCC enrollees, Company 309 S-73, arrived on May 6, 1933, and were followed a short time later by Companies 331 S-116, 1361 S-117,

**Figure 79.** This octagonal log building at Parker Dam was built by the CCC and restored following a tornado in 1985.

and 1380 S-118. The men laid out roads and built bridges, planted thousands of trees, excavated a 20-acre recreational lake, and constructed sandstone Parker Dam, named for William Parker who operated a logging "splash" dam on the site in the 1870s. They erected log and stone picnic pavilions beside the lake (two of these remain); built 16 cabins; and constructed the building that now houses Pennsylvania's CCC Museum. In addition, the original Camp S-73 headquarters building remains as a park educational building, and the American flag still flies from the pole set in place by the enrollees of Company 309.

In 1936, while the CCC was still at work developing the park, it was designated a Pennsylvania recreational preserve. Today, Parker Dam State Park reflects the architectural quality and integrity of the park rustic style emblematic of the New Deal era.

***Additional Information:*** 28 Fairview Road, Penfield, PA 15849 (Figure 80); 814-765-0630; *www.dcnr.state.pa.us/stateparks/parks/parkerdam.* **GPS:** N41.11.97/W78.30.27. Facilities include RV/tent sites, cabins, picnic areas and shelters, Parker Lake with beach and bathhouse, outdoor education cabin, trails, CCC Interpretive Center.

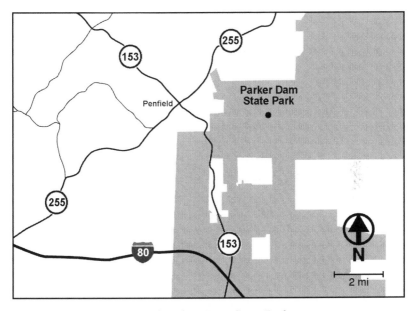

**Figure 80.** The location of Parker Dam State Park.

## Other CCC-Related Parks

## State Parks

**1. Blue Knob State Park,** 124 Park Road, Imler, PA 16655-9207; 814-276-357; *www.dcnr.state.pa.us/stateparks*. **GPS:** N40.16.00/ W78.34.99. **Background:** Like other areas in the Allegheny Mountains, the hills around Johnstown and Altoona were logged for many years. Blue Knob State Park, featuring Pennsylvania's second highest peak, was developed by the CCC and WPA as an RDA. **Facilities:** RV/tent sites, group camp, picnic areas and shelters, trails, pool, Ski Blue Knob. **CCC Company:** 2332 NP-7/SP-14. **CCC Features:** Park roads, picnic areas, trails, group camp.

**2. Cook Forest State Park,** PO Box 120, Cooksburg, PA 16217-0120; 814-744-8407; *www.dcnr.state.pa.us/stateparks*. **GPS:** N41.33.23/W79.20.87. **Background:** Nestled in an area dubbed the "Black Forest," portions of the park's old-growth woodlands are preserved as a National Natural Landmark. CCC enrollees built many park structures from blight-killed American chestnut trees. **Facilities:** Visitor center, RV/tent sites, group campground, cabins, picnic areas and shelters, trails (including section of the North Country National Scenic Trail), pool, winter activities areas, Sawmill Crafts and Performing Arts Center. **CCC Company:** 360 S-100/SP-2. **CCC Features:** Park roads and bridges, trails, picnic shelters, Indian and River Cabins, Log Cabin Inn Environmental Education Center.

**3. FRENCH CREEK STATE PARK,** 843 Park Road, Elverson, PA 19520-9523; 610-582-9680; *www.dcnr.state.pa.us/stateparks*. **GPS:** N40.19.82/W75.79.28. **Background:** Surrounded by farmlands, French Creek was developed as an RDA and preserves stands of forest land featuring Hopewell and Scotts Run lakes. The park is adjacent to Hopewell Furnace National Historic Site where CCC enrollees did some restoration work (*www.nps.gov/hofu*). **Facilities:** RV/tent sites, cabins, group camping area, group cabins, lakes, picnic areas, trails. **CCC Companies:** 2313 SP-7 and 3301V SP-17/NP-4. **CCC Features:** Park roads, trails, Hopewell Lake, Six Penny Day Use Area, group cabin camp.

**4. LAUREL HILL STATE PARK,** 1454 Laurel Hill Park Road, Somerset, PA 15501-5629; 814-445-7725; *www.dcnr.state.pa.us/stateparks*. **GPS:** N40.0.58/W79.13.47. **Background:** Located in the Allegheny Mountains, this heavily logged area was, by the early 1930s, a devastated landscape. Laurel Hill was acquired in 1935 for an RDA. Today, the park's more than 200 CCC-era structures are the most in any Pennsylvania state park. **Facilities:** RV/tent sites, group campground, camping cabins, group cabin camps, picnic areas and shelters, Laurel Hill Lodge, trails (including section of the Potomac Highlands National Scenic Trail), lake. **CCC Companies:** 2332 SP-8 and SP-15. **CCC Features:** Park roads, trails, picnic areas, Laurel Hill Lake, beach house and dam, group cabin camps.

**5. PROMISED LAND STATE PARK,** RR 1, Box 96, Greentown, PA 18426-9735; 570-676-3428; *www.dcnr.state.pa.us/stateparks*. **GPS:** N41.29.90/W75.21.40. **Background:** Once the land of the native Delaware Indians, early Euro-American settlers heavily logged the area leaving it cut-over and eroded. The state purchased the site in 1902 to preserve and restore the forest. The first park facilities were built in 1905, but much of the present park was developed by the CCC. **Facilities:** RV/tent sites, cabins, picnic areas and shelters, Promised Land and Lower Lakes, boating facilities, trails, museum, amphitheatre, historic Whittacker Lodge. **CCC Company:** S-193. **CCC Features:** Bear Wallow Cabins (Plate 9, top), Whittacker Lodge, trails.

**6. Raccoon Creek State Park,** 3000 State Route 18, Hookstown, PA 15050-9416; 724-899-2200; *www.dcnr.state.pa.us/stateparks.* **GPS:** N40.50.36/W80.42.50. **Background:** This park near Pittsburgh was developed by CCC and WPA workers as an RDA. Many CCC-era features remain intact. **Facilities:** RV/tent sites, group campground, cabins, Lakeside Lodge, group cabin camp, picnic areas and shelters, Raccoon Lake, trails, Wildflower Reserve, historic Franklin Springs. **CCC Company:** 2332 SP-6/NP-3. **CCC Features:** Park roads, trails, picnic areas and shelters, group cabin camp.

# National Parks

**7. Fort Necessity National Battlefield Park,** One Washington Parkway, Farmington, PA 15437; 724-329-5512; *www.nps.gov/fone.* **GPS:** N39.48.99/W79.35.32. **Background:** In 1754, a small stockade was erected by the British to protect the frontier from the French and their native allies. Dubbed "Fort Necessity," it was the site of George Washington's first combat — and his only surrender. The Fort Necessity site was set aside as a national memorial in 1931 and Pennsylvania purchased surrounding land for a park. Later the two were combined to create the National Battlefield. CCC developed roads, landscaping, and facilities. **Facilities:** Visitor center, reconstructed fort, picnic areas, Mount Washington Tavern, grave of General Benjamin Braddock. **CCC Companies:** 2326 and 1329 SP-12. **CCC Features:** Park roads, landscaping, picnic area and shelter.

**8. Gettysburg National Military Park,** 97 Taneytown Road, Gettysburg, PA 17325; 717-334-1124; *www.nps.gov/gett.* **GPS:** N39.49.12/W77.13.95. **Background:** Fields and hills near Gettysburg, site of one of the pivotal battles in American history, were preserved in 1895 as the country's second National Military Park. The CCC carried out landscaping work and historic restorations. Enrollees served as guides for visitors to the battle's 75th anniversary commemoration in 1938. This was the site of the only all-black CCC Company, including black military officers, working with NPS. **Facilities:** Visitor center, monuments and historic sites, reconstructed fortifications and structures, picnic areas, trails. **CCC Companies:** 385C NP-1/MP-1 and 1355C NP-2/MP-2. **CCC Features:** Park entrance stations, landscaping, road improvements, bridges, trails, comfort stations, and maintenance structures.

# RHODE ISLAND

## Other CCC-Related Parks

## State Parks

**1. BURLINGAME STATE PARK,** Route 1, Charlestown, RI 02813; 401-322-8910; *www.riparks.com/burlingastatepark.htm.* **GPS:** N41.22.82/ W71.40.59. **Background:** Located among woodlands surrounding Watchaug Pond, land for the park was set aside in 1927. It was named to honor parks commissioner Edwin Burlingame. Early development was carried out by the state's first CCC camp. **Facilities:** RV/tent sites, picnic areas and shelters, swimming, boating, fishing facilities. **CCC Company:** 141 S-51. **CCC Features:** Park roads, trails, picnic areas and shelters.

# VERMONT

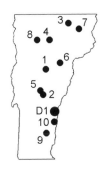

## Destination Parks

### D1. MOUNT ASCUTNEY STATE PARK

*Company 129 is located on the slopes of Mount Ascutney and looking down on the beautiful Connecticut River. It's an ace camp they tell us, going strong.*[20]

— *Happy Days,* September 8, 1934

Despite their conservative political views — Herbert Hoover won the state in the 1932 presidential election — Vermonters embraced the CCC. This happened because, as historian Townsend Anderson noted, the CCC was a social program that involved work in areas with which Vermonters were familiar — that is, "on the land and in the woods." In 1935, the state purchased 1,200 acres surrounding 3,144-foot-high Mount Ascutney in the Connecticut River Valley for a park to be developed by the Corps.

CCC Company 129 SP-1 set up camp near Back Mountain Road (hikers on the Windsor Trail may still see traces of this camp). Among their first projects was construction of a road to a site just beneath the summit and a trail to the top of the mountain. Crews also laid out a campground with stone comfort stations; erected staff residences, offices, and maintenance buildings; constructed a steel-framed fire tower (still standing) with adjacent ranger cabin; and crafted rough stone entrance gates and other distinctive architectural features (Figure 81). CCC enrollees also quarried the prized Ascutney granite used in many park structures.

**Figure 81.** CCC enrollees used Ascutney granite to build the caretaker's cottage and entrance to Mount Ascutney State Park.

At the urging of a few enthusiasts, the CCC also created Vermont's, and possibly New England's, earliest downhill ski trails, laying the foundation for an industry that would explode in popularity following WW II. Under the guidance of state forester Perry Merrill and CCC engineer Charlie Lord, the Corps carved a primitive trail (the two mile-long Bruce Trail) at Mount Mansfield in the fall of 1933. Over the next several years, CCC crews built ski trails at Killington, Mad River Glen, Okemo, and Ascutney (1938) that were among the first in New England and the United States. In his article "The Skiing Legacy of the CCC" which appeared in *Ski Magazine* in December, 1994, David Goodman noted that Merrill once proclaimed "The CCC made Vermont the Ski Capital of the East." Today, Mount Ascutney State Park remains one of numerous excellent examples of CCC work in Vermont's parks and forests. More than a dozen Vermont State Parks owe their origins to both Vermonters' love of the land and the legacy of the CCC.

*Additional Information:* 1826 Back Mountain Road, Windsor, VT 05089 (Figure 82); 802-674-2060; *www.vtstateparks.com/htm/ascutney.htm.* **GPS:** N43.26.25/W72.24.35. Facilities are seasonal and include RV/tent sites, picnic areas and shelters, trails, summit road, winter sports facilities.

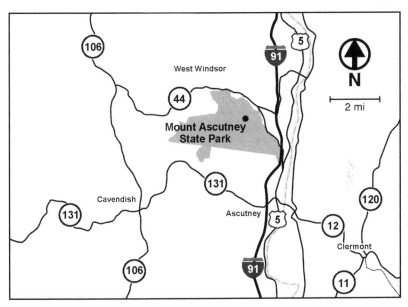

**Figure 82.** The location of Mount Ascutney State Park.

# Other CCC-Related Parks

## State Parks

**1. ALLIS STATE PARK,** 284 Allis State Park Road, Randolph, VT 05060; 802-276-3175; *www.vtstateparks.com.* **GPS:** N44.03.10/W72.37.90. **Background:** Set atop the summit of Bear Mountain, the park was created in the early 1930s from the donation of Bear Mountain Farm by owner Wallace Allis. A summit fire-tower offers views of the surrounding area. **Facilities** (seasonal): RV/tent sites, overnight shelters, picnic area, group pavilion, group camping area, trails. **CCC Company:** 198 S-58. **CCC Features:** Park roads, campground with tables and brick fireplaces, group pavilion, trails, ranger residence, fire tower.

**2. COOLIDGE STATE PARK,** 855 Coolidge State Park Road, Plymouth, VT 05056; 802-672-3612; *www.vtstateparks.com.* **GPS:** N43.33.10/ W72.41.85. **Background:** Located in the Coolidge State Forest, the park is near the village of Plymouth, birthplace of President Calvin Coolidge. CCC "Camp Coolidge" was one of the state's first CCC camps and the former president often visited with the enrollees. **Facilities:** RV/tent sites, overnight shelters, picnic areas, group picnic shelters, trails. **CCC Companies:** 1455 S-52 and 1219 and 1169 S-61. **CCC Features:** Park roads, campground, picnic areas, lean-to shelters, trails, comfort station.

**3.** CRYSTAL LAKE STATE PARK, 96 Bellwater Avenue, Barton, VT 05822; 802-525-6205; *www.vtstateparks.com.* **GPS:** N44.44.72/ W72.10.39. **Background:** Located beside the glacial lake, the park is noted for its unusual bathhouse built by the CCC. **Facilities** (seasonal): Picnic areas, cottage, bathhouse and beach. **CCC Companies:** 1160 SP-3 and SP-9. **CCC Features:** Brick and stone bathhouse and beach area.

**4.** ELMORE STATE PARK, 856 State Route 12, Lake Elmore, VT 05657; 802-888-2982; *www.vtstateparks.com.* **GPS:** N44.32.62/W72.31.77. **Background:** Established in 1936, the park is located in wooded hills between Elmore Mountain and Lake Elmore. **Facilities** (seasonal): RV/tent sites, picnic areas and shelters, group pavilion, water sports facilities, trails. **CCC Companies:** 1208 and 1209 SP-3. **CCC Features:** Bathhouse, pavilion, beach.

**5.** GIFFORD WOODS STATE PARK, 34 Gifford Woods, Killington, VT 05751; 802-775-5354; *www.vtstateparks.com.* **GPS:** N43.40.57/ W72.48.68. **Background:** Established in 1931, this park is located in the heart of Vermont's winter sports area. The Appalachian Trail goes through the park. The adjacent Gifford Woods Natural Area is a National Natural Landmark. **Facilities** (seasonal): RV/tent sites, overnight shelters, cabins, picnic area, trails. **CCC Company:** 145 S-52. **CCC Features:** Campground, picnic area, lean-tos, stone ranger residence and utility buildings.

**6.** GROTON STATE FOREST, c/o Big Deer State Park, 1467 Boulder Beach Road, Groton, VT 05046; 802-584-3822 (summer), 802-479-4280 (winter); *www.vtstateparks.com.* **GPS:** N44.17.22/W72.16.07. **Background:** Heavily logged during the 1800s and devastated by a fire in 1903, the state began purchasing land for restoration in 1919 and continued to acquire new tracts until 1975. CCC enrollees planted millions of trees in the 26,000-acre forest that is now home to six state parks, three of which — New Discovery, Kettle Pond, and Stillwater, were developed by the CCC. **Facilities** (seasonal): Groton: Picnic shelters, summit road and observation shelter, trails, Groton Nature

Center. Big Deer State Park: Campground, lean-to shelters. Boulder Beach State Park: Picnic areas and shelter, beaches on Lake Groton. New Discovery State Park: Campground, lean-to shelters, trails. Kettle Pond State Park: group camp lean-to shelters, lakeside trails. Seyon Lodge State Park: Special events facility on Noyes Pond. Stillwater State Park: Campgrounds, lean-to shelters, picnic areas. Lake Groton beach. **CCC Companies:** 146, 1162, and 1217 S-59. **CCC Features:** Groton: Osmore Ponds Shelter, Owls Head summit road and observation shelter, trails. New Discovery and Stillwater: campgrounds. Kettle Pond: group camp lean-to shelters.

**7.** MAIDSTONE STATE PARK, Route 1, Box 388, Guildhall, VT 05905; 802-676-3930; *www.vtstateparks.com.* **GPS:** N44.38.31/W71.38.60. **Background:** Located in the mountains of the Northeast Kingdom, this is Vermont's most remote park. Established in 1938, the park borders glacier-carved Maidstone Lake. **Facilities** (seasonal)**:** RV/ tent sites, overnight shelter sites, picnic areas, group lodge, beach and bathhouse, trails. **CCC Company:** 1132 P-52. **CCC Features:** Campground with tables and fireplaces, picnic shelter, group lodge.

**8.** MOUNT MANSFIELD STATE FOREST, c/o Underhill State Park, Mountain Road, Underhill Center, VT 05490; 802-899-3022; *www.vtstateparks.com.* **GPS:** N44.31.74/W72.50.57. **Background:** This 38,000-acre forest is Vermont's largest and surrounds 4,393-foot-high Mount Mansfield, the state's highest peak. The forest is home to CCC-developed Underhill and Smugglers Notch state parks, and Little River State Park surrounding CCC-built Waterbury Reservoir. The 830-acre reservoir and dam were the largest project of its kind undertaken by the CCC. **Facilities:** Mount Mansfield: Summit road, ski runs, shelters, summit hut, ski dorm, picnic areas, trails; Underhill (seasonal): Campground, picnic shelter, lean-to shelters, group camp; Smugglers Notch (seasonal): Campground, lean-to shelters, picnic area, trails (including access to the Long Trail), scenic byway; Little River (seasonal): Campground, lake and beach, recreation fields, nature museum, trails. **CCC Companies:** Mansfield, Underhill and Smugglers Notch: 1291 S-67 and 1135 S-60; Little River: 119 CE-10, 1105V CE-14, 1106V CE-11, 1107-V CE-1, 1108V CE-2, 1109V CE-3, 1110V CE-4, 1136 CE-12, and 1181 CE-16. **CCC Features:** Mount Mansfield: Ski runs, ski shelter, stone summit hut, ski dorm (CCC barracks building), picnic areas, summit road, trails; Underhill: Campground, log picnic shelter, ranger residence, trails; Smugglers Notch:

Campground, picnic areas, lean-to shelters, trails; Little River: Waterbury Lake and dam.

**9. TOWNSHEND STATE PARK,** 2755 State Forest Road, Townshend, VT 05353; 802-365-7500; *www.vtstateparks.com.* **GPS:** N43.02.46/ W72.41.56. **Background:** Surrounded by the Townshend State Forest, this park is set along the West River beneath Bald Mountain. **Facilities** (seasonal): RV/tent sites, overnight shelters, picnic areas, nature center and museum, contact station and group shelter, fire tower, trails, nearby Lake Townshend Recreation Area. **CCC Company:** 119 S-54. **CCC Features:** Park roads, bridges, contact station and group shelter, campground, picnic area, trails, fire tower.

**10. WILGUS STATE PARK,** 3985 Route 5, Ascutney, VT 05030; 802-674-5422; *www.vtstateparks.com.* **GPS:** N43.23.40/W72.24.40. **Background:** Created from land donated in 1933 by Colonel and Mrs. William Wilgus, the park is located on the Connecticut River near Mount Ascutney. **Facilities** (seasonal): RV/tent sites, overnight shelters, group camp, cabins, picnic areas and shelters, trails. **CCC Company:** 129 SP-1. **CCC Features:** Picnic areas with stone tables and fireplaces, ranger's quarters/contact station.

# WEST VIRGINIA

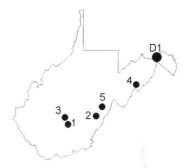

## Destination Parks

### D1. CACAPON RESORT STATE PARK

*The unique details are what amaze me most. The materials used; sandstone from the area, blacksmith made door latches and chandeliers, the hand hewn logs, wormy chestnut paneling.*[21]

— Kelly Smith, Naturalist
Cacapon Resort State Park

Described as the "Emerald of the Eastern Panhandle," Cacapon Resort State Park has been a showcase for West Virginia's parks system since it opened on July 1, 1937. While 2,300-foot-high Cacapon Mountain was the main attraction, it was the CCC that turned the dream of a park into reality. At the onset of the Great Depression, this was a landscape of worn out or abandoned farms and cut-over woodlands. The land was considered practically worthless and its sale to the government for pennies an acre was seen as a "godsend." A request was submitted for a CCC camp to develop the park and enrollees from CCC Company 1523 SP-4, "Camp Morgan," arrived in October 1934; and spent the next seven years building a park that is still considered a "jewel" of the West Virginia State Parks system.

The enrollees, mostly West Virginians, laid out roads, excavated and dammed a five-acre lake, and built a beach, boat docks, and bathhouse. They blazed 27 miles of trails, erected 18 log cabins, and constructed picnic shelters, stables, gatehouse, and superintendent's

161

residence (Figure 83). In addition, the CCC camp's recreation hall and a barracks building remain as park maintenance structures. The CCC's signature project was the Cacapon Inn, now known as the "Old Inn." This rustic, log and stone building features a dining room, kitchen, meeting rooms, stone fireplace, and 11 guest rooms. The inn offered the first overnight accommodations in a West Virginia state park and it remains popular for family reunions, retreats, and other group activities. Park facilities have expanded in recent years and now include a modern lodge with 48 guest rooms, new cabins, tennis courts, a Robert Trent Jones-designed golf course, and a nature center featuring exhibits and artifacts tracing the park's CCC legacy. A short distance away is the village of Berkeley Springs, with its historic springs and spas. In the Shawnee language, Cacapon means "medicinal waters." Certainly, the work done here by the CCC healed both the land and the men.

***Additional Information:*** 818 Cacapon Lodge Drive, Berkeley Springs, WV 25411 (Figure 84); 304-258-1022, *www.cacaponresort.com*. **GPS:** N39.28.79/W78.17.84. Facilities include modern lodge with restaurant and meeting rooms, rustic and modern cabins, group lodge (the "Old Inn"), nature center, stables, picnic areas and shelters, lake with beach and bathhouse, trails, golf course, interpretive programs.

**Figure 83.** CCC enrollees constructed the rustic style Lakeside Shelter in Cacapon Resort State Park.

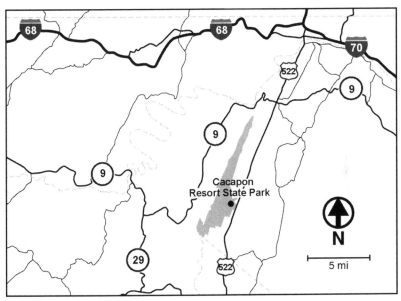

**Figure 84.** The location of Cacapon Resort State Park.

# Other CCC-Related Parks

## State Parks

**1. BABCOCK STATE PARK,** 484 Babcock State Park Road, Clifftop, WV 25831-9801; 304-438-3004; *www.wvstateparks.com.* **GPS:** N37.58.76/W80.56.80. **Background:** Located near New River Gorge National Scenic River, the park land was donated in 1934 by E. V. Babcock. Park attractions include the "Island in the Sky" Trail leading to a gorge overlook, and the Glade Creek Grist Mill assembled in 1976 of parts from old mills. **Background:** RV/tent sites, picnic areas and shelters, cabins, Boley Lake, pool, tennis courts, trails. **CCC Companies:** 532 and 1522 SP-3. **CCC Features:** Park roads, administration building, cabins, picnic areas and shelters, trails, pool, bathhouse.

**2. DROOP MOUNTAIN BATTLEFIELD STATE PARK,** WV Route 219, Hillsboro, WV 24946; 304-653-4254; *www.wvstateparks.com.* **GPS:** N38.06.72/W80.15.99. **Background:** The park preserves the site of the largest Civil War battle fought in West Virginia. Through the efforts of legislator John D. Sutton, a battle veteran, Droop Mountain

163

became the state's first park in 1927. CCC enrollees from nearby Watoga State Park developed the original facilities. The CCC milled blight-killed chestnut wood here for use at Babcock and Watoga state parks. **Facilities:** Museum, picnic areas and shelters, historic sites and structures, trails, summit lookout tower. **CCC Companies:** See Watoga State Park below. **CCC Features:** Park roads, picnic areas and shelters, trails, museum, lookout tower.

**3. HAWKS NEST STATE PARK,** PO Box 857, 177 W. Main Street, Ansted, WV 25812; 304-658-5212; *www.wvstateparks.com*. **GPS:** N38.12.10/ W81.11.82. **Background:** Set along the New River Gorge National Scenic River, the park offers exceptional hiking, rafting, and birding opportunities. Hawks Nest is noted for its CCC structures and stonework. **Facilities:** Lodge, restaurant, pool, picnic areas and shelters, trails, golf course, aerial tramway, rafting and boating (concessionaire). **CCC Company:** 1522 SP-3 (from Babcock). **CCC Features:** Picnic areas, comfort station, and Lower Park Shelter, Hawks Nest Overlook (Plate 9, bottom).

**4. LOST RIVER STATE PARK,** 321 Park Drive, Mathias, WV 26812; 304-897-5372; *www.wvstateparks.com*. **GPS:** N38.53.81/W78.54.83. **Background:** Renowned for its woodlands and waterways, this park is located at the edge of the George Washington National Forest. The CCC developed early park facilities including the stone shelter on the summit of "Cranny Crow." **Facilities:** RV/tent sites, cabins, picnic areas and shelters, pool, bathhouse, tennis courts, stables, trails. **CCC Company:** 1524 SP-2. **CCC Features:** Park roads, administration building, cabins, pool, bathhouse, trails and footbridges, Cranny Crow shelter.

**5. WATOGA STATE PARK,** Beaver Creek Road, Marlinton, WV 24954; 304-799-4087; *www.wvstateparks.com*. **GPS:** N38.06.22/W80.50.64. **Background:** Nestled in the remote Appalachian Highlands, Watoga is the state's largest park. It was developed by the CCC and remains a treasure of rustic architecture. **Facilities:** Visitor center with restaurant and store, RV/tent sites, primitive campground, picnic areas and shelters, cabins, lake with water sports facilities, pool, bathhouse, trails (including sections of the Greenbrier River Rail-Trail), arboretum, recreation building, CCC museum. **CCC Companies:** 1541V and 1535 SP-1; 1525 S-52/SP-5; and 3537 SP-7. **CCC Features:** Park roads, visitor center and restaurant, cabins, pool, bathhouse, trails, lake and dam, CCC camp buildings (used for storage).

# *North Central Region*

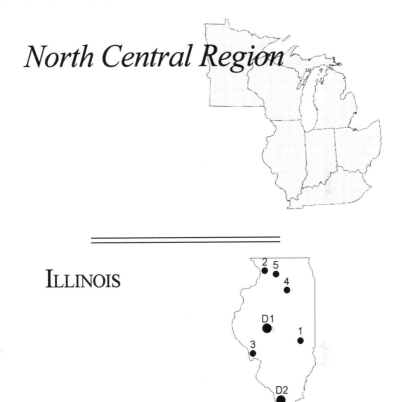

## ILLINOIS

## Destination Parks

### D1. LINCOLN'S NEW SALEM STATE HISTORIC SITE

> *The restoration is being carried out as a memorial to*
> *Abraham Lincoln . . . it consists of the restoration of*
> *cabins, mills, etc. . . . through the cooperation of the*
> *State of Illinois and local participation.*[22]
>
> — Harry Collier, Special Investigator
> 1938 Supplemental Report

Among the thousands of CCC projects around the nation, none was quite like that carried out by Company 1683 SP-45 near Petersburg, Illinois. Beginning in June, 1933, these men spent seven years reconstructing a long vanished pioneer village along the Sangamon River (Figure 85). The village was New Salem, where Abraham Lincoln spent the formative years of his adulthood and developed his lifelong reputation for honesty, integrity, perseverance, and hard work. Here, he clerked in his own store, worked as postmaster, studied law under Mentor Graham, served as Captain of volunteers during the Blackhawk War; and found his first true love, Ann Rutledge. In 1834, villagers chose him for their representative to the state legislature, beginning his career in politics. Many historians believe that the time he spent in New Salem (1831–1837) set him on a path toward the presidency and immortality.

Within a few years of Lincoln's move to the state capital in Springfield, New Salem was declining. Soon little would remain, save a few fading wagon roads and crumbling buildings. In 1917, the Old Salem League was formed to keep alive the story of Lincoln's years in New Salem. They surveyed the site to identify building locations and remnants. Once the sites were marked, a small museum was erected with plans to reconstruct some structures. The Depression brought further development to a halt — until arrival of the CCC.

Enrollees carried out three distinct projects at New Salem. They worked with state archeologists to conduct field work in preparation

**Figure 85.** The CCC built twenty-two Lincoln-era-style buildings at Lincoln's New Salem State Historic Site.

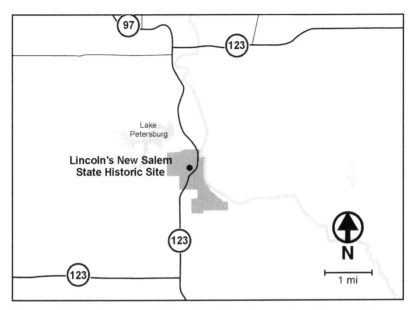

**Figure 86.** The location of Lincoln's New Salem State Historic Site.

for reconstructing houses, mills, stores, and other buildings, and were aided in this work by historical documents and oral histories from the Illinois archives. At the same time, others worked on roads, bridges and trails; installed water lines; planted trees and shrubs; and built comfort stations, picnic areas, and a restaurant. Their final project was careful reconstruction of more than two dozen historic buildings, including the Berry-Lincoln Store, grist and carding mills, Isaac Burner and Isaac Gulhier houses, Alexander and Martin Trent house, and Onstot's Cooper Shop. Today, Lincoln's New Salem State Historic Site features a visitor center and museum, auditorium, outdoor amphitheatre, campground, and picnic shelter. The park stands as testimony to the memory of young Abe Lincoln, and to the men of the CCC who brought his frontier home back to life.

***Additional Information:*** 1555 History Lane, Petersburg, IL 62675; 217-632-4000 (Figure 86); *www.lincolnsnewsalem.com*. **GPS:** N39.58.55/W89.50.51. Facilities include visitor center with museum, auditorium and gift shop, historic sites and structures, RV/tent sites, picnic areas and shelters, trails, interpretive programs and guided tours, Theater in the Park performances in the Kelso Hollow Amphitheater.

---

## D2. GIANT CITY STATE PARK

*Most young men very much enjoyed the CCC life at Giant City's camps, and felt good about being able to financially help their families.*[23]

— Kay Rippelmeyer-Tippy
*A Brief History of the Civilian Conservation Corps
at Giant City State Park*

Tucked into the Shawnee Hills of southern Illinois, Giant City State Park preserves an area of subtle beauty, unique geology, and significant human history. Native Americans occupied this area for centuries, with Woodland Period inhabitants constructing a "stone fort" from river rocks. Later, Euro-American settlers dubbed the towering, glacially carved sandstone formations the "Giant City."

The unusual rock formations have drawn tourists for more than a century (inscriptions in the rocks date to the 1840s) and efforts to set aside the land as a park began with the state's purchase of 1,000 acres in 1927. Active work on the park began in 1933 with the arrival of CCC Company 696 SP-11 of "Camp Giant City" and Company 1657 SP-41 of "Camp Stone Fort." Company 1657 remained only one year, while Company 696, joined briefly by Company 692 DSP-1, worked in the park until 1942. CCC crews laid out roads lined with rough stone walls, carved more than 15 miles of trails, erected 12 rustic cabins (newer cottages now stand on the original foundations), developed picnic areas with covered shelters, and built the stone and timber Giant City Lodge. Located at the park's highest point, the lodge was constructed from randomly placed blocks of native sandstone and massive oak beams (Plate 10). Work on the two-story structure with adjoining single-story wings began in 1935. It was dedicated on August 30, 1936, by Illinois Governor Henry Horner during a ceremony attended by more than 20,000 onlookers.

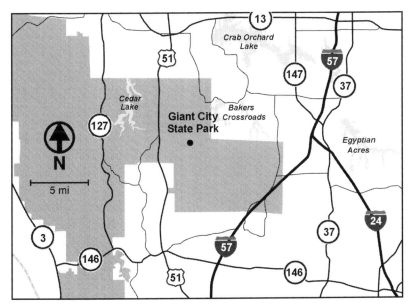

**Figure 87.** The location of Giant City State Park.

Men from Company 696 also crafted furniture for the cabins and lodge, first using California redwood and later fashioning pieces from local oak and pecan. The quality of their work was so highly regarded that the men also crafted furniture for the lodge at Pere Marquette State Park. More than three-quarters of a century after its development, Giant City State Park, now grown to more than 4,000 acres, remains one of southern Illinois' most popular destinations. The park's rock formations have been recognized as a National Natural Landmark, while the lodge is listed on the National Register of Historic Places.

***Additional Information:*** 235 Giant City Road, Makanda, IL 62598 (Figure 87); 618-457-4836; *http://dnr.state.il.us/lands/landmgt/parks/* **GPS:** N37.35.43/W89.11.55. Facilities include visitor center, RV/tent sites, lodge (dining room and meeting facilities), cabins and cottages, picnic areas and shelters, historic sites and structures, unique geological features, Fern Rock Nature Preserve, ponds and Little Grassy Lake, trails, recreation fields.

# Other CCC-Related Parks
## State Parks

**1. Fox Ridge State Park,** 18175 State Park Road, Charleston, IL 61920; 217-345-6416; *http://dnr.state.il.us/lands/landmgt/parks/.* **GPS:** N39.23.81/W88.06.66. **Background:** Development of this park was attributable to the CCC and to the citizens of nearby Charleston, who helped purchase the land. The wooded park has V-shaped valleys with streams meandering to the Embarras River. **Facilities:** RV/tent sites, cabins, picnic areas and shelters, pavilion, water activities. **CCC Companies:** 2657V SP-52 and SP-58 and 2681 SP-58. **CCC Features:** Picnic shelters, Biological Studies Research Laboratory and Lake, superintendent's residence, workshop, trails, bridges.

**2. Mississippi Palisades State Park,** 16372A State Route 84 North, Savanna, IL 61704; 815-273-2731; *http://dnr.state.il.us/lands/landmgt/parks/.* **GPS:** N42.08.69/W90.10.02. **Background:** The "Driftless Area" along the Mississippi River, bypassed during the last glacial period, features remnants of palisade bluffs and ravines. A portion of the park is a National Natural Landmark. **Facilities:** RV/tent sites, picnic areas, water activities on the river, trails. **CCC Companies:** 627 SP-10, side camps from 1678V SP-31 and 2657V SP-57. **CCC Features:** Pump houses, spring access, picnic areas and stone shelter, stone pedestrian bridge, trails.

**3. Pere Marquette State Park,** 13112 Visitor Center Lane, Grafton, IL 62037; 618-786-3323; *http://dnr.state.il.us/lands/landmgt/parks/.* **GPS:** N38.58.35/W90.32.53. **Background:** Situated on the Illinois River, this park is named in honor of the French missionary, Fr. Jacques Marquette, who traveled through the area with Louis Jolliet in 1673. **Facilities:** Visitor center, Pere Marquette Lodge, conference center, cabins, indoor pool and sauna, RV/tent sites, picnic areas, trails, hunting reserves, fishing and boating facilities, youth camp, group camps. **CCC Companies:** 1646V SP-9 and 2646 SP-61. **CCC Features:** Historic lodge, cabins, group camp cabins, dining halls, pools, trails, lookout shelters.

**4. Starved Rock State Park,** IL Route 178, Utica, IL 61373; 815-667-4726; *http://dnr.state.il.us/lands/landmgt/parks/.* **GPS:** N41.19.22/W88.59.93. **Background:** Situated amid bluffs above the Illinois River, the park is renowned for its rock formations and hardwood forests. The park's name is drawn from a war between rival Potawatomi and Illiniwek Indians three centuries ago. **Facilities:** Visitor center, historic Starved Rock Lodge, indoor pool and sauna, RV/tent sites, picnic areas, trails, fishing and boating facilities, youth camp. **CCC Companies:** 614 SP-8 and 1609 SP-23. **CCC Features:** Lodge, cabins, trails, picnic areas.

**5. WHITE PINES FOREST STATE PARK,** 6712 West Pines Road, Mount Morris, IL 61054; 815-946-3717. **GPS:** N41.59.39/W89.27.94. **Background:** Set aside in 1927, this park preserves the last surviving stand of naturally occurring white pines in Illinois, the most southerly occurrence in the nation. The park borders the historic old Chicago-Iowa Trail, a 19th century western migration route. **Facilities:** Lodge, cabins, RV/tent sites, picnic area, trails. **CCC Company:** 1678V SP-57. **CCC Features:** Historic White Pines Inn and Restaurant, log cabins, picnic areas, trails.

# INDIANA

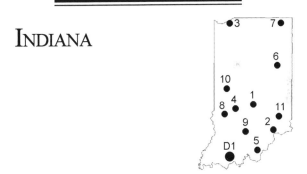

# Destination Parks

## D1. LINCOLN BOYHOOD NATIONAL MEMORIAL AND LINCOLN STATE PARK

*Khaki clad youths stood with bared heads at the grave of Nancy Hanks Lincoln today at a brief ceremony commemorating the birth of her son, Abraham Lincoln.*[24]

— "CCC Youths Bare Heads at Nancy Lincoln's Grave"
*The Indianapolis News,* February 12, 1934

The story of these two parks begins in 1816 when Thomas Lincoln brought his family to the Indiana frontier. Abe, only 7 years old, helped his father build a crude cabin in these woods. Two years later Abe helped craft a simple coffin for his mother, Nancy Hanks, following her death from "milk sickness." In 1828, Abe's sister, Sarah, died in childbirth and was buried in the nearby Pigeon Creek Baptist Church cemetery. When asked to describe his Indiana youth, Lincoln responded simply, "Here, I grew up."

In 1879, Nancy Hanks Lincoln's unmarked grave was identified and Spencer County purchased a half-acre of land around it. Additional land was acquired and the site was fenced in 1900. A stone memorial was added in 1917 and the Nancy Hanks Lincoln Burial Ground was dedicated in 1925. At the urging of Indiana parks director Richard Lieber, the Indiana Lincoln Union (ILU) was established in 1926 to raise funds for a larger memorial park to be designed by Frederick Law Olmsted, Jr.

In 1933, Lincoln State Park was established as an ECW project to provide recreational facilities for visitors. After setting up camp, CCC Company 1543V SP-2 removed unwanted structures, planted trees, developed a campground, built picnic shelters, excavated Lake Lincoln, built a ranger cabin, and carved a road to the Pigeon Creek church (Figure 88). Crews also assisted in archeological excavations around the Lincoln cabin site. During this work, the men unearthed

**Figure 88.** This lakeside cabin in Lincoln State Park is a quiet retreat.

what was believed to have been hearth and foundation stones from the original structure. The decision was made to not reconstruct the cabin, but to reproduce the artifacts in a bronze casting that was dedicated during a ceremony in 1935 (Plate 11, top). In 1940, CCC Company 553 SP-15 arrived to work with the WPA on landscaping and the placement of signs and markers. At the same time, NPS architect Richard Bishop was commissioned to design a memorial building in harmony with the park's landscape and historical significance. In 1944, Indiana sculptor E. H. Daniels added five commemorative exterior limestone panels depicting stages of Abraham Lincoln's life.

President John F. Kennedy signed legislation in 1962 transferring 115 acres of the memorial park to the NPS for the Lincoln Boyhood National Memorial. Today, the two parks commemorate the frontier youth of Abraham Lincoln and the legacy of the men of the CCC. The Lincoln Bicentennial Plaza opened in the state park in 2009 and the park's amphitheater hosts the outdoor drama *Lincoln* each summer.

***Additional Information:*** Lincoln Boyhood National Memorial: 2916 E. South Street, Lincoln City, IN 47552 (Figure 89); 812-937-4541; *www.nps.gov/libo*. **GPS:** N38.06.70/W86.59.89. Facilities include visitor center, historic sites and structures, picnic area, trails, interpretive programs. Lincoln State Park: State Highway 162, PO Box 216, Lincoln City, IN 47552; 812-937-4710; *www.in.gov/dnr/parklake*. **GPS:** N38.06.70/W86.59.89. Facilities include RV/tent sites, cabins, group camp, picnic areas and shelters, historic sites and structures, trails, Lake Lincoln water activities, amphitheater, interpretive programs.

# Other CCC-Related Parks
## State Parks

1. BROWN COUNTY STATE PARK, 1405 State Road 46 West, Nashville, IN 47448; 812-988-6406; *www.in.gov/dnr/parklake*. **GPS:** N39.11.56/W86.12.99. **Background:** Indiana's largest state park opened as a game preserve in 1929. Additional land was acquired and consolidated into the park in 1941. The CCC developed many park structures and recreational features. **Facilities:** RV/tent sites, horse camp, Abe Martin Lodge, cabins, picnic areas and shelters, Ogle and Strahl lakes, nature center, pool, tennis courts, recreation fields, barn,

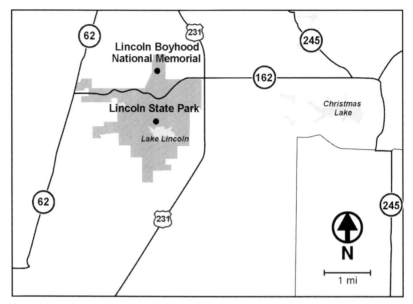

**Figure 89.** The location of Lincoln Boyhood National Memorial and Lincoln State Park.

amphitheaters, lookout tower, trails, Ogle Hollow Nature Preserve. **CCC Companies:** 1557V SP-9 and 1561V S-53A. **CCC Features:** Park roads and gatehouses, picnic areas and shelters, cook-ovens, west lookout tower, trails, saddle barn, administrative structures.

**2. CLIFTY FALLS STATE PARK,** 2221 Clifty Drive, Madison, IN 47250; 812-273-8885; *www.in.gov/dnr/parklake*. **GPS:** N38.45.59/ W85.24.99. **Background:** Established in 1920, the park is located where Clifty Creek flows through canyons and over cascades into the Ohio River. **Facilities:** RV/tent sites, Clifty Falls Inn, restaurant, conference center, picnic areas and shelters, pool, amphitheater, tennis courts, trails. **CCC Companies:** 540 and 1597 SP-6. **CCC Features:** Park roads and gatehouses, picnic areas and shelters, trails.

**3. INDIANA DUNES STATE PARK,** 1600 North 25 East, Chesterton, IN 46304; 219-926-1952; *www.in.gov/dnr/parklake*. **GPS:** N41.39.39/ W87.03.76. **Background:** Botanist Dr. Henry Cowles described this site along Lake Michigan as a "common meeting ground of trees and wildflowers from all directions." Initial consideration was given to setting aside the area as a national park, but Colonel Richard Lieber, founding director of Indiana's state parks system, urged establishment of a state park that opened in 1926. Forty years later additional lands would be set aside to create the surrounding Indiana Dunes National Lakeshore *www.nps.gov/indu*. **Facilities:** RV/tent sites, youth camp, trails, picnic areas and shelters, beach pavilion, nature center. **CCC Companies:** 563 and 1563 DSP-1/SP-5. **CCC Features:** Park roads, trails, picnic areas.

**4. McCormicks Creek State Park,** 250 McCormicks Creek Park Road, Spencer, IN 47460; 812-829-2235; *www.in.gov/dnr/parklake*. **GPS:** N39.17.07/W86.43.60. **Background:** In 1888, Dr. Frederick Denkewalter purchased this property of canyons, streams, and waterfalls and built a sanitarium on the site. After his death, the land was sold to the state and, on July 4, 1916, it became Indiana's first state park. In the 1920s, the sanitarium was remodeled as the Canyon Inn. The inn has been remodeled many times and only foundations remain from the original structure. **Facilities:** RV/tent sites, cabins, group camp, youth camp, nature center, picnic areas and shelters, trails, saddle barn, Canyon Inn, restaurant, conference facilities, Wolf Cave, **CCC Company:** 589 SP-4. **CCC Features:** Park roads and gatehouses, picnic shelters, arched stone bridge, fire tower, CCC Recreation Hall (converted to nature center by WPA).

**5. O'Bannon Woods State Park,** 7240 Old Forest Road, Corydon, IN 47112; 812-738-8232; *www.in.gov/dnr/parklake*. **GPS:** N38.11.97/ W86.15.65. **Background:** This area is renowned for its native chert once prized by natives, and for its karst topography and abundant caves. Areas along the Ohio River were settled in the 1800s and were worn out and eroded farmlands when the site was set aside as the Harrison-Crawford State Forest in 1932. CCC performed reforestation and restoration work. Wyandotte Woods State Recreation Area was added in the 1960s, and the park was renamed for the pioneer family of late Governor Frank O'Bannon in 2004. **Facilities:** RV/tent sites, group camp, picnic areas and shelters, restored 1830s farmstead, nature center, trails, Post Oak Cedar Nature Preserve. **CCC Company:** 517C S-86. **CCC Features:** Reforested landscape, Shelter No. 2, manager's residence, trails, stone walls.

**6. Ouabache State Park,** 4930 E. State Road 201, Bluffton, IN 46714; 260-824-0926; *www.in.gov/dnr/parklake*. **GPS:** N40.43.22/ W85.05.79. **Background:** Long the home of the native Miami Indians, this land along the Wabash River was settled in the mid-19th century. In 1930, the eroded land was acquired for Wells County State Forest and Game Preserve. The site became a state park in 1962. Reforestation and development work was carried out by CCC and WPA. **Facilities:** RV/tent sites, youth campground, picnic areas and shelters, group lodge, Kunkel Lake, pool, recreation field, tennis courts, trails. **CCC Company:** 1592 S-93. **CCC Features:** Park roads, landscape rehabilitation, picnic areas and shelters, trails, Kunkel Lake.

**7. POKAGON STATE PARK,** 450 Lane 100 Lake James, Angola, IN 46703; 260-833-2012; *www.in.gov/dnr/parklake*. **GPS:** N41.42.50/ W85.01.34. **Background:** This area of glacial lakes, marshes, fens, and woodlands was donated to the state for a park in 1925 and the Potawatomi Inn opened in 1928. **Facilities:** RV/tent sites, group camp, youth camp, nature center, Potawatomi Inn with restaurant and conference facilities, picnic areas and shelters, trails, saddle barn, toboggan run in winter, nearby Lake James and Snow Lake. **CCC Company:** 556 SP-7. **CCC Features:** Park roads, gate house, reforested areas, campground, reforested areas, beach, beach house, CCC shelter, Spring Shelter, group camp dining hall, saddle barn, administration building.

**8. SHAKAMAK STATE PARK,** 6265 West State Road 48, Jasonville, IN 47438; 812-665-2158; *www.in.gov/dnr/parklake*. **GPS:** N39.10.57/ W87.14.08. **Background:** The woodlands, man-made lakes, and abandoned strip mines along the Shakamak River were donated to the state in 1929 as an experiment in restoration of heavily-used lands for recreation. The name, from the Kickapoo language, means "river of the long fish (eels)." **Facilities:** RV/tent sites, cabins, group camp with amphitheater, picnic areas with shelters, lakes, trails, tennis court, pool, saddle barn. **CCC Company:** 522 SP-3. **CCC Features:** Park roads and gatehouse, cabins, trails, picnic shelters, saddle barn, nature center (formerly the bathhouse built by CCC and WPA), administrative and maintenance structures.

**9. SPRING MILL STATE PARK,** 3333 State Road 600 East, Mitchell, IN 47446; 812-849-4129; *www.in.gov/dnr/parklake*. **GPS:** N38.43.88/ W86.24.18. **Background:** Noted for its setting amid limestone caves and woodlands, the park also features a restored Pioneer Village, Spring Mill Inn, Spring Mill Lake, and the Gus Grissom Memorial, dedicated to the Indiana man who was America's second astronaut. **Facilities:** RV/tent sites, youth camp, picnic areas and shelters, Pioneer Village, Spring Mill Inn, lake, Twin Caves, pool, trails. **CCC**

**Companies:** 1526 and 1536 SP-1 and 6539C SP-10. **CCC Features:** Park roads, campgrounds, trails, picnic shelters, comfort stations, triple-arch bridge, restored Bullitt House in village, nature center (formerly the bathhouse built by CCC and WPA), landscaping around historic Spring Mill Inn.

**10.** TURKEY RUN STATE PARK, 8121 East Park Road, Marshall, IN 47859; 765-597-2635; *www.in.gov/dnr/parklake*. **GPS:** N39.53.03/ W87.12.16. **Background:** Established in 1916 as Indiana's second state park, this area of hemlock groves and ravines carved by Sugar Creek was acquired by public subscription to prevent development by timber interests. Historic structures include the Turkey Run Inn (ca. 1919 but remodeled many times), 1871 log church (relocated to the park in 1923), the 19th century Salmon Lusk Home and the Richard Lieber Memorial Cabin, relocated to park and dedicated to Colonel Lieber, "father" of Indiana State Parks. Lieber's grave is located in the park. **Facilities:** RV/tent sites, youth camp, nature center and planetarium, trails, picnic areas and shelters, Turkey Run Inn, restaurant and conference center, pool, tennis court, Rocky Hollow Falls Nature Preserve, covered bridge. **CCC Companies:** 1543V and 2580 SP-8. **CCC Features:** Park roads and gatehouses, trails with rock work, shelter houses, comfort stations, nature center (formerly the saddle barn), administrative structures.

**11.** VERSAILLES STATE PARK, 1387 E. US 50, Versailles, IN 47042; 812-689-6424; *www.in.gov/dnr/parklake*. **GPS:** N39.04.08/ W85.14.23. **Background:** Established from abandoned farmland as an RDA, this park is the second largest in the state. Workers from the Federal Emergency Relief Administration (FERA) carried out initial park development. They were followed by CCC and WPA workers who completed the project. **Facilities:** RV/tent sites, group camp, picnic areas with shelters, trails, 230-acre lake. **CCC Company:** 596 NP-1/SP-11. **CCC Features:** Reforested areas, group camp trails, picnic areas, shelters and maintenance buildings (nearly all work carried out in collaboration with WPA).

# KENTUCKY

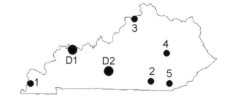

## Destination Parks

### D1. JOHN JAMES AUDUBON STATE PARK

*I was one of eight kids and my dad was out of work. Joining the CCC was a Godsend for me and my family.*[25]

— Clyde "Tubby" Littrell, CCC veteran
Audubon State Park

In 1932, Emma Guy Cromwell was appointed director for Kentucky's new state parks system. Shortly after Franklin D. Roosevelt was elected to the presidency, Cromwell applied to the ECW program for CCC camps to aid in developing the state's fledgling parks. Henderson, Kentucky, librarian Susan Towles urged Cromwell to consider a park and museum along the Ohio River where naturalist and illustrator John James Audubon had lived more than a century before. In 1934, the state acquired 300 acres in the Wolf Hills east of Henderson for the planned park. The next year, CCC Company 1540 SP-9 arrived in the new park. Recognizing the support from the director of Kentucky's state parks, the enrollees dubbed their new home "Camp Cromwell."

Over the next four years, the men drained swamps, built roads and trails, and dug two lakes — one a secluded wilderness pond, the other a recreational lake. They quarried stone and milled timber used to construct log and stone buildings, including picnic shelters and cottages. Working with WPA craftsmen, enrollees assisted in building an English country-style tea house and the park's centerpiece, the John James Audubon Museum (Figure 90).

The museum was designed in the French Norman style reminiscent of Audubon's childhood home in France. It houses the world's

PLATE 1

**Top:** The fieldstone visitor center, built by the CCC at Franklin D. Roosevelt State Park, Georgia, was visited occasionally by FDR when he stayed at the Little White House in nearby Warm Springs. **Bottom:** Group camps, like this one at Chopawamsic RDA, now Prince William Forest Park, Virginia, were built near cities so that children could get exercise and camping experiences in the fresh air of summer.

PLATE 2

Bunker Tower, built by the CCC in Cheaha State Park, Alabama, was an important fire tower located atop the highest point in Alabama.

PLATE 3

The *Spirit of the CCC* statue at Highlands Hammock State Park, Florida, depicts a proud CCC enrollee ready to tackle any task. This statue is one of fifty-four placed by CCC veterans and supporters, in association with the CCC Legacy Foundation, at sites across the country. New statues are being added. Visit *www.ccclegacy.org* for the most current list of statue locations.

PLATE 4

**Top:** A heart-shaped stone was placed in the wall of the observation tower at Georgia's Fort Mountain State Park in 1935. It was carved by CCC stonemason and foreman Arnold Bailey to honor his fiancée, Margaret. **Bottom:** The Art Moderne-style visitor center at Ocmulgee National Monument near Macon, Georgia, is one of the more distinctive buildings constructed by the CCC.

PLATE 5

The entrance to Tishomingo State Park in Mississippi is marked one of many handcrafted metal signs created by a CCC enrollee, Ernest Clausel, and displayed at the park.

PLATE 6

**Top:** The arched bridge and dam at Cumberland Mountain State Park, Tennessee, is the largest masonry structure built by the CCC. **Bottom:** Cabins built by the CCC at Fairy Stone State Park in Virginia display a rustic style. The use of hand-hewn logs and chinking is reminiscent of pioneer days.

PLATE 7

**Top:** These exhibits are in the CCC Museum for Virginia at Pocahontas State Park. **Bottom:** African-American CCC workers restored miles of canals, locks, and towpaths in Chesapeake and Ohio Canal National Historical Park in Maryland and the District of Columbia.

PLATE 8

**Top:** The rustic Bascom Lodge near the summit of Mount Greylock in Massachusetts was constructed by the CCC. **Bottom:** This Colonial-era cannon overlooks the fields and forests of Saratoga National Military Park in New York. CCC enrollees restored the park's woodlands and meadows to appear as they did at the time of the battles of Saratoga in 1777.

PLATE 9

**Top:** This log cabin in Pennsylvania's Promised Land State Park is an excellent example of the Park Rustic architectural style characteristic of many CCC structures. **Bottom:** A visitor enjoys the panoramic view of the New River from the CCC-built overlook in Hawks Nest State Park, West Virginia.

PLATE 10

The soaring interior lobby of the Giant City State Park Lodge reflects the fine craftsmanship of CCC workers.

PLATE 11

**Top:** The bronze casting marks the foundation of the Lincoln family's cabin at the Lincoln Boyhood National Memorial in Indiana. **Bottom:** An early color photograph shows the check-in station at the east entrance of Minnesota's Itasca State Park shortly after it was built by the CCC.

PLATE 12

Thunderbird Lodge in Washington State Park, Missouri, displays the building's distinctive effigy carving.

PLATE 13

**Top:** The CCC built portions of the scenic highway in Theodore Roosevelt National Park in North Dakota. **Bottom:** This stone check-in station, constructed by the CCC, stood at the east entrance to the South Unit of Theodore Roosevelt National Park. The entrance was moved to nearby Medora and the building is no longer in use but may be seen by following a short foot trail from the park's scenic highway.

PLATE 14

**Top:** The Southwestern-Pueblo-style visitor center and adjacent administration buildings at New Mexico's Bandelier National Monument was one of the largest building projects undertaken by the CCC in the national parks. **Bottom:** This 1930s color postcard shows the recently built pool enclosing historic San Solomon Springs in Texas's Balmorhea State Park. The CCC camp may be seen in the upper part of the image.

PLATE 15

**Top:** Constructed by the CCC of native stone and terra cotta tile, this distinctive comfort station is located in the Texas Springs picnic area at Death Valley National Park in California. **Bottom:** Massive Ship Rock and Creation Rock form a natural amphitheater at Red Rocks Park and Amphitheatre near Denver, Colorado. The CCC constructed the seating and stages for what is now one of the nation's premier outdoor performing-arts venues.

PLATE 16

**Top:** The former CCC cottages at Valley of Fire State Park in Nevada have been preserved as a historic site and picnic area. **Bottom:** This shelter at Oregon's Silver Falls State Park, constructed by the CCC of native stone and logs, has been carefully restored.

**Figure 90.** The museum at John James Audubon State Park was a joint project of the CCC and WPA. It features one of the world's largest collections of drawings by naturalist John James Audubon.

largest collection of memorabilia relating to John James Audubon, including his four-volume set *The Birds of America*. The collection was placed on loan to the museum by Alice Tyler, widow of the artist's great-grandson. The local historical society, under Susan Towles' direction, collected other museum pieces and the Friends of Audubon continues to add objects to the collection. In 1994, the Friends group and the State purchased much of the Tyler collection to secure it for the museum permanently.

In 1938, work was completed on the stone picnic shelters and Wilderness Lake. In June, 1940, the park cottages, tea house, and the 28-acre lake opened to the public (Figure 91). The tea house was a popular gathering place for both locals and tourists until it shuttered its doors during WW II. After the war, the building reopened as the park's visitor center and office.

While Audubon has expanded with the addition of a nine-hole golf course, much of the park retains the imprint of the work performed by the CCC and WPA.

**Figure 91.** CCC Company 1540 placed this stone in the wall of a building at John James Audubon State Park.

***Additional Information:*** PO Box 576, 3100 US Highway 41 North, Henderson, KY 42419 (Figure 92); 270-826-2247; *www.parks.ky.gov.* **GPS:** N37.52.89/W87.33.43. Facilities include visitor center, museum and nature center, meeting rooms, RV/tent sites, cabins, picnic areas and shelters, lakes, trails, tennis courts, nature preserve, boat rentals, interpretive programs.

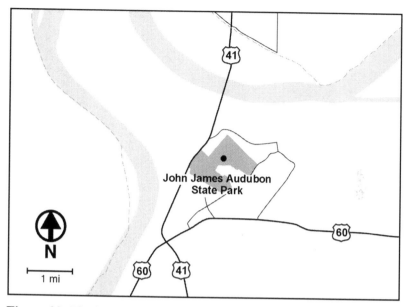

**Figure 92.** The location of John James Audubon State Park.

## D2. MAMMOTH CAVE NATIONAL PARK

*Superintendent reports conditions for carrying out work during winter months most favorable. Can work unlimited number of men underground where it is warm and dry.*[26]

— T. J. McVey, Special Investigator
Camp Report, 1934

This geological wonder in the limestone hills of central Kentucky has been a tourist destination since curiosity seekers first arrived in the early 19th century. In 1926, President Calvin Coolidge signed legislation designating Mammoth Cave as America's 26th national park. Designation was only the beginning of a long process of transforming the area's eroded farmland into a park. Unlike western parks, the land above Mammoth Cave was privately owned and had to be purchased through the combined efforts of the state and thousands of private citizens. Even with onset of the Depression, enough funds were raised to acquire more than 50,000 acres.

The work of restoring the land began with the arrival of CCC Company 501C NP-1 in May, 1933. Setting up camp on Flint Ridge at the site of an abandoned country club, enrollees went to work building trails both within the cave and on the surface. In November, they were joined by Company 543 NP-2 that set up camp near the historic cave entrance. Within a year, two more units, Company 582 NP-3 (Joppa Ridge) and Company 516 NP-4 (near present Maple Springs Group Camp) joined the work effort (figures 19 and 93). Every company spent time inside the cave with crews alternating so that no company spent all of its time underground. In addition, Company 501C handled erosion control and tree planting assignments; Company 543 removed hundreds of undesirable buildings, installed cave entrance gates, built furniture, and transported supplies and equipment to men in the field; Company 582 constructed and staffed two fire towers and removed miles of old farm fences; and Company 516 operated a quarry providing stone for roads and other uses, as well as installing water and sewer systems. Workers also constructed many park buildings, from staff residences to Mammoth Cave Hotel's cottages and summer cabins.

**Figure 93.** Lantern light was used by CCC enrollees to work inside Mammoth Cave National Park.

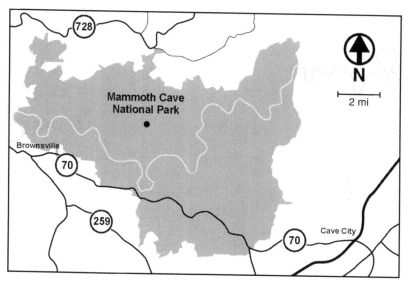

**Figure 94.** The location of Mammoth Cave National Park.

Mammoth Cave National Park, from its tunnel trails and summer cabins to campgrounds and towering shade trees, remains a tangible legacy of CCC craftsmanship and resources restoration.

*Additional Information:* 1 Mammoth Cave Parkway, Mammoth Cave, Kentucky; 270-758-2180 (Figure 94); *www.nps.gov/maca.* **GPS:** N37.11.13/W86.06.05. Facilities include visitor center, historic structures, RV/tent sites, motel and cottages, Maple Springs group camp and research center, picnic areas, cave and surface trails, cave and boat tours, interpretive programs.

# Other CCC-Related Parks

## State Parks

**1. COLUMBUS-BELMONT STATE PARK,** 350 Park Road, Columbus, KY 42032-0009; 270-677-2327; *www.kystateparks.ky.gov.* **GPS:** N36.45.72/W89.06.42. **Background:** Situated on bluffs overlooking the Mississippi River, the park preserves the site of a Confederate fort referred to as the "Gibraltar of the West." The CCC developed facilities and stabilized historic features and structures. **Facilities:** RV/tent sites, group camp, gift shop, trails, picnic area, museum, historic fortifications. **CCC Company:** 583 SP-8. **CCC Features:** Stabilized Civil War fortifications, preserved historic structures, trails, picnic area.

**2.** CUMBERLAND FALLS STATE RESORT PARK, 7351 Highway 90, Corbin, KY 40701-8857; 606-528-4121; *www.kystateparks.ky.gov.* **GPS:** N36.50.33/W84.20.60. **Background:** This park surrounds the 125-foot-high cascade of the Cumberland River, often called the "Niagara of the South." **Facilities:** RV/tent sites, group camp, cabins, lodge and conference center, restaurant, pool, trails, picnic areas, museum, water sports facilities. **CCC Companies:** 509 and 1578 SP-1 and 563 SP-7. **CCC Features:** Park roads, trails, picnic areas, cabins, fire tower, DuPont Lodge.

**3.** GENERAL BUTLER STATE RESORT PARK, 1608 Highway 227, Carrollton, KY 41008-0325; 502-732-4384; *www.kystateparks.ky.gov.* **GPS:** N38.40.16/W85.09.05. **Background:** Located at the confluence of the Ohio and Kentucky Rivers, the park preserves the natural beauty of the area, as well as the historic 19th century home of General William O. Butler. **Facilities:** RV/tent sites, cabins, lodge and conference center, restaurant, group camp, pool, trails, picnic areas, lake, golf course, museum. **CCC Company:** 592 SP-6. **CCC Features:** Park roads, trails, shelter house, Ohio River Valley Overlook.

**4.** NATURAL BRIDGE STATE RESORT PARK, 2135 Natural Bridge Road, Slade, KY 40376-9701; 606-663-2214; *www.kystateparks.ky.gov.* **GPS:** N37.46.49/W83.40.70. **Background**: Located in the Daniel Boone National Forest, the park preserves an ancient 78-foot-long, 65-foot-high sandstone arch and other unique geological features. **Facilities:** RV/tent sites, cabins, group camp, lodge, cottages, lake, trails, pool, trails, picnic areas, museum. **CCC Company:** 567 SP-2. **CCC Features:** Park roads and bridge, roadside stone-work, trails and trail steps, trail shelters.

**5.** PINE MOUNTAIN STATE RESORT PARK, 1050 State Park Road, Pineville, KY 40977-0610; 606-337-3066; *www.kystateparks.ky.gov.* **GPS:** N36.44.23/W83.44.19. **Background:** Established in 1924 on scenic land adjacent to Kentucky Ridge State Forest, Pine Mountain is the state's oldest park. It preserves the largest number of CCC-era facilities in the system. **Facilities:** RV/tent sites, cabins, group camp, historic chestnut-log lodge and dining room, pool, trails, picnic areas, golf course. **CCC Companies:** 548 SP-3 and 563 SP-10. **CCC Features:** Park ranger station, arched roadway bridge, scenic overlooks on park roads, interpretive center, log cabins, campground picnic shelter, Hemlock Garden and Lower Laurel Cove shelters, Little Amphitheatre, Laurel Cove Amphitheater and Reflecting Pool, stone grills in Hemlock Garden, Honeymoon Falls Trail reservoir, lodge upper lobby and porch, park manager's residence, utility buildings.

# MICHIGAN

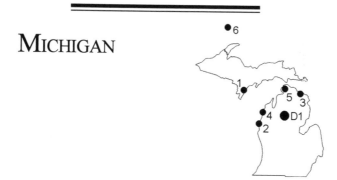

## Destination Parks

### D1. NORTH AND SOUTH HIGGINS LAKE AND HARTWICK PINES STATE PARKS

*Michigan's CCC camps have disappeared, but the legacy of the Corps — the forests, parks, and conservation efforts — remains.*[27]

— Roger N. Rosentreter
"Roosevelt's Tree Army: Michigan's Civilian Conservation Corps"

More than 100,000 men worked in CCC camps across Michigan, the third largest enrollment in the nation. Two parks in the heart of the state preserve the legacy of these CCC enrollees' enduring contributions to their state and to the country. The state operated a tree nursery on North Higgins Lake when CCC Company 672 S-52 arrived in May, 1933. For nine years, these men, joined by WW I veterans from Company 1670V S-108/95, managed seedling and tree plots that provided raw materials for reforestation projects across Michigan.

The men also constructed a log and stone meeting facility with surrounding cabins for the Department of Conservation's training school. Now known as the Ralph A. MacMullan Conference Center, the facility continues to offer conference space for civic and non-profit groups.

In 1965, the nursery closed briefly before reopening as North Higgins Lake State Park with trails, picnic areas, and campground. A popular destination in the park is the CCC Museum complex tracing the story of the CCC in Michigan (Figure 95). The main building, erected in 1986, recreates a typical CCC barracks and includes original materials from Battle Creek's "Camp Custer." The site also features historic seedling and tree nurseries and a reconstructed fire tower. Nearby, 962-acre South Higgins Lake State Park, established in 1927, offers campgrounds, picnic areas, trails, and more than a mile of lakefront.

A few miles north of Higgins Lake is Hartwick Pines State Park, established in 1927 from a donation of 49 acres of old growth pine forest by Karen M. Hartwick in memory of her husband, Major Edward Hartwick, killed in WW I. Today, the park has grown to 9,000 acres and is the largest on the Lower Peninsula. Much of this park's development began in June, 1933, with the arrival of CCC Company 674 SP-8. In 1938, that company was replaced by companies 2690 and 2960V SP-8. These men completed reforestation, trail construction, and building construction projects. Two of these CCC-built structures now house the Michigan Logging Museum, tracing the importance of this industry in Michigan history (Figure 96).

***Additional Information:*** North Higgins Lake: 11747 N. Higgins Lake Drive, Roscommon, MI 48653 (Figure 97); 989-821-6125. **GPS:** N44.30.82/W84.45.54. Facilities include RV/tent sites, picnic areas and shelters, Ralph A. MacMullan Conference Center, trails, Higgins Lake water activities, CCC Museum (seasonal). South Higgins Lake: 106 State Park Drive, Roscommon, MI 48653; 989-821-6374; *www.michigan.gov/dnr*. **GPS:** N44.25.79/W84.40.25. Facilities include RV/tent sites, picnic areas and shelters, trails, Higgins and Marl lakes, bathhouse. Hartwick Pines: 4216 Ranger Road, Grayling, MI 49738; 989-348-7068. **GPS:** N44.44.64/W84.39.31. Facilities include RV/tent sites, picnic areas and shelters, trails, logging museum (seasonal).

**Figure 95.** A restored barracks building at North Higgins Lake State Park houses Michigan's CCC Museum.

**Figure 96.** The Michigan Logging Museum is located in a former CCC building in Hartwick Pines State Park.

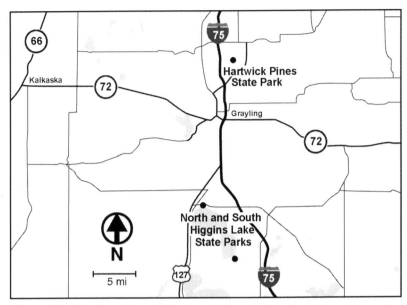

**Figure 97.** The location of North and South Higgins Lake state parks and Hartwick Pines State Park.

# Other CCC-Related Parks

## State Parks

**1. J. W. WELLS STATE PARK,** N7670 Highway M-35, Cedar River MI 49887; 906-863-9747; *www.michigan.gov/dnr*. **GPS:** N45.23.50/ W87.21.94. **Background:** Located on Green Bay, the park stretches along three miles of Lake Michigan shoreline. The land was donated to the state in 1925 by the family of John Walter Wells, a lumber executive and mayor of nearby Menominee. **Facilities:** RV/tent sites, cabins, picnic areas and shelters, trails, beach and bathhouse, Bay Stone Lodge group cabin. **CCC Companies:** 676, 1612 and 3615 SP-9. **CCC Features:** Park roads, log signs and kiosks campground pump house and comfort station/laundry building, day use area pump house, Washington Cabin, bathhouse, Bay Stone Lodge (formerly the superintendent's residence), stone trail shelters.

**2. LUDINGTON STATE PARK, 8800** W. M-116, Ludington, MI 49431; 231-843-2423; *www.michigan.gov/dnr*. **GPS:** N44.02.07/W86.30.11. **Background:** Tucked between Hamlin Lake and Lake Michigan, this park features recreation facilities and trails through dunes, marsh, and forest. **Facilities:** Visitor center, RV/tent sites, hike-in campground, cabins, picnic areas and shelters, trails, canoe trail, bathhouse, boating facilities. **CCC Company:** 1666 SP-2. **CCC Features:** Park entrance road, lighthouse road, day use parking area, original Beechwood and Pines campground loops, trails, Lake Michigan Bathhouse and seawall, trail-side shelters (3), old manager's residence and office/utility building.

**3. ORCHARD BEACH STATE PARK,** 2064 North Lakeshore Road, Manistee, MI 49660; 231-723-7422; *www.michigan.gov/dnr*. **GPS:** N44.16.76/W86.18.87. **Background:** In 1939, a crew of CCC enrollees from nearby Ludington State Park began work on development of this park along a bluff overlooking Lake Michigan. **Facilities:** RV/tent sites, picnic areas and shelters, nature trail, beach. **CCC Company:** 1666 SP-2. **CCC Features:** Entrance road, landscaping and log fencing, limestone picnic shelter, water sumps and pump house in campground, line house, comfort station.

**4. P. H. HOEFT STATE PARK,** 5001 US 23 North, Rogers City, MI 49779; 989-734-2543; *www.michigan.gov/dnr*. **GPS:** N45.27.91/W83.52.95. **Background:** This small park, located along Lake Huron, was one of Michigan's first parks. Land for the park was donated by timber executive P. H. Hoeft in 1922 and the CCC carried out early development of the park. **Facilities:** RV/tent sites, picnic area and shelter, cabin, trails, beach. **CCC Company:** 1667V S-77. **CCC Features:** Park entrance, original campground, comfort station, day use parking area, picnic area and shelter, bathhouse/shelter, staff garage and artesian well.

**5. WILDERNESS STATE PARK,** 903 Wilderness Park Drive, Carp Lake MI 49718; 231-436-5381; *www.michigan.gov/dnr*. **GPS:** N45.44.72/W84.53.97. **Background:** Covering nearly 26 miles of Lake Michigan shoreline, the park preserves a landscape of evergreens and hardwoods, meadows, ponds, marshlands and dunes. **Facilities:** RV/tent sites, cabins, group bunkhouses (WPA), picnic areas, beaches, trails including a section of the North Country Trail, boat launches. **CCC Company:** 1617 SP-4. **CCC Features:** Lake Shore Campground, Wayside Shelter with stone fireplace, Station Point, Sturgeon Bay and Nebo cabins, CCC camp pump house, Pines Campground (site of CCC camp), trails, Goose Pond.

## National Parks

**6. ISLE ROYALE NATIONAL PARK,** 800 East Lakeshore Drive, Houghton, MI 49931-1896; 906-482-0984; *www.nps.gov/isro*. **GPS:** N48.07.45/ W88.32.02. **Background:** Created by retreating glaciers, the Isle Royale archipelago has been restored as a vestige of remote wilderness after many years of commercial logging. The park was authorized in 1931 and established in 1940. CCC enrollees battled a 1936 fire that burned nearly a third of the island. **Facilities:** Visitor centers at Houghton (mainland), Windigo, and Rock Harbor, campgrounds and back-country campsites, trails, interpretive activities, boat transportation. **CCC Companies:** 2613 and 3686 NP-1, 634 NP-2, 3686 NP-3. **CCC Features:** Park trails, reforested areas from 1936 fire, Mott Island Headquarters residential and support buildings, foundations and ruins of Daisy Farm CCC camp.

# MINNESOTA

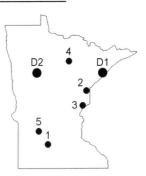

## Destination Parks

### D1. GOOSEBERRY FALLS STATE PARK

> *The lack of prior development, the dramatic setting, the long tenure of the camp, and the skill of the camp members combined to make Gooseberry a showcase of what the New Deal agencies could accomplish.*[28]
>
> — David R. Benson
> *Stories in Log and Stone: The Legacy of the New Deal in Minnesota State Parks*

Overlooking the Gooseberry River where it flows into Lake Superior, 640-acre Gooseberry Falls State Park is rich in natural beauty and historical significance. Set aside in 1933 as a joint project of the Minnesota Highway and Conservation Departments, Gooseberry Falls was originally established as a game refuge featuring exceptional views of the river and the broad expanse of Lake Superior. Park development began with the arrival of CCC Company 1720 SP-5 in May, 1934, and Company 2710 SP-10 the following September. The park was dedicated in 1937.

Work on park projects began in the spring of 1935 with the construction of Lady Slipper Lodge, Lake View Shelter, and Falls View Shelter (Figure 98). Each of these structures, along with several other buildings, was constructed of native stone noted for distinctive hues of red and blue. The red stone was quarried near Duluth; while the blue came from East Beaver Bay. By far the most impressive CCC-built structure at Gooseberry Falls is the Concourse along Minnesota Highway 61. Often referred to as "the Castle in the Park," the concourse is 12 feet wide at the base, at places 25 feet high, and nearly 300 feet long. Work on this project and others in the park, was overseen by Italian stonemasons John Berini and Joe Cattaneo. In his book, *Stories in Log and Stone: The Legacy of the New Deal in Minnesota State Parks*, David Benson noted that the masons boasted that "if all

**Figure 98.** The rough-hewn stone Lady Slipper Lodge at Gooseberry Falls State Park features red granite blocks quarried near Duluth, Minnesota.

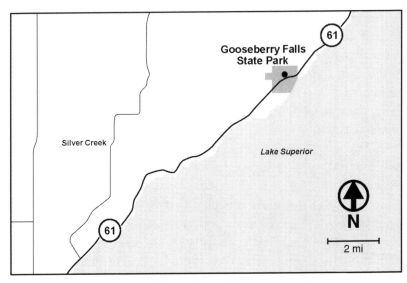

**Figure 99.** The location of Gooseberry Falls State Park.

the mortar were removed from the walls, the buildings would still stand."[1] Today, the Concourse anchors the park's Gateway Plaza.

CCC workers also graded roads, blazed trails, laid out camp-grounds and picnic areas, and crafted stone picnic tables. Gooseberry Falls features more than 80 CCC-built structures and the park's original 640 acre site is listed on the National Register of Historic Places. Following the CCC camp's closure in 1941, a local newspaper published the accolade, "Here lies a park that will live in the years to come as a tribute to the nation's Civilian Conservation Corps and a monument to Company 2710, its officers, and its boys."

***Additional Information:*** 3206 Highway 61 East, Two Harbors, MN 55616 (Figure 99); 218-834-3855; *www.dnr.state.mn.us/state_parks*. **GPS:** N47.08.54/W91.28.11. Facilities include visitor center and nature store, RV/tent sites, picnic areas and shelters, trails including sections of the Lake Superior Trail, beach and Lake Superior Water Trail.

## D2. ITASCA STATE PARK

*The extensive New Deal development here changed the
face of Itasca.*[29]

— David R. Benson
*Stories in Log and Stone: The Legacy of the
New Deal in Minnesota State Parks*

Following the Louisiana Purchase, explorers sought the headwaters of the Mississippi River to mark the nation's western boundary. In 1832, led by Anishinabe guide Ozawindib, Henry R. Schoolcraft
stood by a remote lake in Minnesota that he believed was the river's
source. He named it "Itasca," merging the Latin "verITAS" (true) and
"CAput" (head). Over the next half century, the surrounding forests
were logged leaving behind a scarred landscape. In the 1880s, surveyor Jacob Brower urged the state to save remaining stands of virgin
pines surrounding Lake Itasca. Despite opposition, Itasca became
Minnesota's first state park in April, 1891, but threats to the lake did
not end. In 1903, park manager Mary Gibbs opposed the closing of
gates on a nearby dam that would flood the park. Despite threats from
timber company officials, she stood firm and Itasca was again saved
from devastation. Her memory is honored in the park's Mary Gibbs
Mississippi Headwaters Center.

While the park's Douglas Lodge (1905) and the Clubhouse (1911)
date from the early years, Itasca is the work of the CCC. Company
1764 SP-1/SP-19, the first in a Minnesota park, arrived on June 27,
1933. Among their first projects was the "Old Timer's Cabin," crafted
from massive logs and described in the NPS book *Park and Recreation Structures* as "almost humorous in its scale" (Figure 100). The
men also erected cabin #12 across the lake, laid out roads, picnic
areas, and campgrounds, and constructed a stepping-stones dam across
the Mississippi headwaters. With assistance from two other CCC companies, 724 S-57 and 788 S-70, the enrollees completed work on the
log and stone Forest Inn, one of the largest CCC-structures in the
Minnesota parks system; built the Fourplex shelter, graded the ten-
mile-long Wilderness Drive, and blazed hiking and cross-country ski

**Figure 100.** The whimsical Old Timer's Cabin in Itasca State Park was constructed of oversized logs.

trails. On July 15, 1942, Camp SP-19 became the last CCC camp in the nation to close. Today, 32,000-acre Itasca State Park, featuring more than 70 New Deal-era structures, is listed on the National Register of Historic Places (Plate 11, bottom).

Visitors interested in seeing an intact CCC camp, one of the few still in existence, may travel about 70 miles north of Itasca State Park to Blackduck, Minnesota, to see "Camp Rabideau" in the Chippewa National Forest.

***Additional Information:*** 36750 Main Park Drive, Park Rapids, MN 56470 (Figure 101); 218-699-7251; *www.dnr.state.mn.us/state_parks/ itasca.* **GPS:** N47.11.56/W95.09.89. Facilities include Jacob Brower Visitor Center, Mary Gibbs Mississippi Headwaters Center, historic structures, RV/tent sites, cabins, picnic areas and shelters, lakes and ponds with water sports facilities, trails, Itasca Wilderness Sanctuary.

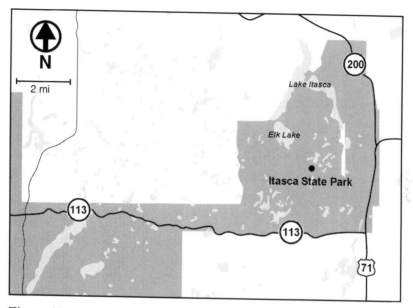

**Figure 101.** The location of Itasca State Park.

# Other CCC-Related Parks

## State Parks

**1. Fort Ridgely State Park,** 72158 County Road 30, Fairfax, MN 55332-9601; 507-426-7840; *http://www.dnr.state.mn.us/state_parks*. **GPS:** N44.27.12/W94.43.91. **Background:** Located near the Minnesota River, Fort Ridgely was established in 1855, remaining active until 1872. In 1911, the site was designated a memorial park for the soldiers who served there. The Minnesota Historical Society supervised CCC enrollees excavating and preserving fort ruins. **Facilities:** RV/tent sites, horse camp, group camp, picnic areas and shelters, trails, winter activities areas, golf course, fort ruins and interpretive center. **CCC Companies:** 2709 DSP-4, 2712 SP-4, and 2713V SP-12. **CCC Features:** Fort ruins and restored commissary, picnic area and fireplaces, campground and comfort station, water tower, utility buildings.

**2. Jay Cooke State Park,** 780 Highway 210, Carlton, MN 55718; 218-384-4610; *http://www.dnr.state.mn.us/state_parks*. **GPS:** N46.39.27/92.22.30. **Background:** This landscape of forests and exposed bedrock along the Saint Louis River was donated to the state in 1915. CCC and WPA carried out initial park development. **Facilities:** RV/tent sites, picnic areas and shelters, River Inn shelter, group camp, cabin, trails. **CCC Companies:** 1712 SP-2 and 2711 SP-21. **CCC Features:** River Inn Lodge, swinging bridge, Oldenburg Point Shelter, picnic shelter, custodian's cabin, water tower and comfort station.

**3. SAINT CROIX STATE PARK,** 30065 Saint Croix Road, Hinckley, MN 55037; 320-384-6591; *http://www.dnr.state.mn.us/state_parks*. **GPS:** N45.56.78/W92.36.36. **Background:** Developed as Minnesota's only RDA and the second largest in the nation (South Dakota's Custer State Park was the largest), Saint Croix offered public campgrounds, recreation along the Saint Croix National Scenic River, and group camps for companies, girls, boys, and disabled children. The park features more than 150 New Deal-era structures and is a National Historic Landmark. **Facilities:** RV, tent sites, group camps, guest houses, cabins, interpretive center, trails. **CCC Company:** 3715 NP-1/SP-5. **CCC Features:** Park entrance portals and roads, Riverview campground, cabins, Saint Croix Lodge and Interpretive Center (Figure 102), group camps (in collaboration with WPA), CCC camp ruins and interpretive trail, water tower, administrative structures.

**4. SCENIC STATE PARK,** 56956 Scenic Highway 7, Bigfork, MN 56628; 218-743-3362; *http://www.dnr.state.mn.us/state_parks*. **GPS:**

**Figure 102.** The Riverview Campground Lodge is in Saint Croix State Park.

**Figure 103.** CCC men prepare chicken for dinner in Sibley State Park.

N47.42.81/W93.34.26. **Background:** This park preserves an area of virgin forests and lakes acquired by the state in 1921. **Facilities:** RV/tent sites, picnic areas, Coon and Sandwick lakes facilities, beach, day lodge, trails. **CCC Companies:** 2713V and 1722 SP-3. **CCC Features:** Scenic State Park Lodge with furniture and decorations, naturalist's cabin, picnic shelter, water tower, maintenance structures.

**5. SIBLEY STATE PARK,** 800 Sibley Road, NE, New London, MN 56273-9664; 320-354-2055; *http://www.dnr.state.mn.us/state_parks*. **GPS:** N45.18.82/95.01.94. **Background:** This landscape of forested hills, prairies, and lakes was set aside as a game preserve in 1917, then designated a state park in 1919. **Facilities:** RV/tent sites, horse camp, group camps, picnic areas and shelters, winter sports and water sports facilities, trails. **CCC Company:** 1785V SP-7. **CCC Features:** Park roads, Lakeview campground, comfort stations, Cedar Hill picnic area and shelters, beach and bathhouse, trails, water tower, fish-cleaning house, custodian's cabin, administrative structures (Figure 103).

# OHIO

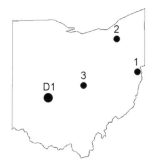

## Destination Parks

### D1. JOHN BRYAN STATE PARK

*The most obvious features . . . point to the CCC's and
their phenomenal craftsmanship are the stone structures
throughout the park.*[30]
— Rachel Stout-O'Connor, Park Historian

Located in gorge and canyon country along the Little Miami National Scenic River, John Bryan State Park has been described as the "most scenic state park in western Ohio." The portion of the river gorge in the park also has been designated a National Natural Landmark. The park owes its origins to John Bryan, a local businessman and civic leader, and an eccentric. In 1896, he purchased 335 acres along the Little Miami River Gorge for his "Riverside Farm." The next year, Bryan began construction of the "world's largest" barn on the property. When completed, it stood four stories tall, 206 feet long and 120 feet wide. It was demolished in 1967 and the park campground now occupies the site.

Bryan bequeathed the land to the state on condition that "no religious services be held on the property and that no well-behaved person be excluded because of race or color." Remarkably, two governors refused the gift under these conditions. In 1923, the legislature intervened, enacting a bill accepting the property. Two years later, John Bryan became Ohio's first state forest park. Additional land was later donated in memory of Edward Orton, former president of nearby

Antioch College and first president of The Ohio State University. In 1972, the Clifton Gorge National Natural Landmark Area was established along the river on land adjacent to the park.

With establishment of the ECW program in 1933, resources became available to develop facilities for the park. CCC Company 553 SP-16 arrived at John Bryan in June, 1935, to begin six years of work. The men laid out roads and blazed miles of trails, including the Pittsburgh–Cincinnati Stagecoach Trail which preserves portions of a 19th century wagon-road. Also, enrollees built two foot-bridges across the Little Miami River. One bridge featured a dam that, when closed, created a "swimming hole." In addition, the workers erected the park office, two picnic shelters (Figure 104), and a log and stone "Day Lodge" with two fireplaces, kitchen, and dining area.

Steven Klissaroff, a CCC enrollee at John Bryan and a gifted artist, painted more than 80 scenes of the park during his time in the Corps. Today, several of his works are on display in the park.

***Additional Information:*** 3790 State Route 370; Yellow Springs, OH 45387 (Figure 105); 937-767-1274; *www.ohiodnr.com/parks.*

**Figure 104.** This hand-hewn, fieldstone shelter is nestled among shade trees at John Bryan State Park.

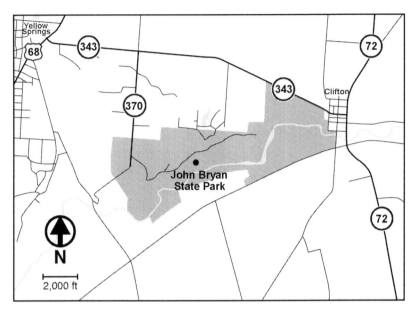

**Figure 105.** The location of John Bryan State Park.

**GPS:** N39.47.42/W83.51.96. Facilities include RV/tent sites, group camp, picnic areas and shelters, trails, water activities, Clifton Gorge Natural Area.

# Other CCC-Related Parks
## State Parks

**1. JEFFERSON LAKE STATE PARK,** 501 TWSP Road, 261A, Richmond, OH 43944-9710; 740-765-4459; *www.ohiodnr.com/parks*. **GPS:** N40.27.97/W80.48.41. **Background:** Located in Ohio's Appalachian Highlands, the park preserves stands of hardwood trees. **Facilities:** RV/tent sites, picnic areas and shelters, Jefferson Lake, beach and bathhouse, trails, nature center. **CCC Company:** 580C SP-9. **CCC Features:** picnic areas, trails, Jefferson Lake Dam.

## National Parks

**2. CUYAHOGA VALLEY NATIONAL PARK,** 15610 Vaughn Road, Brecksville, OH 44141; 800-257-9477; *www.nps.gov/cuva*. **GPS:** N41.13.86/W81.30.50. **Background:** Established as a National

Recreation Area in 1974 and designated a National Park in 2000, the Cuyahoga River Valley is rich in both scenic and historic value. Within the 33,000-acre park are 200-year old farms, preserved remains of the Ohio and Erie Canal, and miles of trails and public recreation areas. The national park was created through the consolidation of Virginia Kendall State Park and public park land from the nearby cities of Cleveland and Akron. The CCC developed several early structures, especially in Kendall State Park. **Facilities:** Visitor centers, museums, Ohio and Erie Canal and Towpath, Cuyahoga Valley Scenic Railroad, trails, picnic areas and shelters, recreation fields, lodging, lakes, Blossom Music Center (summer home of Cleveland Symphony). **CCC Companies:** 576 SP-4 and SP-5, 577 SP-6, 3518 SP-19. **CCC Features:** Happy Days Camp Lodge visitor center; Octagon Shelter; Kendall Lake, dam, and bathhouse; Kendall Park toboggan slide; Furnace Run Lake, dam, and bathhouse; Kendall Park trails and stone work.

## Other Parks

**3.** GREAT CIRCLE EARTHWORKS, 99 Cooper Avenue, Newark, OH 43055; 800-589-8224; *http://ohsweb.ohiohistory.org/places/c08/greatcircle.shtml.* **GPS:** N40.04.07/W82.42.87. **Background:** Built by the Hopewell Culture nearly 2,000 years ago, the Great Circle and nearby Octagon earthworks and adjoining mounds and trenches were restored by the CCC as Mound Builders State Memorial. The site is now operated by the Ohio Historical Society (*www.ohiohistory.org*). **Facilities:** Museum, earthworks, trails. **CCC Company:** 1544V SP-18. **CCC Features:** Restored mounds, earthworks, superintendent's house.

# WISCONSIN

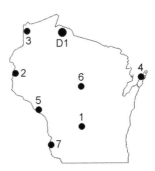

## Destination Parks

### D1. COPPER FALLS STATE PARK

*The buildings are Rustic handcrafted masterpieces belonging to this historic period in our state and national heritage that remain as symbols of hope, perseverance and fortitude of the American spirit during the Great Depression.*[31]

— Mary Schueller, daughter of a Copper Falls CCC Veteran
*Rustic Reflections of Copper Falls State Park*

In the half century following Wisconsin's 1848 admission to the Union, the state's north-country was logged and mined to fuel the nation's westward expansion. By the early 20th century, much of this area was called the "cutover" in reference to its denuded appearance. Conservationists urged preservation of remaining vestiges of Wisconsin's natural heritage. In 1907 the state became one of the first to establish a parks commission; the new agency was headed by landscape architect John Nolen. The commission identified several possible park sites, including one near the confluence of the Tyler and Bad rivers where water flowed through steep canyons and over Copper, Tyler (now Brownstone), and Red Granite falls, the latter added to the park in 1973.

The land belonged to the Lake Superior Power Company, and had been acquired for impoundment to generate hydroelectric power. However, difficult access made development impractical. In 1925, the Wisconsin parks commission leased the land with option to buy it once funds were approved. In 1929, 520 acres were acquired for the proposed Copper Falls State Park. However, with onset of the Depression, park development ceased. In 1934, funding became available for CCC camps to work in Wisconsin's state parks and Copper Falls was chosen as one of the first to be assigned a camp. On November 4, 1935, Company D-692 SP-7 arrived on the banks of the Bad River to begin work at Copper Falls. The men, relocated from Giant City State Park in Illinois, had experience in drainage and erosion control (the letter "D" in the Company designation was for experience in drainage work), as well as skills in carpentry, masonry, blacksmithing, furniture-making, and other essential trades.

Workers graded roads and blazed trails, erected steel footbridges over the Bad River and Tyler Forks, and began construction of the contact station, pump house, and observation tower. Their signature project was the Combination Building (concession-shelter), a large log structure featuring an indoor meeting and concession space and a covered gathering space, each highlighted by stone fireplaces (Figure 106) . The CCC camp closed late in 1937 and unfinished projects were completed by local WPA workers. Sadly, some original CCC structures were lost during catastrophic floods in 1941 and 1946, yet the park's historical integrity and its linkage to the CCC, led to its placement on the National Register of Historic Places.

***Additional Information:*** 36764 Copper Falls Road, Mellen, WI 54546 (Figure 107); 715-274-5123; *www.dnr.state.wi.us/Org/land/parks*. **GPS:** N46.20.52/W90.38.34. Facilities include RV/tent sites, backcountry camp sites, cabin, group camp, picnic areas and shelters, Bad River, Loon Lake and Murphy Lake, recreation fields, trails (including a section of the North Country National Scenic Trail).

# Other CCC-Related Parks

## State Parks

**1. Devils Lake State Park,** South 5975 Park Road, Baraboo, WI 53913-9299; 608-356-8301; *www.dnr.state.wi.us/Org/land/parks*. **GPS:** N43.26.03/W89.44.19. **Background:** This park preserves forested hills, high eroded bluffs, and glacier-carved rock outcrops. Devils

**Figure 106.** The rustic log-and-stone Combination Building is one of the CCC's most recognized projects in Copper Falls State Park.

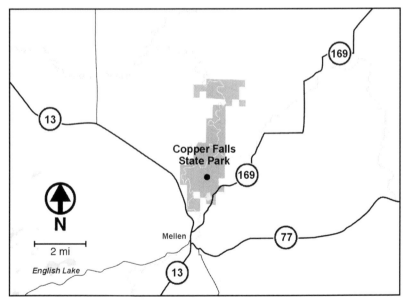

**Figure 107.** The location of Copper Falls State Park.

Lake, the centerpiece of the park, was created more than 10,000 years ago by the retreating ice sheet. A section of the Ice Age National Scenic Trail follows a path through the park. **Facilities:** Visitor center, RV/tent sites, group camp, picnic areas and shelters, lake with water sports facilities, trails. **CCC Company:** 2669 SP-12. **CCC Features:** Campground, comfort stations, nature center, beaches, chateau.

**2. INTERSTATE STATE PARK,** State Route 35, Box 703, Saint Croix Falls, WI 54024; 715-483-3747; *www.dnr.state.wi.us/Org/land/parks.* **GPS:** N45.23.35/W92.38.26. **Background:** Established in 1900 along the Saint Croix River boundary between Minnesota and Wisconsin, this is Wisconsin's oldest state park. The site preserves basalt cliffs, woodlands, ponds, glacial potholes, and a lake formed by melt-water from retreating glaciers. The park is part of the Ice Age National Scientific Reserve. In 1936, CCC crews unearthed ancient bison bones that may be seen in the Ice Age Interpretive Center. CCC and WPA collaborated in the park's development. **Facilities:** Interpretive Center, RV/tent sites, picnic areas and shelters, Lake O' the Dalles and Saint Croix River, beach, stone bathhouse, amphitheater, trails (including the western terminus of the Ice Age National Scenic Trail). **CCC Companies:** 633 and 4610 SP-13. **CCC Features:** Campgrounds, picnic areas and stone shelters, Lake O' the Dalles, beach and stone bathhouse, trails.

**3. PATTISON STATE PARK,** 6294 S. State Road 35, Superior, WI 54880-8326; 715-399-3111; *www.dnr.state.wi.us/Org/land/parks.* **GPS:** N46.32.13/W92.07.12. **Background:** Named for Martin Pattison, lumberman and miner, who purchased the land to save it from destruction by a proposed dam project. He donated it for a park in 1918. **Facilities:** RV/tent sites, picnic areas, group shelter, trails, nature center. **CCC Company:** 3663 SP-11. **CCC Features:** Park roads, campground with pedestrian underpass, group shelter, beach, bathhouses, nature center, trails.

**4. PENINSULA STATE PARK,** 9462 Shore Road, Box 218, Fish Creek, WI 54212-0218; 920-868-3258; *www.dnr.state.wi.us/Org/land/parks.* **GPS:** N45.07.40/W87.14.12. **Background:** Established in 1909, the park follows eight miles of Lake Michigan shoreline with bluffs that cut across a northern hardwood forest and abandoned farm fields. Within the park are the historic Eagle Bluff Lighthouse (ca. 1868), two historic cemeteries, burial site of Potawatomi chief Kaquados, and an amphitheater that is home to the American Folklore Theater.

**Facilities:** RV/tent sites, picnic areas and shelters, trails, pier, tennis courts, Eagle Lookout Tower, lighthouse, golf course, nature center. **CCC Company:** 3648 SP-10. **CCC Features:** Eagle Terrace, Eagle Tower (rebuilt by CCC), Shore Road stone curbing, bathhouse, trails, old ski jump and toboggan run (near the present nature center), maintenance buildings.

**5. PERROT STATE PARK,** Route 1, Box 407, Trempealeau, WI 54661-0407; 608-534-6409; *www.dnr.state.wi.us/Org/land/parks.* **GPS:** N44.01.59/W91.28.93. **Background:** Located at the confluence of the Trempealeau and Mississippi rivers, this park features high bluffs with views of the river and countryside. The site was set aside for a park in 1918 and the CCC carried out much of the park's development. **Facilities:** RV/tent sites, picnic areas, boating facilities, trails (including access to Great River State Trail), nature center. **CCC Company:** 2606 SP-16. **CCC Features:** Park roads, campground, picnic area, shelter, trails.

**6. RIB MOUNTAIN STATE PARK,** 4200 Park Road, Wausau, WI 54401; 715-842-2522; *www.dnr.state.wi.us/Org/land/parks.* **GPS:** N44.55.11/W89.40.49. **Background:** Rib Mountain, a ridge of ancient rock more than a billion years old, is among the oldest geological landforms in the United States. The park preserves the mountain and the surrounding landscape. **Facilities:** RV/tent sites, picnic areas and shelter, trails, amphitheater, lookout tower, Granite Peak downhill ski area. **CCC Companies:** 3649 and 3652 SP-15. **CCC Features:** Park roads, campground, picnic areas, gazebo, trails with stone steps, original ski chalet and ski runs.

**7. WYALUSING STATE PARK,** 13081 State Park Lane, Bagley WI 53801; 608-996-2261; *www.dnr.state.wi.us/Org/land/parks.* **GPS:** N42.58.67/W91.07.39. **Background:** Established in 1917 as Nelson Dewey State Park, this park was named for Wisconsin's first governor. The park's name was changed to Wyalusing in 1937, because in 1935 a new park, Nelson Dewey Memorial Park, was created to preserve his home and further honor his name. Wyalusing, drawn from the Munsee-Delaware Indian language, means "place where the holy man dwells." The site preserves sandstone hills and woodlands at the confluence of the Wisconsin and Mississippi rivers. **Facilities:** RV/tent sites, group camps, picnic areas and shelters, trails, observation points, astronomy center. **CCC Company:** 2972 SP-6. **CCC Features:** Park roads, trails, Peterson Shelter (finished by WPA).

# *Midwest Region*

## IOWA

## Destination Parks

### D1. BACKBONE STATE PARK

*We hope that the Mount Vernon camp will like Back-
bone State Park and greet the members of Company 781
as friends.*[32]

— Editorial in *Backbone Lyre*
April 25, 1934

Amid northeastern Iowa's farmlands, Backbone State Park is a
geological and scenic treasure. A century ago, geologist Samuel Calvin
eloquently wrote of this area, "Its sides are in places precipitous, the
rocky cliffs rising sheer for more than 80 feet. Erosion and secular
decay have carved the rocks into picturesque columns, towers, castles,
battlements, and flying buttresses."

In 1920, the Iowa legislature set aside nearly 1,400 acres along a horseshoe bend of the Maquoketa River for the state's first park, but little development had been done when the Depression brought work to a halt. In 1931, Governor John Hammill created the Iowa State Planning Board to provide recommendations for conserving the state's natural resources, and to improve or provide greater recreational opportunities. With establishment of the ECW program in 1933, the planning board's findings provided opportunities for parks projects to be carried out by the CCC. Backbone State Park was among the first of more than twenty Iowa parks to benefit from the Corps' labors.

CCC Company 1756 SP-2 arrived at Backbone in June, 1933; and was followed in April, 1934, by Company 781 SP-17. Over the next eight years, the men built dams on the Maquoketa River to create Backbone Lake; constructed a bathhouse and boathouse; laid out park roads, bridges, and hiking trails; hand-crafted eight cabins from native stone and timber; built an auditorium for special events; and developed picnic areas, shelters, and comfort stations (Figure 108). Their landmark structure was a large Stone Lodge overlooking Backbone Lake. Today, portions of Backbone State Park, including the

**Figure 108.** The CCC built this bridge over the Makuoketa River in Backbone State Park.

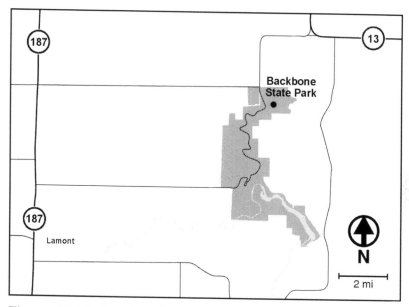

**Figure 109.** The location of Backbone State Park.

CCC cabins and Stone Lodge, have been listed on the National Register of Historic Places. In addition to the park's historic structures and its integrity of design, Backbone also is home to the Iowa Civilian Conservation Corps Museum which features exhibits and artifacts tracing the rich legacy of the CCC's work at Backbone State Park and across the state.

***Additional Information:*** 1347 129th Street, Dundee, IA 52038 (Figure 109); 563-924-2000; *www.iowadnr.gov.* **GPS:** N42.37.07/ W91.33.74. Facilities include RV/tent sites, cabins, CCC museum (seasonal), picnic areas and shelters, lake with boathouse and bathhouse, trails, adjacent state forest (hunting).

# Other CCC-Related Parks

## State Parks

**1. BEEDS LAKE STATE PARK,** 1422 165th Street, Hampton, IA 50441; 641-456-2047; *www.iowadnr.gov.* **GPS:** N42.46.08/W93.14.52. **Background:** In 1857, T. K. Hansbury dammed Sandy Creek to form a lake that would supply water to operate nearby mills. In 1864, William Beed purchased the property and constructed the earthen causeway across the lake. The land was later acquired by the state for a park that opened in 1934. **Facilities:** RV/tent sites, picnic areas and shelters, lake, beach, lodge, boating facilities. **CCC Company:** 2717 DSP-4/SP-22. **CCC Features:** Beach building, spillway, picnic areas, trails.

**2. BLACK HAWK STATE PARK,** 228 South Blossom, Lake View, IA 51450; 712-657-8712; *www.iowadnr.gov.* **GPS:** N42.18.02/ W95.02.83. **Background:** Named for Chief Black Hawk, whose refusal to leave his tribe's ancestral lands led to the Black Hawk War in 1832. The land adjacent to Black Hawk Lake was set aside for a park in 1935. **Facilities:** RV/tent sites, picnic areas and shelters, cabin, trails including Sauk Bike Trail, lake with boat ramps, beach, and shelter. **CCC Company:** 1776V SP-6. **CCC Features:** Trails, beach and shelter, family cabin.

**3. DOLLIVER MEMORIAL STATE PARK,** 2757 Dolliver Park Avenue, Lehigh, IA 50557; 515-359-2539; *www.iowadnr.gov.* **GPS:** N42.23.45/ W94.04.85. **Background:** This area of bluffs and woodlands along the Des Moines River was set aside as a park in 1925. The park is a geological treasure with the sandstone Copperas Beds revealing 100 million years of natural history. **Facilities:** RV/tent sites, group camp, trails, picnic areas and shelters, boating and fishing facilities. **CCC Companies:** 2725V DSP-3 and 1776V SP-6. **CCC Features:** Park roads, trails, two log and stone day lodges.

**4. LAKE MACBRIDE STATE PARK,** 3525 Highway 382 NE, Solon, IA 52333; 319-624-2200; *www.iowadnr.gov.* **GPS:** N41.49.29/ W91.37.42. **Background:** This park opened in 1937 through the efforts of the Iowa City Chamber of Commerce and Iowa conservationist J. N. "Ding" Darling. It is named for Dr. Thomas McBride, longtime president of the University of Iowa and the state's "father" of conservation. **Facilities:** RV/tent sites, picnic areas and shelters, day lodge, lake with beach, bathhouse and boat ramps. Nearby is the McBride Recreation Area Raptor Center. **CCC Company:** 782 PE-60/ SP-19. **CCC Features:** Day Lodge, beach building, picnic shelters, trails, campground.

**5. LAKE WAPELLO STATE PARK,** 15248 Campground Road, Drakesville, IA 52552; 641-722-3371; *www.iowadnr.gov.* **GPS:** N40.49.34/ W92.34.48. **Background:** Surrounding Lake Wapello, the park offers year round recreational activities. **Facilities:** RV/tent sites, cabins, trails, picnic areas and shelters, lake with beach pavilion and restaurant, Camp Wapello Group Camp. **CCC Company:** 773 SP-14. **CCC Features:** Beach pavilion and restaurant, trails, picnic shelters.

**6. LEDGES STATE PARK,** 1515 P Avenue, Madrid, IA 50156; 515-432-1852; *www.iowadnr.gov.* **GPS:** N41.59.73/W93.52.75. **Background:** One of Iowa's first parks, the woodlands and canyons along Peas Creek were first carved by retreating glaciers more than 13,000 years ago. **Facilities:** RV/tent sites, picnic areas and shelters, day lodge, trails, Des Moines River, M. L. Hutton Memorial (dedicated to first director of Iowa State Conservation Commission, 1935). **CCC Company:** 2723 DSP-5/SP-26. **CCC Features:** Park roads, arched-stone bridge, Oak Woods Shelter, Lower Ledges Shelter, picnic areas, trails.

**7. PALISADES-KEPLER STATE PARK,** 700 Kepler Drive, Mount Vernon, IA 52314; 319-895-6039; *www.iowadnr.gov.* **GPS:** N41.54.64/ W91.30.22. **Background:** Known for its landscape of river bluffs, ravines, and hardwood forests, the park was originally the site of a summer resort developed in the 1890s. The land was acquired by the state and the park was established in 1922. **Facilities:** RV/tent sites, cabins, picnic areas and shelters, trails, Cedar River boating and fishing facilities. **CCC Company:** 2722 DSP-1/SP-1. **CCC Features:** Park roads, trails, entry portals, Day Lodge, utility structures.

**8. PILOT KNOB STATE PARK,** 2148 340th Street, Forest City, IA 50436; 641-581-4835; *www.iowadnr.gov.* **GPS:** N43.15.09/W93.33.59. **Background:** Established in 1923, the park preserves Pilot Knob, the second highest point in Iowa. The rocky promontory, rising above the glacier-carved landscape, was a landmark for westward-bound settlers. The summit-top observation tower was built by the CCC. **Facilities:** RV/tent sites, picnic areas and shelters, trails, Dead Mans Lake (bog), man-made lake, winter sports facilities. **CCC Company:** 1757 SP-16. **CCC Features:** Picnic shelter #3, observation tower, trails.

**9. PINE LAKE STATE PARK,** 22620 County Highway S56, Eldora, IA 50627-8010; 641-858-5832; *www.iowadnr.gov.* **GPS:** N42.22.24/ W93.04.73. **Background:** Located east of the Iowa River amid stands of pines, the park features CCC structures and two lakes. Pine Lake is a terminal point for the Lake to Lake Bike Trail. **Facilities:** RV/tent sites, cabins, picnic areas and shelters, trails, Upper and Lower Pine Lakes. **CCC Company:** 1755 SP-10. **CCC Features:** Cabins, stone and timber day lodge, trails, picnic areas.

**10. SPRINGBROOK STATE PARK,** 2437 160th Road, Guthrie Center, IA 50115; 641-747-3591; *www.iowadnr.gov*. **GPS:** N41.46.36/ W94.27.94. **Background:** Established in 1926, the park is situated amid woodlands and prairies along the Raccoon River and Springbrook Creek. Springbrook State Park is a link on the Central Iowa State Bike Trail. **Facilities:** RV/tent sites, cabins, trails, picnic areas and shelters, lake, Conservation Education Center, Forestry Demonstration Areas. **CCC Company:** 779 SP-7. **CCC Features:** Picnic areas and shelter, trails, lake and dam, cabins.

**11. STONE STATE PARK,** 5001 Talbot Road, Sioux City, IA 51003; 712-255-4698; *www.iowadnr.gov*. **GPS:** N42.33.27/W96.27.83. **Background:** Located in the wooded loess hills of western Iowa, the park owes its origins to Thomas J. Stone who acquired the property in 1895. His son Edgar developed the land as a park and zoo which was purchased by Sioux City in 1912 and sold to the state in 1935. **Facilities:** RV/tent sites, picnic areas, day lodge, trails, Dorothy Pecaut Nature Center. **CCC Company:** 2725V SP-23. **CCC Features:** Campground, entrance portals and roads, picnic areas, trails, staff residences, Calumet Shelter, Stone Lodge.

# KANSAS

## Other CCC-Related Parks

## State Parks

**1. CRAWFORD STATE PARK,** 1 Lake Road, Farlington, KS 66734; 620-362-3671; *www.kdwp.state.ks.us/state_parks*. **GPS:** N37.37.86/W94.48.88. **Background:** Located in southeastern Kansas on the edge of the Ozark Mountains, this wooded park surrounds the shores of 150-acre Crawford Lake which was constructed by the CCC in 1935. The park features the CCC Memorial Trail that includes exhibits about the Corps' work and a "Spirit of the CCC" statue; as well as the Deer Run Trail that links the park with the nearby Farlington Fish Hatchery, also built by the CCC. **Facilities:** RV/tent sites, cabins, bathhouses and boat ramps, beach, playgrounds, historic archeological sites. **Company:** 788 SCS-10. **CCC Features:** Lake, trail, fish hatchery.

# MISSOURI

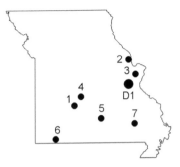

## Destination Parks

### D1. MERAMEC STATE PARK AND WASHINGTON STATE PARK

*The Civilian Conservation Corps (CCC) and the Works Progress Administration (WPA) changed the face of the fledgling Missouri state park system and propelled it forward toward the enviable position it now holds as one of the best in the nation.*[33]

— Lynn Morrow
"Grand Buildings of the Thirties," *Ozarks Watch Magazine*

These two Ozark parks, located only 33 miles apart, preserve some of the finest examples of CCC landscape work and structural design. Missouri created a parks system in 1917 and, by the late 1920s, nearly a dozen sites had been set aside. However, onset of the Depression brought work in these parks to a halt. The ECW program and the CCC ushered in an era of dramatic growth for Missouri's parks as has been noted by historian James Denny, writing in the Spring 1994 issue of *Ozarks Watch Magazine*. "Although the Great Depression is rightfully viewed as an era of hard times . . . it proved to be a golden age for the [Missouri] state park system."

CCC Company 739 SP-3 arrived in Meramec State Park in June, 1933. Set on the banks of the Meramec River, the park is known for its many caves. The largest, Fisher Cave, had been a tourist attraction for more than a century before CCC workers improved walkways, bridges, and stairways within the cave (Figure 110). They blazed woodland trails; built more than a dozen cabins (one duplex is a preserved CCC barracks); and constructed a lookout tower, shelter house, and administrative structures. The Corps' most notable project in the park was construction of the log and stone Dining Lodge perched atop a wooded ridge.

A few miles away, Washington State Park was set aside in 1932 to preserve the site's beauty and Native American history. Washington is exceptional both for its ancient Indian petroglyphs, and for its many well-preserved CCC buildings. Company 1743C SP-11 arrived in the park in the spring of 1934 and remained for five years. Composed of young African Americans, the men dubbed their home "Camp Thunderbird" to honor the area's native history. In the company were several stone masons and their craftsmanship is evident in the picnic shelters and pavilions, rock guard-walls along park roads, as well as in the carefully cut stone slabs of the 1000 Steps Trail (Figure 111). Their finest work was Thunderbird Lodge, featuring a symbolic Thunderbird carved into the chimney and wrought-iron hardware

**Figure 110.** CCC enrollees pose in front of Fisher Cave at Meramec State Park.

**Figure 111.** This unusual octagonal shelter is in Washington State Park.

throughout (Plate 12). They also built an octagonal-shaped overlook shelter in the nearby hills. Today, the CCC structures at Meramec and Washington state parks, along with those in other Missouri parks, are listed on the National Register of Historic Places.

***Additional Information:*** Meramec: 115 Meramec Park Drive, Sullivan, MO 63080 (Figure 112); 573-468-6072; *www.mostateparks.com.* **GPS:** N38.12.82/W91.05.54. Facilities include visitor center, RV/tent sites, cabins, motel, gift shop and grill, picnic areas and shelters, trails, Fisher Cave tours, water activities. Washington: 13041 State Highway 104, De Soto, MO 63020; 636-586-0322; *www.mostateparks.com.* **GPS:** N38.05.29/W90.41.34. Facilities include visitor center, historic sites, RV/tent sites, group camp, cabins, picnic areas and shelters, pool, trails.

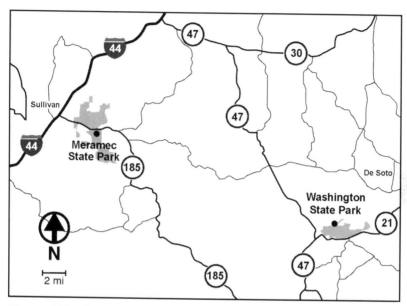

**Figure 112.** The location of Meramec State Park and Washington State Park.

# Other CCC-Related Parks
## State Parks

**1. BENNETT SPRING STATE PARK,** 26250 Highway 64A, Lebanon, MO 65536-6797; 417-532-4338; *www.mostateparks.com.* **GPS:** N37.43.56/W92.51.42. **Background:** With its abundance of spring water, the area was a 19th-century milling center. Among the most successful millers was Peter Bennett. In 1924, the state acquired land along the river, including Bennetts Spring, for one of Missouri's first parks. **Facilities:** RV/tent sites, cabins, motel, picnic areas and shelters, dining lodge, pool, boating facilities, trails, nature center. **CCC Company:** 1772V SP-7. **CCC Features:** Park roads, arched bridge, cabins, shelters, trails, dining lodge.

**2. CUIVRE RIVER STATE PARK,** 678 State Route 147, Troy, MO 63379; 636-528-7247; *www.mostateparks.com.* **GPS:** N39.0.46/W90.55.22. **Background:** This land of hardwood forests, glades, and tall grass prairie was set aside as an RDA. It became a Missouri state park in 1946. CCC and WPA developed the group camps and other facilities.

**Facilities:** Visitor center, RV/tent sites, three group camps, picnic areas and shelter, Lake Lincoln, trails. **CCC Company:** 3771 NP-1/SP-13. **CCC Features:** Park roads, bridges, trails, group camps, picnic shelter.

**3. Dr. Edmund Babler Memorial State Park,** 800 Guy Park Drive, Wildwood, MO 63005; 636-458-3813; *www.mostateparks.com.* **GPS:** N38.37.05/W91.41.30. **Background:** Created in 1937 from a gift of 880 acres by Jacob Babler to honor his brother, Saint Louis surgeon Edmund Babler, M.D., the park preserves forests and fields near Saint Louis. A centerpiece of the park is a life-size statue of Dr. Babler unveiled by Interior Secretary Harold Ickes during the park's 1938 dedication. A park feature is the Jacob Babler Outdoor Education Center, an ADA-accessible group camp for children and adults. **Facilities:** River Hill Visitor Center, RV/tent sites, group camp, picnic areas, pool, recreation fields, trails. **CCC Companies:** 2729 SP-2, 3763 SP-22, and 2730 SCS-32. **CCC Features:** Park entrance; roads; Alta, Cochran and Walnut Grove picnic shelters.

**4. Lake of the Ozarks State Park,** 403 State Route 134, Kaiser, MO 65047; 573-348-2694; *www.mostateparks.com.* **GPS:** N38.07.45/ W92.33.67. **Background:** Created in 1934 as an RDA following impoundment of the Osage River, this is the state's largest park. The park is known for its CCC-built structures. **Facilities:** RV/tent sites, cabins, four group camps, picnic areas and shelters, marinas, beaches, bathhouses, stables, trails, amphitheater, Fort Leonard Wood Recreation Area, Ozark Caverns (guided tours). **CCC Companies:** 1712 NP-2/SP-20, 1756 NP-3/SP-11, and 1726 SP-12. **CCC Features:** Park roads, Pin Oak Hollow Bridge, stone dams, cabins, comfort stations, group camp, Rising Sun and McCubbin Point picnic shelters, beach, administrative buildings.

**5. Montauk State Park,** 345 County Road 6670, Salem, MO 65560; 573-548-2201; *www.mostateparks.com.* **GPS:** N37.27.35/W91.40.99. **Background:** Acquired by the state in 1926, the park preserves some of the Ozark Region's finest trout fishing along the Jacks Fork and Current national scenic rivers. The park also preserves an old mill (ca. 1896), a vestige of the area's flour-milling heritage. The CCC built the spillway dam, fish hatchery, and other park structures. **Facilities:** RV/tent sites, cabins, motel, dining lodge, picnic areas and shelter, trails. **CCC Company:** 1770V SP-1. **Significant CCC Features:** Spillway dam, fish hatchery, old picnic shelter, cabins, naturalist's office, old mill restoration, administrative structures.

**6. ROARING RIVER STATE PARK,** 12716 Farm Road 2239, Cassville, MO 65625; 417-847-2539; *www.mostateparks.com.* **GPS:** N36.35.17/W93.50.23. **Background:** Located in the Ozark Mountains, Roaring River preserves a landscape of wooded hills and valleys along Roaring River. In 1928, Saint Louis business leader Thomas Sayman purchased land and donated it for the park. **Facilities:** RV/tent sites, cabins, group camp, pool, trails, fire tower, Roaring River Hills Natural Area, Emory Melton Inn and Conference Center. **CCC Company:** 1713 SP-4. **CCC Features:** Camp Smokey Group Camp, bathhouse, dam and spillway, cabins, Deer Leap Trail, Kitchen Shelter No. 2, CCC Lodge (park store).

**7. SAM A. BAKER STATE PARK,** MO Route 143, Patterson, MO 63956; 573-856-4411; *www.mostateparks.com.* **GPS:** N37.15.15/W90.30.32. **Background:** The ancient landscape of the Saint Francois Mountains, a remnant of Precambrian volcanoes, is among the oldest exposed rocks in North America. The land was acquired for a park in 1926 through the efforts of Governor Samuel Baker. Development was carried out by CCC and WPA. **Facilities:** Visitor center, RV/tent sites, equestrian camp, cabins, dining lodge, picnic areas and shelters, nature center, Saint Francois River water sports facilities, trails (including a section of the paved Ozark Trail), Mudlick Natural Area. **CCC Company:** 740 SP-5. **CCC Features:** Park roads, dining lodge, cabins.

# NEBRASKA

D1

1

## Destination Parks

### D1. SCOTTS BLUFF NATIONAL MONUMENT

*Scotts Bluff National Monument is unique as a park site as everything (except the entrance booth and the residence) was constructed by the CCC and is still in use today.*[34]

— Eric Haugland, Park Ranger
Scotts Bluff National Monument

Rising nearly 800 feet above the North Platte River, Scotts Bluff is a 60-million-year-old erosional remnant of the ancient Great Plains. The promontory, named for Hiram Scott, a mountain man who had the misfortune to die at its base in 1828, served for decades as a landmark for pioneers traveling along the Oregon, California, and Mormon trails. The bluff's role as a westward compass ended with the opening of the Transcontinental Railroad in 1869. Scotts Bluff's importance in American history was acknowledged through its designation as a National Monument in 1919; however, few funds were appropriated for its development. In 1931, a survey team assessed the feasibility of constructing a road to the summit, but with the nation in the grip of the Depression, the project was cancelled.

Much changed with the election of President Franklin Roosevelt. In the fall of 1933, local Civil Works Administration (CWA) crews began the Summit Road project and continued it until funds ran out. In June, 1934, monument "custodian" Dr. Harold Cook arranged for a CCC camp at Scotts Bluff. CCC Company 762 NM-1 arrived in May, 1935, to begin three years of work. During this time, the men

**Figure 113.** The national park visitor center at Scotts Bluff National Monument lies in the shadow of the landform that was an important landmark along the Oregon Trail.

completed the Summit Road, finished work on Saddle Rock Trail, cleared land for picnic grounds, expanded the WPA-constructed Oregon Trail Museum, and crafted museum exhibits and dioramas that remain on display. In addition, they erected a custodian's residence (now offices), comfort stations, and other structures, most made from adobe bricks manufactured on site (Figure 113).

In his history of Scotts Bluff, Ron Cockrell wrote that the monument was set aside as a memorial to "those brave souls who moved the spirit of America westward." It also remains a legacy to the men of the CCC who helped to renew that spirit during some of the nation's darkest days.

*Additional Information:* 190276 Old Oregon Trail, Gering, NE 69341 (Figure 114); 308-436-9700; *www.nps.gov/scbl.* **GPS:** N41.49.91/ W103.42.56. Facilities include visitor center and Oregon Trail Museum, historic sites, picnic area, Saddle Rock and Oregon trails, Summit Road (seasonal shuttle service available), interpretive programs.

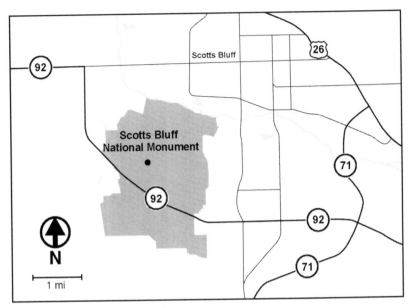

**Figure 114.** The location of Scotts Bluff National Monument.

# Other CCC-Related Parks

## State Parks

**1.** PONCA STATE PARK, 88090 Spur 26E, Ponca, NE 68770; 402-755-2284; *http://outdoornebraska.ne.gov/parks/*. **GPS:** N42.35.70/W96.41.95. **Background:** Established from lands donated in 1934, the park preserves woodlands along the Missouri River. The CCC developed facilities, including the Corps of Discovery Trail commemorating the passage of Lewis and Clark in 1804. The park is a gateway to the Missouri National Recreational River. **Facilities:** RV/tent sites, picnic areas and shelters, trails, water sports facilities, golf course, Missouri National Recreational River Resource and Education Center. **CCC Company:** 2736 DSP-1/SP-5. **CCC Features:** Park roads, picnic areas and shelters, comfort stations, landscaping, trails.

# North Dakota

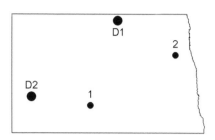

## Destination Parks

### D1. INTERNATIONAL PEACE GARDEN

*We did it with plain old manpower. I have fond memories of the boys who were there.*[35]

— George Warren, CCC veteran
International Peace Garden

On July 14, 1932, 50,000 people gathered along the North Dakota-Manitoba border to dedicate a garden that did not yet exist. A stone cairn unveiled that day was inscribed with these words: "To God and His Glory, we two nations dedicate this Garden, and pledge ourselves, that as long as man shall live we will not take up arms against one another." This "International Peace Garden" was the dream of Canadian horticulturist Henry Moore, who proposed creating a garden along the world's longest "unfortified border" at a 1928 conference.

Readily endorsed, a committee searched for a site. Niagara Falls was an early favorite, but when Moore toured the Turtle Mountains of North Dakota and Manitoba, he wrote, "Those undulating hills rising out of the limitless prairies are filled with lakes and streams. On the south, wheat everywhere, and on the north, the Manitoba Forest Reserve. What a place for a Garden."[1]

Manitoba donated Crown Lands and North Dakota purchased property for the proposed 2,339-acre botanical preserve. Creation of the ECW program provided resources for development on the United States' side of the park, while Manitoba's government hired unemployed local men to carry out work north of the border. CCC Company 794 SP-1 of "Camp Borderline" arrived at the Garden in the spring of

**Figure 115.** This large CCC Lodge at the International Peace Garden is filled, each summer, with group-camp participants.

1934 and worked at the site, even through frigid winters, until 1941. The men laid out roads and stone bridges, erected a lodge of North Dakota granite and Manitoba timber, and built cabins, comfort stations, and picnic shelters; and excavated Lake Udall, named for Manitoba newspaper editor W. V. Udall (figures 115 and 116). Work ceased during WW II and did not resume until the 1950s. The Peace Towers that now dominate the site were a gift from the United States on the Garden's 50th anniversary, and the 9-11 Memorial, composed of girders from the World Trade Center, was dedicated on September 11, 2002. Plans are under consideration for a Peace Hall of Fame to be erected in the Gardens.

Exhibits in the Garden's Interpretive Center chronicle the park's history, including the role of the CCC in its creation. While much has changed from the fields and woods the CCC enrollees found, their legacy is preserved in this botanical paradise.

***Additional Information:*** 10939 US Highway 281, Dunseith, ND 58329 (Figure 117); 701-263-4390; *www.peacegarden.com.* **GPS:** N48.59.57/W100.03.10. Facilities include visitor center, RV/tent sites, group camps, picnic areas and shelters, lakes Udall and Stormon, trails, chapel, floral clock, gift shop, dining services, Peace Tower, bell tower, amphitheatre, auditorium, Game Warden Museum, International Center for Peace and Conflict Resolution (planned), interpretive programs.

**Figure 116.** Vertical logs were used by the CCC to build this rustic comfort station at the International Peace Garden.

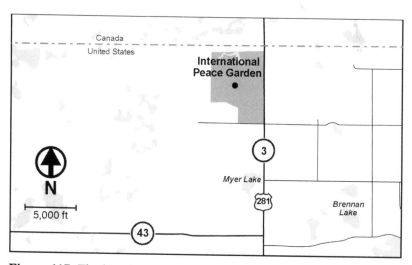

**Figure 117.** The location of International Peace Garden.

## D2. THEODORE ROOSEVELT NATIONAL PARK AND
## CHATEAU DE MORES STATE HISTORIC SITE

*We built the entry gate, the rock cairns, the flagstone walks and rock walls. We sat down with a piece of paper and designed it rock by rock. A group of us cut, shaped and built rock walls that are still standing.*[36]

— Jack Krank, CCC veteran
Theodore Roosevelt National Park

In the early 1920s, a group of North Dakotans promoted a national park in the badlands to honor President Theodore Roosevelt for his leadership and conservation legacy. In the 1880s, Roosevelt had spent several seasons in the Dakota Territory as a rancher and hunter. He remarked several times, "I never would have been President if it had not been for my experiences in North Dakota." While advocates of the North Dakota park saw it becoming one more destination along a highway that was envisioned to link several other western parks, the federal government was not interested. During the Depression, advocates persuaded the Resettlement Administration to set aside a portion of recently acquired marginal lands for a park. This was done, and much of the remainder would later become part of the Little Missouri National Grasslands. In 1934, an agreement was reached among the Resettlement Administration, ECW Program, NPS, and state. Originally, NPS proposed a state park, but the North Dakota Historical Society was unprepared to manage a park of the planned size. Nonetheless, the society agreed to sponsor three CCC camps.

CCC Company 2767 DSP-7 arrived in July 1934, and set up camp on the banks of the Little Missouri River near the present South Unit of the park. Two other companies, 2771 DSP-5 and 2772 SP-7, established camps along the river in the future North Unit. Company 2771 remained only a year; while Company 2772 worked until 1939, when it moved to the South Unit. During their years in "Roosevelt Regional State Park," enrollees built roads and trails, laid out picnic areas and campgrounds, and erected shelters and administrative buildings. Notable examples of their work include miles 7 to 13 of the South Unit

Scenic Drive (Plate 13, top), the old East Entrance Station (Plate 13, bottom) (now abandoned but accessible by a foot trail), and many stone culverts. In the North Unit, there are several CCC picnic shelters including the dramatic River Bend Overlook Shelter that sits high above the Little Missouri River (Figure 118). Through the perseverance of Representative William Lemke, "Theodore Roosevelt National Memorial Park," was established in 1947. It was elevated to national park status in 1978.

While in the park, the CCC aided WPA workers in restoring the home of the Marquis de Mores, a French entrepreneur and founder of Medora, named for his wife, in 1883. His home, where "TR" was often a guest, and packing plant, where Chimney Park is now located, along with CCC-era buildings are now part of the Chateau de Mores State Historic Site (Figure 119).

***Additional Information:*** Theodore Roosevelt National Park: 315 Second Avenue, Medora, ND 58645-0007 (Figure 120); 701-623-4730; *www.nps.gov/thro*. **GPS:** N46.55.20/W103.31.56. Facilities include Painted Canyon, South Unit and North Unit visitor centers, historic sites and structures (including Roosevelt's Maltese Cross cabin), RV/tent sites, group camp, picnic areas and shelters, trails, stables, scenic drives, interpretive programs. Chateau de Mores State Historic Site:

**Figure 118.** This rough-hewn stone shelter above the Little Missouri River in Theodore Roosevelt National Park invites the visitors to take in the grandeur of the rugged landscape.

**Figure 119.** CCC workers constructed this administrative building at Chateau de Mores State Historic Site.

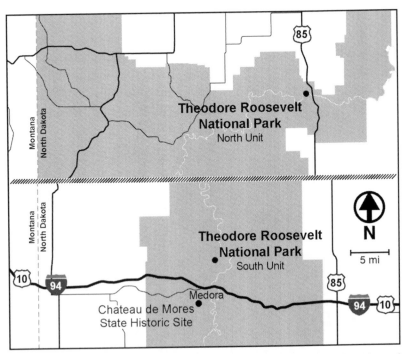

**Figure 120.** The location of Theodore Roosevelt National Park and Chateau de Mores State Historic Site. The South Unit of the national park and the state historic site are located near Medora. The North Unit of the national park is located about 70 miles north of Medora.

228

Chateau Road, Medora, ND 58645; 701-623-4355; *http://history.nd.gov/historicsites/chateau.* Visitor center, historic sites and structures, picnic areas, interpretive programs.

## Other CCC-Related Parks

## State Parks

**1. FORT ABRAHAM LINCOLN STATE PARK,** 4480 Fort Lincoln Road, Mandan, ND 58554; 701-667-6340; *www.ndparks.com.* **GPS:** N46.46.04/W100.50.98. **Background:** Late in the 16th century, the native Mandan constructed On-A-Slant village on the slopes above the Missouri River and lived there for nearly two centuries before disease forced them to abandon the area. In 1804, Lewis and Clark's Corps of Discovery paused here. After the Civil War, the Army built infantry Fort McKeen on the bluffs above the old Mandan village. In 1872, this fort was renamed "Abraham Lincoln" and served as the home of the 7th Cavalry, commanded by Lieutenant Colonel George A. Custer. In May, 1876, Custer led his troopers from here to the Battle of the Little Big Horn. The fort closed in 1891 and later became a state park. CCC enrollees restored historic structures and built a visitor

**Figure 121.** The visitor center and museum were built by the CCC at Fort Abraham Lincoln State Park.

229

**Figure 122.** This rustic log and stone shelter is part of Turtle River State Park.

center (Figure 121), trails, and picnic areas. **Facilities:** Visitor center and museum, historic structures, RV/tent sites, primitive campground, picnic areas, shelters and trails. **CCC Company:** 2775 SP-3. **CCC Features:** Visitor center and museum, restored and reconstructed lodges and blockhouses, foundation markers, picnic shelters, trails.

**2. TURTLE RIVER STATE PARK,** 3084 Park Avenue, Arvilla, ND 58214; 701-343-2992; *www.ndparks.com.* **GPS:** N47.56.01/W97.29.84. **Background:** Located in a scenic valley, the park preserves woodlands and marshes along the Turtle River. **Facilities:** RV/tent sites, group camp, cabins, chalet, picnic areas and shelter, Woodland Lodge, trails (including a portion of the Northern Star Mountain Bike Trail). **CCC Companies:** 2770 DSP-4, 764 and 4727 SP-5. **CCC Features:** Park roads, bridges, Woodland Lodge (relocated and reconstructed), CCC picnic shelter (Figure 122), trails, abandoned gatehouse.

# SOUTH DAKOTA

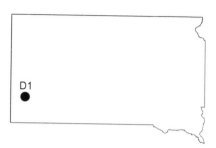

## Destination Parks

### D1. CUSTER STATE PARK AND WIND CAVE NATIONAL PARK

*The marriage of man and nature is demonstrated throughout the park with buildings, bridges and structures. The detailed craftsmanship is displayed in a manner that complements the stated goals.*[37]

— Bradley Block, Chief of Interpretation
Custer State Park

Rising above the desolate Badlands, the forested Black Hills are sacred to the native Lakota who fought unsuccessfully for them following the discovery of gold there in 1874. In only a few years, gold seekers were replaced by tourists anxious to explore the scenic landscape. In 1912, South Dakota established the Custer State Forest, and Governor Peter Norbeck set aside a game preserve as habitat for elk, bison, bighorn sheep, and other wildlife. The name of the site was changed to Custer State Park in 1919. Over time, the preserve expanded to 71,000 acres, making it one of the largest state parks in the nation. Even before its designation, the park was home to one of the first Black Hills resorts — Sylvan Lake Lodge. Blue Bell, Legion Lake, and State Game lodges were established in the 1920s and 1930s; the latter served as President Calvin Coolidge's "Summer White House" in 1927.

Much development of this area occurred during the New Deal when the CCC operated several camps. Company 1793 SP-1 at "Camp Pine Creek," arrived in 1933; followed by companies 1795 and 2766

SP-2 at "Camp Doran." A year later, Company 2757 SP-3 at "Camp Narrows," and companies 2755 and 795 SP-4 at "Camp Lodge" joined the work. Among the buildings erected or restored by the CCC were the Peter Norbeck Visitor Center (Figure 123), the "Herdsman's Home" (now the Wildlife Station Visitor Center), Mount Coolidge and Harney Peak lookout towers and a replica of the 1870s Gordon Stockade. Crews developed picnic grounds and shelters; dammed streams creating Doran, Center, and Sylvan lakes; carved trails and improved roads, including work on Iron Mountain and Needles highways; and built or renovated cabins at the Blue Bell and Sylvan Lake resorts. The present Black Hills Playhouse includes structures once part of Camp Lodge. No CCC camps worked at nearby Mount Rushmore National Memorial but enrollees did participate in the park's 1936 dedication.

Nearby Wind Cave was first explored in 1881, but success as a tourist attraction became mired in legal disputes and family feuds. In 1903, the caverns were set aside as Wind Cave National Park, however visitor facilities remained primitive. In July, 1934, CCC Company 2754 NP-1 began work in the park. The men replaced wooden cave stairs with cement steps and metal hand-rails; widened cave trails and installed an elevator; constructed the visitor center (Figure 124),

**Figure 123.** This 1930s image shows the Peter Norbeck Visitor Center under construction in Custer State Park.

**Figure 124.** The CCC built this elaborate visitor center and administration building at Wind Cave National Park.

and developed the first campground (now the headquarters picnic area). A side camp carried out projects in nearby Jewel Cave National Monument.

*Additional Information:* Custer: 13329 US Highway 16A, Custer, SD 57730 (Figure 125); 605-255-4515; *http://gfp.sd.gov/state-parks/directory/custer*. **GPS:** N43.45.89/W103.22.83. Facilities include visitor center, RV/tent sites, cabins, resort lodges, restaurant, lakes with water activities, trails, scenic roads, bison herds. Wind Cave: 26611 US Highway 385, Hot Springs, SD 57747-9430; 605-745-4600; *www.nps.gov/wica*. **GPS:** N43.33.30/W103.28.45. Facilities include visitor center, RV/tent sites, picnic areas, surface and cave trails, cave tours and interpretive programs.

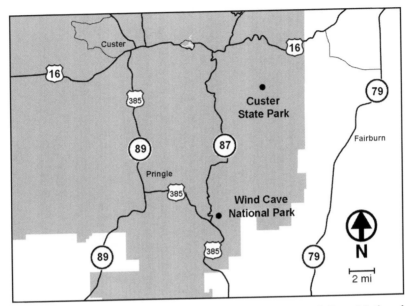

**Figure 125.** The location of Custer State Park and Wind Cave National Park.

# Southwest Region

## ARIZONA

## Destination Parks

### D1. GRAND CANYON NATIONAL PARK

> *Grand Canyon National Park owes a great debt to the Civilian Conservation Corps . . . projects which we had contemplated but were unable to execute through lack of funds, are now being done in a highly acceptable manner by enrolled men.*[38]
>
> — M. R. Tillotson, CCC-era Superintendent
> Grand Canyon National Park

One of the world's natural wonders, the Grand Canyon of the Colorado River was long known to Native Americans. Spanish explorers glimpsed its expanse in the 16th century, but it was Colonel John Wesley Powell's 1869–1870 expedition down the Colorado that riveted the nation's attention to this magnificent landscape. The Grand Canyon was set aside as a forest reserve in 1893 and named a national monument by President Theodore Roosevelt in 1908. It became a national park in 1919. Early tourists arrived by train and by the 1920s thousands were visiting by automobile, placing enormous strain on limited facilities. Plans for development were soon halted by the onset of the Depression, but the CCC gave the Grand Canyon projects new life.

The first Corps enrollees arrived at Grand Canyon in 1933 and, over the next nine years, six CCC Camps, NP-1–6, operated in the park. Some crews worked only a few seasons, while others remained for extended tours. Two companies, 818 NP-1 and 819 NP-2, remained the longest. Company 818, had the full experience — working in the canyon's depths in winter and remote North Rim in summer. An inspector once described their North Rim camp as "probably the most isolated camp in the U.S."

The greatest concentration of CCC features in Grand Canyon National Park may be found in Canyon Village. These include low stone walls along the canyon's edge, the rustic Community Building, footpaths and a hand-hewn wooden bridge, and stone steps beneath Kolb Studio. Near Bright Angel Lodge, a plaque commemorates a remarkable feat — the CCC's stringing of the Trans-Canyon Telephone Line in 1934 (Figure 126). The men also built or improved roads, among them the Old Desert View Highway. They carried out extensive trail work that included widening the Bright Angel Trailhead and constructing two stone shelters; blasting a path connecting Bright Angel and Kaibab trails; blazing Clear Creek Trail; and laying out paths leading to Ribbon Falls and Upper Ribbon Falls (Figure 127). Company 818, working near Phantom Ranch, built a mule corral, ranger station, and Rock House Bridge; planted cottonwood trees; and dug a pool for ranch guests (traces remain). Enrollees also assisted scientists with research projects and developed museum and wayside exhibits, including a display of fossils at Cedar Ridge on the South Kaibab Trail. Throughout the park, the CCC carried out many fire suppression and landscaping projects.

In summing up their contributions, park ranger Pam Cox wrote in the summer 2003 *Canyon View* newsletter that "throughout

**Figure 126.** A CCC enrollee is installing the first telephone lines to span the Grand Canyon.

**Figure 127.** Work by the CCC created trails along the North Rim of Grand Canyon National Park.

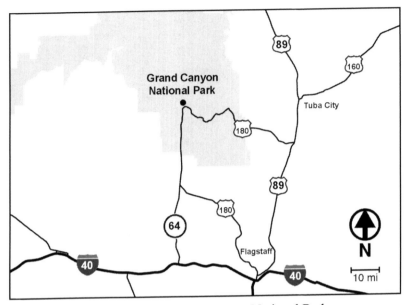

**Figure 128.** The location of Grand Canyon National Park.

Grand Canyon National Park, the fruits of the CCC workers' labors can be seen."

***Additional Information:*** Village Loop Road, Grand Canyon, AZ 86023 (Figure 128); 928-638-7888; *www.nps.gov/grca.* **GPS:** N36.03.32/W112.08.33. Facilities include visitor centers, museums, historic sites and structures, shops, restaurants, RV/tent sites, lodgings, picnic areas, trails, interpretive programs, guide services.

---

## D2. Colossal Cave Mountain Park

*Colossal Cave owes an enormous debt to the Civilian Conservation Corps for its handsome headquarters buildings, to say nothing of the installation of the lighting, walkways, and handrails in the cave.*[39]

— Mattie K. Maierhauser and E. Lendell Cockrum
Colossal Cave Mountain Park Research Library

238

Colossal Cave, located in the Rincon Mountains near Tucson, is considered one of the largest "dry" (dormant) limestone caves in the world. Created by eons of groundwater seeping through Escabrosa limestone, the cave contains nearly 40 miles of charted passages. Solomon Lick, owner of the nearby Mountain Springs Hotel, discovered the cave in 1879 while searching for stray cattle, but did not publicize his early explorations. While the cavern did not attract tourists, it did draw a different clientele in the 1880s when it became a hideout for bandits and train-robbers.

In 1917, Dr. Byron Cummings, archeologist with the Arizona State Museum and future president of the University of Arizona, first mapped the cave, identified geological formations, and gathered evidence of human habitation going back more than a thousand years. In 1922, Frank Schmidt leased the property and offered guided tours. A decade later, cattleman Charles Day purchased nearby Mountain Springs Ranch and renamed it "La Posta Quemada," (burnt station) — in reference to a fire in the 1870s that destroyed a railway stop at the site. In 1934, Schmidt ceded the lease to the state, paving the way for the CCC to develop a park. Company 858 SP-10 arrived that summer and set up camp near the ranch. Camp buildings still in existence include a bathhouse, now used as a barn; and the camp office, an adobe structure that now houses the park's museum (Figure 129). In October, 1935, Company 2851 SP-10 replaced the earlier crew. These men constructed the park headquarters that appears to cling to the mountainside, enlarged the cave entrance, widened passageways and installed electric lights, built a stone ramada (pavilion) at La Sevilla picnic ground, and laid out campgrounds, picnic areas and roads. Skilled wood-workers and craftsmen also produced furniture and fixtures that are still in daily use.

In 1991, the Pima County Parklands Foundation took over management of Colossal Cave and La Posta Quemada Ranch, creating a 2,000-acre park. Today, with acknowledgment of the CCC's contributions, the park is listed on the National Register of Historic Places.

***Additional Information:*** 16721 East Old Spanish Trail, Vail, AZ 85641 (Figure 130); 520-647-7275; *www.colossalcave.com.* **GPS:** N32.03.75/W110.38.02. Facilities include RV/tent sites, picnic areas and shelters, trails, cave tours, gardens, Native American historic sites.

**Figure 129.** Rough-hewn stone was used to construct the Combination Building at Colossal Cave Mountain Park.

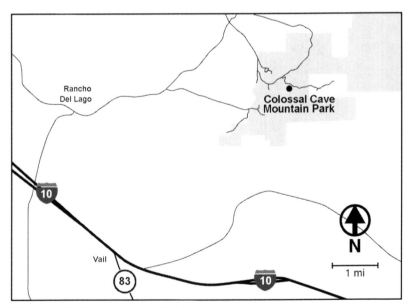

**Figure 130.** The location of Colossal Cave Mountain Park.

**Figure 131.** This shelter in Chiricahua National Monument was built with locally quarried stone.

# Other CCC-Related Parks
## National Parks

**1.** CHIRICAHUA NATIONAL MONUMENT, 13063 East Bonita Canyon Road, Willcox, AZ 85643-9737; 520-824-3560 x 302; *www.nps.gov/ chir.* **GPS:** N32.00.30/W109.21.43. **Background:** Located in southeastern Arizona's high desert, the monument preserves unusual geological formations and Native American history. **Facilities:** Visitor center, campground, picnic areas, trails, wilderness area, historic Faraway Ranch. **CCC Company:** 828 NM-2A. **CCC Features:** Bonita Canyon Road, Echo Canyon Trail shelter, CCC camp ruins (Figure 131).

**2.** PETRIFIED FOREST NATIONAL PARK, 1 Park Road, Petrified Forest, AZ 86028; 928-524-6228; *www.nps.gov/pefo.* **GPS:** N35.04.94/ W109.47.20. **Background:** The site was set aside in 1906 to preserve mineralized wood and other fossils from the Mesozoic and Triassic periods, as well as ancient dwellings and petroglyphs. It became a national park in 1962. **Facilities:** Visitor center, Rainbow Forest and Painted Desert Inn museums, ancient pueblos, trails, picnic areas. **CCC Companies:** 3342 NP-7 and 1837 NP-8. **CCC Features:** Staff residences, roads, trails, stabilized Agate House and Puerco Pueblos, Rainbow Forest and Painted Desert Inn museums (Figure 132).

**Figure 132.** The CCC constructed the historic Painted Desert Inn in Petrified Forest National Park.

**3. SAGUARO NATIONAL PARK,** 3693 South Old Spanish Trail, Tucson, AZ 85730-5601; 520-733-5153; *www.nps.gov/sagu.* **GPS:** N32.10.80/ W110.44.14. **Background:** Set aside as a National Monument in 1933 and designated a National Park in 1994, the park is composed of two units: Rincon Mountain (east) and Tucson Mountain (west). The park protects the natural beauty of the Sonoran Desert and the Saguaro cactus ecosystem. **Facilities:** Visitor centers, picnic facilities, trails, backcountry campsites, archeological sites. **CCC Companies:** 1837 SP-6 and 2862 SP-11/NM-3. **CCC Features:** Historic Cactus Forest Drive with stone retaining walls, bridges and culverts (east), picnic facilities (west), trails.

**4. WUPATKI AND SUNSET CRATER VOLCANIC NATIONAL MONUMENTS,** Flagstaff Area National Monuments, 6400 North Highway 89, Flagstaff, AZ 86004; 928-526-1157; *www.nps.gov/wupa* and *www.nps.gov/ sucr.* **GPS:** N35.32.69/W111.23.92. **Background:** These two national monuments were established to preserve ancient Puebloan cultural sites and the site of a volcanic eruption 900 years ago. CCC enrollees carried out development and site stabilization. **Facilities:** Wupatki and Sunset Crater visitor centers, campground (Forest Service), picnic areas, trails. **CCC Company:** 3838 NP-12/NM-5. **CCC Features:** Roads, ranger residence, stabilized ruins.

**Figure 133.** CCC crews are grading roads at Papago Park.

## Other Parks

**5. PAPAGO PARK,** 625 N. Galvin Parkway, Tempe, AZ 85008; 602-495-5458; *http://phoenix.gov/parks.* **GPS:** N33.26.87/W111.56.62. **Background:** This landscape of sandstone buttes and desert was set aside as Papago Sahuaro National Monument in 1914. In 1930, the monument was returned to the state for development as a park. During WW II, the park housed German POWs. In 1959, the park was purchased by the City of Phoenix. **Facilities:** Picnic areas, trails, fishing ponds, 18-hole golf course, Desert Botanical Garden, Phoenix Zoo, Phoenix Municipal Stadium (baseball), Hunt's Tomb (grave of first governor), amphitheater, softball complex. **CCC Companies:** 2849 BR-19 and 2860 SP-4. **CCC Features:** Ramadas (shelters), 3,500-seat amphitheater, trails, roads, picnic sites, fishing ponds (Figure 133).

# ARKANSAS

## Destination Parks

### D1. PETIT JEAN STATE PARK

*The spirit of the Ozarks has been awakened in Petit Jean State Park, Arkansas. Here the completion of a community building has proved the medium for revival.*[40]

— 1937 Yearbook: Parks and Recreation Program
US Department of the Interior, National Park Service

Nestled between the Ozark and Ouachita national forests, Petit Jean State Park is a land of wooded hills overlooking Cedar Creek and the Arkansas River. The park's unusual name comes from the story of a tragic affair between a French explorer and his fiancée who, disguised as a cabin-boy nicknamed 'Petit Jean,' followed him to a mountain towering above the Arkansas River. Only after she fell ill was she recognized. She died and was buried near the summit of the mountain that now bears her "name."

For more than a century, the forests of this area were logged to fuel the nation's growth westward. In 1907, Fort Smith Lumber Company officials gathered in an area called "Seven Hollows" to assess the timber's profitability. They concluded that the rugged terrain around Petit Jean Mountain made commercial use unprofitable and the land was eventually offered to the government for use as a "national park." In 1921, company agent Dr. T. W. Hardison met with NPS Director Stephen Mather to promote the site. Mather appreciated its scenic value but concluded that the site was too small for a national park. Hardison took his case to the Arkansas legislature where, in 1923, a bill was passed designating Petit Jean Mountain and adjacent Cedar Creek Canyon as Arkansas's first state park.

Little development took place until 1933 when CCC Company 1781V SP-1, composed of WW I veterans, arrived in the park. The crew included experienced carpenters, masons, and artisans who accomplished projects of exceptional quality and craftsmanship. They blazed Cedar Falls, Seven Hollows, Cedar Creek, and Canyon trails; carved stone steps leading to an overlook of 95-foot-high Cedar Falls; and quarried stone for a dam impounding 170-acre Lake Bailey. In addition to nine log and stone cottages and a distinctive water tower, the men erected the rustic Mather Lodge (Figure 134), named for Stephen Mather, located on a bluff overlooking Cedar Creek Canyon and the surrounding hills. In recognition of the lasting quality and integrity of the CCC work performed at Petit Jean, the park includes three National Historic Register districts featuring more than 80 structures and trails.

**Figure 134.** The large timbers support the rustic log and stone Mather Lodge in Petit Jean State Park.

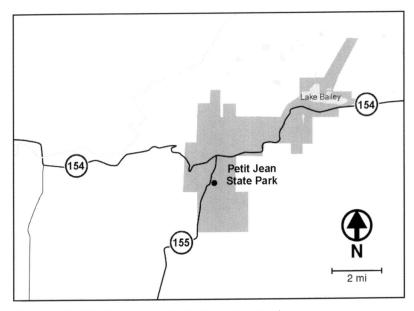

**Figure 135.** The location of Petit Jean State Park.

*Additional Information:* 1285 Petit Jean Road, Morrilton, AR 72110 (Figure 135); 501-727-5441; *www.petitjeanstatepark.com.* **GPS:** N35.07.65/W92.55.44. Facilities including visitor center, RV/tent sites, cabins, Mather Lodge, restaurant, picnic areas and shelters, lakes Roosevelt and Bailey, boathouse, bathhouse, pool, tennis court, trails, Red Bluff scenic drive.

# Other CCC-Related Parks

## State Parks

**1.** CROWLEYS RIDGE STATE PARK, 2092 Highway 168 North, Paragould, AR 72450; 870-573-6751; *www.arkansasstateparks.com.* **GPS:** N36.02.67/W90.35.95. **Background:** The park is located in a geologically significant highland area rising above broad valleys. **Facilities:** Visitor center, RV/tent sites, cabins, group lodge, lakes, picnic areas and pavilions, trails. **CCC Companies:** 1727 and 3799 SP-4. **CCC Features:** CCC Pavilion and bathhouse on Ponder Lake, group camp, amphitheater, trails with CCC interpretive markers, picnic area.

**2. DEVILS DEN STATE PARK,** 11333 West Arkansas Highway 74, West Fork, AR 72774; 479-761-3325; *www.arkansasstateparks.com.* **GPS:** N35.46.96/W94.15.15. **Background:** Situated near Lee Creek Valley in the Boston Mountains area of the Ozarks, the park is a geologically diverse area of water, woodlands, and limestone caves in the Ozark National Forest. **Facilities:** Visitor center, RV/tent sites, lake, café, park store, pool, group camp, horse camp, trails. **CCC Companies:** 754 SP-5 and 3777 SP-5. **CCC Features:** Cabins, picnic areas and shelters, trails, stone dam impounding Devils Lake, pavilion and restaurant (Figure 136).

**3. LAKE CATHERINE STATE PARK,** 1200 Catherine Park Road, Hot Springs, AR 71913; 501-844-4176; *www.arkansasstateparks.com.* **GPS:** N34.26.14/W92.54.82. **Background:** Located on the banks of Lake Catherine in the Ouachita Mountains, this park is a short distance from Hot Springs. **Facilities:** Visitor center, RV/tent sites, cabins, picnic areas, marina, amphitheater, trails. **CCC Companies:** 3777 SP-9 and SP-10. **CCC Features:** Cabins, nature center with CCC exhibits, trails, picnic areas.

**4. MOUNT NEBO STATE PARK,** 16728 W. State Highway 155, Dardanelle, AR 72834; 479-229-3655; *www.arkansasstateparks.com.*

**Figure 136.** Inviting views welcome visitors to this CCC-built shelter at Devils Den State Park.

**GPS:** N35.13.21/W93.15.16. **Background:** Established in 1927, the park is set on the slopes of Mount Nebo offering views of the Arkansas River Valley, nearby Lake Dardanelle, and the Ozark National Forest. **Facilities:** Visitor center, RV/tent sites, cabins, trails, pool, bathhouse, tennis courts, recreation fields. **CCC Companies:** 1780V and 3779C SP-2. **CCC Features:** Cabins, roads and bridges, trails, pavilions, stone work around historic springs and Fern Lake.

# National Parks

**5.** BUFFALO NATIONAL RIVER, 402 North Walnut, Suite 136, Harrison, AR 72601; 870-439-2502; *www.nps.gov/buff.* **GPS:** N35.59.22/ W107.58.53. **Background:** More than 130 miles of the Buffalo River were set aside as a preserve in 1972. The lower river section near Buffalo Point incorporates the former Buffalo River State Park, developed by the CCC. **Facilities:** Tyler Bend Visitor Center, campgrounds, picnic areas, historic structures, concession services (cabins, restaurant). **CCC Company:** 4733 SP-13. **CCC Features:** Historic district roads, trails, stone work, picnic pavilion, lodge, cabins.

# NEW MEXICO

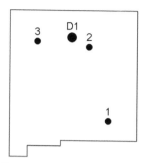

## Destination Parks

### D1. BANDELIER NATIONAL MONUMENT

*Frijoles Canyon witnessed a building boom — the first in 600 years.*[41]

> — T. J. Priehs and Therese Burton
> *Bandelier National Monument*

Bandelier National Monument surrounds Frijoles Canyon, an oasis nestled in New Mexico's high desert near Santa Fe and the once "secret city" of Los Alamos, home to "Site Y" of WW II's Manhattan Project. While this park seems an unlikely place to find evidence of the CCC's finest work, Bandelier preserves a treasure of remarkable structures built by the Corps.

Focal points of the monument are the 600–800-year-old cliff dwellings and other ancient features found in the tree-lined canyon along Frijoles Creek. Built by Ancestral Pueblo people and occupied for nearly 400 years, the dwellings were first described in 1880 by anthropologist Adolph Bandelier. His observations, followed by field reports from archaeologist Edgar Lee Hewett, led to establishment of Bandelier National Monument in 1916. Early tourists, arriving by foot or horseback, were guests in a lodge built in 1909. The original lodge was later replaced by a CCC-built inn that operated, under the same manager, until 1977. During WW II, the inn served as a retreat for Manhattan Project scientists from nearby Los Alamos.

In 1932, Bandelier was transferred to the NPS under supervision of Frank "Boss" Pinkley, who requested funds to improve access to the site. The recently established CCC provided the resources he needed, and enrollees from Company 815 NP-3/ NM-1, "Camp Bandelier," arrived that fall (Figure 137). The men first went to work building a gravel "truck trail" down into Frijoles Canyon. Today's park entrance road still follows this original three-mile route. During the next eight years, CCC men stabilized archeological sites, blazed trails, and built 31 structures, most in low profile Pueblo Revival style, utilizing the same volcanic "tuff" stone the Ancestral Pueblo used centuries before. Today, the visitor center, Frijoles Canyon Lodge (now used for staff housing), offices, gift shop and snack bar, administrative offices, old campground picnic area, comfort station, and several other structures comprise Bandelier's National Historic Landmark District (Plate 14, top). Extensive renovations commenced at the visitor center in 2009 that, when completed, will preserve the original CCC-era structure in a modern facility. In addition to the well-preserved buildings, CCC artisans crafted furniture and stamped-tin fixtures, many of which remain in daily use. Today's visitor to Bandelier National Monument will note the remarkable building skills

**Figure 137.** The CCC camp at Bandelier National Monument was located beneath the cliff dwellings.

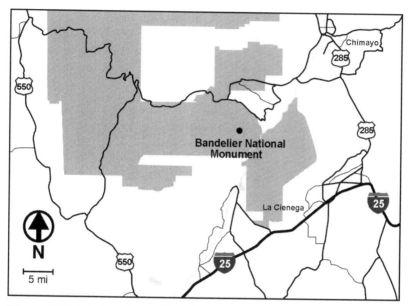

**Figure 138.** The location of Bandelier National Monument.

and superb craftsmanship of both the Ancestral Pueblo People and the CCC.

*Additional Information:* 15 Entrance Road, Los Alamos, New Mexico 87544-9701 (Figure 138); 505-672-3861 x 517; *www.nps.gov/band.* **GPS:** N35.46.72/W106.16.31. Facilities include visitor center and museum, book store, restaurant and gift shop, stabilized and restored historic sites and structures, RV/tent sites, picnic areas, trails, interpretive programs; remote Tsankawi Section of park with trails and petroglyphs.

# Other CCC-Related Parks
## State Parks

**1. BOTTOMLESS LAKES STATE PARK,** HC 12, Box 1200, Roswell, NM 88201; 575-624-6058; *http://www.emnrd.state.nm.us/PRD/.* **GPS:** N33.20.32/W104.20.13. **Background:** Bottomless Lakes is a geological oddity created from collapsed sinkholes amid gypsum hills. Small lakes of green-tinted artesian well water stand in contrast to reddish bluffs. Acquired in 1933, this was New Mexico's first state park. **Facilities:** Visitor center, RV/tent sites, picnic areas and shelters, Lea Lake Recreation Building, beach, small boat facilities. **CCC Company:** 881 SP-3. **Significant CCC Features:** Lake recreation building, beach, Lea Lake Tower.

**2.** HYDE MEMORIAL STATE PARK, 740 Hyde Park Road, Santa Fe, NM 87501; 505-983-7175; *http://www.emnrd.state.nm.us/PRD/*. **GPS:** N35.44.22/W105.50.15. **Background:** In 1927, Benjamin Hyde purchased this land in the Sangre de Cristo Mountains for the first Boy Scout camp in the Southwest. Following his death in 1933, his wife bequeathed the property to the state to educate the public, especially children, about the outdoors. Developed by the CCC, the park opened in 1938. **Facilities:** Visitor center, RV/tent sites, picnic areas and shelters, Hyde Park Lodge, winter sports facilities, trails. **CCC Companies:** 833 and 835 SP-1. **CCC Features:** Park roads and bridges, Hyde Park Lodge, skiing tow-cable building, picnic areas and shelters, trails, staff residence, utility buildings.

**Figure 139.** CCC enrollees assisted in preserving and stabilizing ruins at Chaco Culture National Historical Park.

# National Parks

**3. Chaco Culture National Historical Park,** PO Box 280, Nageezi, NM 87037; 505-786-7014; *www.nps.gov/chcu.* **GPS:** N36.04.13/ W107.58.53. **Background:** Set aside as a National Monument in 1907, the park preserves the sacred lands and structures of Chaco Canyon, ancestral home to the Puebloan people of New Mexico, the Hopi of Arizona, and Navajo from across the American southwest. Native American CCC enrollees carried out soil conservation and landscaping work, including planting more than 10,000 cottonwood, tamarisk, plum, and willow trees. Navajo CCC stonemasons excavated and repaired ancient Chacoan structures (Figure 139). The site was designated a National Historical Park in 1980 and a World Heritage Site in 1987. **Facilities:** Visitor center, historic structures and sites, RV/tent sites, picnic areas, trails, interpretive programs. **CCC Companies:** 2354 and 4819 NP-2. **CCC Features:** Park roads, trails, landscaping, preserved and restored historic structures.

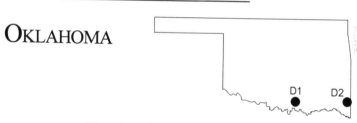

Oklahoma

## Destination Parks

**D1. Chickasaw National Recreation Area and**

**Lake Murray State Park**

*The citizens of Oklahoma are fortunate to have the large number of National Park Service' designed CCC structures and park landscapes that remain.*[42]

— Kris Marek, Director
Oklahoma Tourism and Recreation Planning

Located only forty miles apart, Chickasaw National Recreation Area (NRA) and Lake Murray State Park are renowned for both their beauty and their links to the CCC. Once lands granted to the Chickasaw and Choctaw following their removal along the "Trail of Tears" in the 1830s, Chickasaw NRA originated with the 1902 sale of 640 acres to the government to save the site's mineral springs from development. In 1906, the preserve was designated Platt National Park to honor recently deceased Senator Orville Platt of Connecticut.

Following establishment of the ECW program, CCC Company 808 NP-1, "Camp Branch," began work in the park. At Platt, the CCC designed and built a complete park infrastructure centered on the springs and water (Figure 140). A network of roads and trails connected the camp and picnic grounds, and maintenance and residential areas. Over 300 landscape structures were crafted of timber and/or native stone, the most notable include the Buffalo Spring enclosure, Pavilion Springs Shelter, Old Park Headquarters, chief ranger's office, and the Bromide Pavilion. The park, renamed Chickasaw NRA in 1976, now includes 343-acre Veterans Lake (WPA) and 3,127-acre Arbuckle Lake. The original park, designated the Platt Historic District, preserves much of the original CCC design and construction. The park's Travertine Nature Center features exhibits on the park's natural and cultural history.

**Figure 140.** This rustic pavilion was built by the CCC at Bromide Springs in Chickasaw National Recreation Area.

**Figure 141.** CCC enrollees are laying stone foundations for buildings in Lake Murray State Park.

**Figure 142.** An example of the hand-work used in constructing a stone cottage in Lake Murray State Park.

Two years after work began at Platt, enrollees arrived at Lake Murray to begin work on Oklahoma's first and largest state park. The WPA had begun construction of the 6,500-acre lake in 1933; and CCC Companies 1818 SP-9, 3814-V SP-11, and 849 SP-13 spent six years constructing scenic roads, trails, cabins, picnic pavilions, group camp "bunkhouses," and administrative buildings (figures 141 and 142).

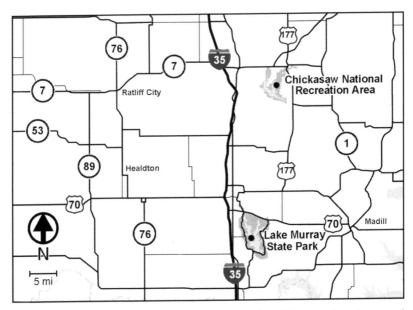

**Figure 143.** The location of Chickasaw National Recreation Area and Lake Murray State Park.

Among the park's most notable CCC-structures are the Colston Cabin (originally a concessions building) and the sandstone Buzzard Roost Pavilion. Lake Murray's most notable structure, Tucker Tower, stands on a cliff overlooking the Lake. Built by the WPA in 1935, it served as a retreat for Oklahoma Governor William "Alfalfa Bill" Murray. Today the tower houses a museum and nature center.

***Additional Information:*** Chickasaw NRA: 1008 West Second Street, Sulphur, OK 73086 (Figure 143); 580-622-3161; *www.nps.gov/chci.* **GPS:** N34.27.69/W97.0.20. Facilities include Travertine Information and Nature Center, RV/tent sites, picnic areas and shelters, mineral springs, lakes, trails, interpretive programs. Lake Murray: 18407 Scenic State Hwy 77, Ardmore, OK 73401; 580-223-4044; *www.touroklahoma.com.* **GPS:** N34.05.73/W97.04.65. Facilities include Tucker Tower Nature Center, RV/tent sites, lodge and restaurant, picnic areas and shelters, lake with marina, trails.

## D2. BEAVERS BEND STATE PARK

*This New Deal legacy is still enjoyed in the twenty-first century by millions of Oklahomans who swim, boat, camp, and hike in parks across the state.*[43]

— Suzanne H. Schrems
Oklahoma Historical Society

Nestled in Oklahoma's Ouachita Mountains, the highest range between the Appalachians and the Rockies, Beavers Bend State Park is an area rich in natural beauty and steeped in the enduring legacy of the CCC. Along the South Mountain Fork River below Broken Bow Lake, 7,200-acre Beavers Bend State Park is one of the state's most visited recreation destinations. As one of Oklahoma's original parks, Beavers Bend was developed between 1935 and 1941 by CCC Company 2815 SP-20. During that time, the CCC men laid out campgrounds and picnic areas; built stone and log shelters and comfort stations; erected 18 cabins (all still in use); blazed hiking trails; constructed a boat dock, swimming area, and bathhouse (now the Nature Center), as well as park administrative and residential facilities (Figure 144). The story of the CCC at Beavers Bend, and across Oklahoma, is

**Figure 144.** CCC workers pose in front of a building, under construction at Beavers Bend State Park.

told through exhibits in the Oklahoma Forest Heritage Center and Museum located within the park. Museum displays also trace the rich history of the scenic Ouachita Mountains and surrounding National Forest.

The original Beavers Bend State Park now has expanded to include the western shores of Broken Bow Lake, as well as the Cedar Creek Golf Course. The park features campgrounds, picnic areas, boat docks, and the 40-room Lakeview Lodge.

Visitors may extend their journey with explorations of scenic byways and trails of the 1.8 million acre Ouachita National Forest. Established in 1907 as the Arkansas National Forest, it is the oldest National Forest in the South. Several CCC crews worked in the forest and visitors will find CCC-built campgrounds, lakes, and picnic areas. Areas convenient to Beavers Bend include CCC-developed Cedar Lake Recreation Area, located within the exceptionally beautiful Winding Stair Mountain National Recreation Area; and the Talimena National Scenic Byway meandering through the heart of the mountains.

***Additional Information:*** PO Box 10, Highway 259A, Broken Bow, OK 74728 (Figure 145); 580-494-6625; *www.beaversbend.com.* **GPS:**

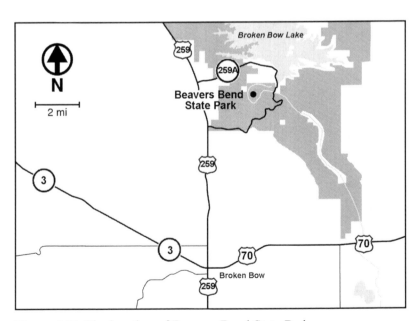

**Figure 145.** The location of Beavers Bend State Park.

N34.08.03/W94.41.36. Facilities including RV/tent sites, cabins, lodge and restaurant, picnic areas and shelters, lake with beach, bathhouse, golf course, Forest Heritage Center and CCC Museum.

# TEXAS

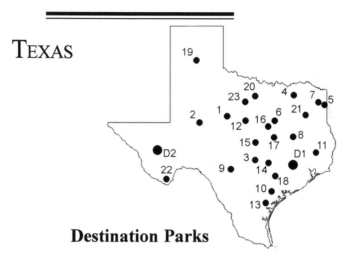

## Destination Parks

### D1. BASTROP STATE PARK AND BUESCHER STATE PARK

> *If one park could be singled out as an example of the CCC's impact, perhaps Bastrop State Park... would be the best.*[44]
>
> — Jim Fox
> "CCC: Fond Memories From a Time of National Hardship"

Located near Austin, Bastrop and Buescher state parks are enduring examples of CCC work in Texas state parks. Beginning in autumn 1933, CCC companies 1811 SP-21 and 1805 SP-22 worked to develop these parks now linked by a scenic byway through the "Lost Pines" region of eastern Texas. Noted for its tracts of loblolly pine that are the westernmost stands of their kind in the United States; the forest was separated from the main pine belt during the last Ice Age. CCC workers found a region devastated by a century of timber cutting and erosion. They began immediately to re-seed the dwindling forest and construct recreational facilities. Three-quarters of a century later, their work has recreated the pine lands of the past.

**Figure 146.** The rustic log and stone cottages at Bastrop State Park are renowned for their enduring craftsmanship.

Set on 3,503 wooded acres, land for Bastrop State Park was a gift from the nearby town of Bastrop, named for a German Baron who received a grant from the Mexican Government to establish a colony there in the 1820s. Due to its proximity to the state capital, Bastrop became a model for parks across Texas. Facility designs and construction methods, endorsed by renowned NPS architect Herbert Maier, were highly regarded for creative use of local materials and integration with the landscape (Figure 146). Today, Bastrop remains true to its original design. Visitors enjoy the park's CCC-built roadways, picnic areas, campgrounds, and other recreational facilities. Other agencies laid out a golf course and built the park's swimming pool. Especially notable structures include the large refectory featuring a massive beamed ceiling and banquet area with bas-relief sculpture mounted over a large fireplace; and more than a dozen rough-stone and log cottages overlooking a lake. Bastrop is one of five Texas state parks listed as National Historic Landmarks.

Located a dozen miles southeast of Bastrop, Buescher State Park was created from land donated by Emil and Elizabeth Buescher and the nearby town of Smithville. The 1,700-acre park opened in 1940

**Figure 147.** A rustic stone and log footbridge crosses a stream at Buescher State Park.

following development by the CCC companies from nearby Bastrop. The men laid out roads and bridges, group pavilion, comfort stations, campground, staff residential facilities, and a small lake (Figure 147). A portion of the original park was later deeded to the University of Texas M. D. Anderson Cancer Center.

*Additional Information:* Bastrop: 3005 TX Highway 21 East, Bastrop, TX 78602-0518 (Figure 148); 512-321-2101; *www.tpwd.state.tx.us.* **GPS:** N30.06.36/W97.17.13. Facilities include RV/tent sites, cabins, group camp, picnic areas and shelters, lake, trails, pool, golf course. Buescher: 100 Park Road 1E, Smithville, TX 78957-0075; 512-237-**2241;** *www.tpwd.state.tx.us.* **GPS:** N30.02.21/W97.09.29. Facilities include RV/tent sites, cabins, picnic areas and shelters, recreation hall, lake, trails. *www.tpwd.state.tx.us.*

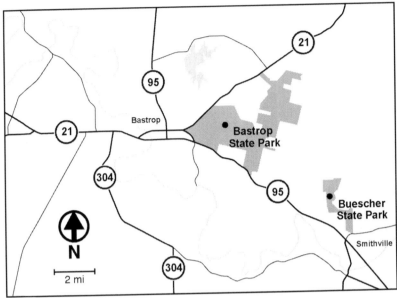

**Figure 148.** The location of Bastrop State Park and Buescher State Park.

---

## D2. BALMORHEA STATE PARK AND DAVIS MOUNTAINS STATE PARK

*Balmorhea's huge spring-fed swimming pool, also rare in the vast Trans Pecos region, attracted enough business to inspire 'development of tourist camps and stores."*[45]

— James Wright Steely
*Parks for Texas: Enduring Landscapes of the New Deal*

Located only thirty-five miles apart, Balmorhea and Davis Mountains state parks, two of 31 state parks in Texas developed by the CCC, preserve some of the Corps' most significant accomplishments.

Balmorhea, located around the artesian San Solomon Springs, was dubbed the "great oasis of the Chihuahuan Desert." Once known as "Mescalero Springs" for the Mescalero Apaches that traveled through west Texas, they were renamed "San Solomon" by early-19th-century Mexican farmers. In 1933, local landowners deeded more than 900 acres for a park at the springs. Later legal issues led to divestiture of all but the park's current 49 acres. CCC Company 1856 SP-47 arrived that year to begin work on the park's distinctive facilities. The centerpiece was the 1.75-acre stone-lined, spring-fed swimming pool, the largest of its type in the world (Plate 14, bottom). This was complemented by the 18-room Spanish Colonial style San Solomon Courts Inn, limestone concession building, two bathhouses, adobe-brick superintendent's residence, canals linking the springs to an underground wetlands viewing area, and park entry portals, roads, and bridges.

Davis Mountains State Park, located in the heart of the largest mountain range in Texas, also benefited from the CCC. In 1933 and early 1934, companies 879 SP-4 and 881 SP-5, supervised by NPS architects and craftsmen, built the remarkable Indian Lodge, a 15-room inn constructed of 18-inch-thick walls of hand-made adobe bricks, cottonwood timbers from nearby Keesy Canyon, and reed-ceilings woven of stalks from the banks of the Rio Grande (Figure 149). Original cedar furniture, some still in use, was hand-crafted by

**Figure 149.** This historic Indian Lodge, a nationally renowned destination in the Chihuahuan Desert, is part of Davis Mountains State Park.

CCC workers at Bastrop State Park. Widely regarded for its elegance amid rugged surroundings, Indian Lodge is recognized as one of the nation's most distinctive inns. Now expanded to 39 rooms, the lodge has been ranked among the top-rated accommodation in Texas. In addition to this structure, enrollees laid out park roads and erected a mountain-top pavilion. The two parks are convenient to Fort Davis National Historic Site, preserving the ruins of a frontier cavalry fort; the University of Texas' McDonald Observatory, one of the premiere astronomical observatories in the nation; and Big Bend National Park, also developed by the CCC.

***Additional Information:*** Balmorhea: TX Highway 17, Toyohvale, TX 79786; 432-375-2370 (Figure 150); *www.tpwd.state.tx.us*. **GPS:** N30.58.68/W103.47.13. Facilities include RV/tent sites, motel, picnic areas and shelters, pool with bathhouse, concession building. Davis Mountains: TX Highway 118N, Fort Davis, TX 79734; 432-426-3337; *www.tpwd.state.tx.us*. **GPS:** N30.35.72/W103.55.96. Facilities include interpretive center, RV/tent sites, lodge, picnic areas and shelters, trails, amphitheatre, Limpia Creek Primitive Area. Indian Lodge: 432-426-3254.

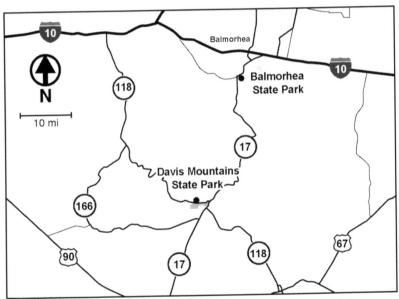

**Figure 150.** The location of Balmorhea State Park and Davis Mountains State Park.

# Other CCC-Related Parks

## State Parks

**1. ABILENE STATE PARK,** 150 Park Road 32, Tuscola, TX 79562; 325-572-3204; *www.tpwd.state.tx.us.* **GPS:** N32.14.26/W99.52.44. **Background:** Established in 1934 through a land gift by the City of Abilene, the park is home to a portion of Texas's official longhorn herd. **Facilities:** RV/tent sites, picnic areas and shelters, pool, concession building, trails. **CCC Company:** 1823V SP-26. **CCC Features:** Park roads, stonework, pool, concession building, picnic areas and shelters, water tower.

**2. BIG SPRING STATE PARK,** 1 Scenic Drive, Big Spring, TX 79720; 432-263-4931; *www.tpwd.state.tx.us.* **GPS:** N32.13.96/W101.29.38. **Background:** Set atop a limestone bluff called Scenic Mountain, the park is named for a long-known natural spring. Developed by the CCC, the park opened in 1936. **Facilities:** Campgrounds with shelters, group pavilion, trails, scenic road, seasonal interpretive center. **CCC Company:** 1857 DSP-11/SP-45. **CCC Features:** Park entrance and scenic loop road, stonework, mountain summit group pavilion, headquarters (concession building), staff residence, spring pump house.

**3. BLANCO STATE PARK,** Park Road 23, Blanco, TX 78606; 830-833-4333; *www.tpwd.state.tx.us.* **GPS:** N30.05.18/W98.25.62. **Background:** This park, along the Blanco River in the hill country near San Antonio, was established in 1934. **Facilities:** RV/tent sites, swimming area, picnic grounds and shelters, trails. **CCC Company:** 854 SP-7. **CCC Features:** Park entrance station and staff residence, dams on Blanco River, stone bridge, picnic areas, CCC "Clubhouse" (group picnic pavilion).

**4. BONHAM STATE PARK,** 1363 State Park 24, Bonham, TX 75418-9285; 903-583-5022; *www.tpwd.state.tx.us.* **GPS:** N33.32.83/W96.08.93. **Background:** Preserving vestiges of Blackland Prairie grasslands, Bonham was developed by CCC enrollees with support from local congressman and future Speaker of the House Sam Rayburn. **Facilities:** RV/tent sites, group camp, picnic area and shelters, lake. **CCC Company:** 894 SP-18. **CCC Features:** Park roads and bridges, entrance portals, bridges, picnic areas and shelters, lake and dam, boathouse, bathhouse, water tower.

**5. CADDO LAKE STATE PARK,** 245 Park Road 2, Karnack, TX 75661; 903-679-3351; *www.tpwd.state.tx.us.* **GPS:** N32.41.49/W94.10.74. **Background:** Located near the Louisiana border, the park is named for Texas's only natural lake. It is composed of ponds, bayous, Cypress swamps, and wetlands that may have been created by the 1811 New Madrid earthquake. **Facilities:** Interpretive center, RV/tent sites, group camp, picnic areas and shelters, trails. **CCC Companies:** 889 SP-1 and 857 SP-40. **CCC Features:** Park entrance portals and roads, cabins, group camp (includes CCC camp barracks and recreation hall).

**6. CLEBURNE STATE PARK,** 5800 Park Road 21, Cleburne, TX 76031; 817-645-4215; *www.tpwd.state.tx.us.* **GPS:** N32.15.71/W97.33.45. **Background:** The park, created from land donated by the City of Cleburne, preserves woodlands that were once the historic route of a 19th century trail followed by Comanche warriors. **Facilities:** RV/tent sites, picnic areas, shelters, group camp with barracks and dining hall, youth camp, trails, boating facilities, swimming area, bathhouse. **CCC Company:** 3804 SP-53. **CCC Features:** Park roads including scenic drive, lake and dam with rock spillway, outdoor fireplaces. WPA completed concession/bathhouse, staff residence, water system.

**7. DAINGERFIELD STATE PARK,** 455 Park Road 17, Daingerfield, TX 75638; 903-645-2921; *www.tpwd.state.tx.us.* **GPS:** N33.0.54/W94.41.90. **Background:** Nestled in wooded hills of northeastern Texas, this park includes Daingerfield Lake. Developed by the CCC, the park opened in 1938. **Facilities:** RV/tent sites, cabins, Bass Lodge, picnic areas, lake trails. **CCC Companies:** 1801C and 2891 SP-49. **CCC Features:** Park roads, lake and dam, cabins, group pavilion.

**8. FORT PARKER STATE PARK,** 194 Park Road 28, Mexia, TX 76667; 254-562-5751; *www.tpwd.state.tx.us.* **GPS:** N31.36.03/W96.32.15. **Background:** Created in 1935, the park preserves historic Old Fort Parker and surrounding land. The fort, located near the park, was built in 1833 and reconstructed by CCC in 1937. The park is located on CCC-built Fort Parker Lake. **Facilities:** RV/tent sites, group camp, youth camp, trails, picnic areas and shelters, group pavilion, lake, old cemetery. **CCC Company:** 3807C SP-44. **CCC Features:** Park roads, concession/bathhouse building, lake and dam, CCC camp infirmary, Old Fort Parker reconstruction (managed by City of Groesbeck).

**9. GARNER STATE PARK,** 234 Rural Route 1050, Concan, TX 78838; 830-232-6132; *www.tpwd.state.tx.us.* **GPS:** N29.35.47/W99.44.43. **Background:** Set in a landscape of canyons, cliffs, and cedar-filled valleys along the Frio River, the park is named for John Nance Garner, Vice President under Franklin D. Roosevelt. **Facilities:** RV/tent sites, cabins, picnic areas and shelters, group pavilion, concession building, Frio River water sports facilities, miniature golf course, Cowboy Theatre. **CCC Company:** 879 SP-42. **CCC Features:** Park entrance portals and roads, stonework, cabins, trails, refectory, staff residential and service structures.

**10. GOLIAD STATE PARK,** 108 Park Road 6, Goliad, TX 77963-3206; 361-645-3405; *www.tpwd.state.tx.us.* **GPS:** N28.39.38/W97.23.23. **Background:** Centerpiece of this park is reconstructed Mission Nuestra Senôra Espiritu Santo de Zuniga State Historic Site. Built on this site in 1749, the church and other buildings were reconstructed by CCC and WPA. **Facilities:** Historic sites, picnic areas, trails. **CCC Company:** 3822V SP-43. **CCC Features:** Restored mission church, furnishings, outbuildings, staff residential complex.

**11. HUNTSVILLE STATE PARK,** Park Road 40, Huntsville, TX 77342-0508; 936-295-5644; *www.tpwd.state.tx.us.* **GPS:** N30.37.07/W95.31.98. **Background:** Notable for its terrain and stands of virgin pines, the park was developed by the CCC and opened in 1938. Torrential rains flooded the site in 1940 and the park remained closed until 1956. **Facilities:** RV/tent sites, overnight shelters, group picnic pavilion, recreation hall, trails, Lake Raven. **CCC Company:** 1823CV SP-61. **CCC Features:** Park roads, bridges, stonework, lake and dam, concession building.

**12. LAKE BROWNWOOD STATE PARK,** 200 State Highway Park Road 15, Lake Brownwood, TX 76801; 325-784-5223; *www.tpwd.state.tx.us.* **GPS:** N31.51.45/W99.01.23. **Background:** Created by damming Pecan Bayou, a tributary of the Colorado River, Lake Brownwood is the centerpiece of the park developed from a 1934 land gift. **Facilities:** RV/tent sites, group camp, recreation building, cabins, picnic areas and shelters, lake, trails. **CCC Company:** 849 and 872 SP-36. **CCC Features:** Park roads and stonework, lake and dam, cabins, refectory, cabins, boat dock and shelter, fisherman's lodge, staff residences.

**13. LAKE CORPUS CHRISTI STATE PARK,** Park Road 25, Mathis, TX 78368; 361-547-2635; *www.tpwd.state.tx.us.* **GPS:** N28.03.73/W97.52.18. **Background:** Nestled in a cove along the banks of Lake Corpus Christi, the park was created in 1934. The large refectory (pavilion) on a ridge above the lake is considered one of the finest examples of CCC work. **Facilities:** RV/tent sites, picnic areas, shelters, refectory, lake, trails. **CCC Company: 886 SP-32. CCC Features**: Park roads and bridges, refectory and interpretive center, boathouses, bathhouse, staff residence.

**14.** LOCKHART STATE PARK, 4179 State Park Road, Lockhart, TX 78644-9716; 512-398-3479; *www.tpwd.state.tx.us*. **GPS:** N29.51.12/ W97.41.89. **Background:** Shaded by pecan trees, this park on the Blackland Prairie was developed in 1934. CCC work included, with some controversy, a 9-hole golf course. The site was leased to a country club until the park opened to the public in 1948. **Facilities:** RV/ tent sites, picnic area, group picnic shelter, recreation hall, pool, trails, golf course, rodeo area, Clear Fork Creek. **CCC Company:** 3803 SP-51. **CCC Features:** Park roads and Clear Fork Creek Bridge, rock dams on Clear Fork Creek, refectory, golf course, pool, staff residence and maintenance facilities.

**15.** LONGHORN CAVERN STATE PARK, Park Road 4, Burnet, TX 78611; 830-598-2283; *www.tpwd.state.tx.us*. **GPS:** N30.41.05/W98.21.09. **Background:** Recognized for its geology, Longhorn Cavern was created by water dissolving bedrock limestone over thousands of years. The elaborate cavern administration building was constructed by the CCC (Figure 151). **Facilities:** Visitor center, picnic areas, cavern trails, guided tours. **CCC Company:** 854 SP-35. **CCC Features:** Park

**Figure 151.** The CCC built this native stone structure at Longhorn Cavern State Park. The building serves as the visitor center and the entrance to the cave.

entrance and stonework, old Administration Building visitor center with CCC exhibits, cave entrance, trails and lighting system, shelter, water tower, cabin.

**16. MERIDIAN STATE PARK,** 173 Park Road 7, Meridian, TX 76665; 254-435-2536; *www.tpwd.state.tx.us.* **GPS:** N31.53.26/W97.41.51. **Background:** Tucked into hills near Waco, the park land borders CCC-built Lake Meridian. Notable for fossils found in its limestone outcroppings, the park opened in 1935. **Facilities:** RV/tent sites, group camp, youth camp, picnic areas and shelters, beach, trails. **CCC Company:** 1827V SP-12. **CCC Features:** Park entrance, roads and bridges, lake and dam, refectory, trails.

**17. MOTHER NEFF STATE PARK,** 1680 State Highway 36, Moody, TX 76557-3317; 254-853-2389; *www.tpwd.state.tx.us.* **GPS:** N31.19.38/W97.28.18. **Background:** Considered Texas's first state park, the original six acres of land along the Leon River were donated by Isabella Eleanor "Mother" Neff in 1916. Neff's son, Pat M. Neff, served as Texas's governor from 1921–1925 and was responsible for creating the Texas state parks system. **Facilities:** RV/tent sites, youth campground, picnic areas, group pavilions, trails. **CCC Company:** 817 SP-38. **CCC Facilities:** Park entrance portals, roads and stonework, refectory, staff residence, Clubhouse pavilion, Tabernacle pavilion, Rock Tower (water tower), picnic areas, trails.

**18. PALMETTO STATE PARK,** 78 Park Road 11 South, Gonzales, TX 78629-5180; 830-672-3266; *www.tpwd.state.tx.us.* **GPS:** N29.35.39/W97.35.08. **Background:** Located along the banks of the San Marcos River, this park is named for the dwarf palmetto plant found in abundance throughout the area. **Facilities:** RV/tent sites, group campground, picnic grounds and shelters, refectory, trails. **CCC Companies:** 873, 886, and 1823CV SP-29. **CCC Features:** Park entrance portals and roads, picnic areas, refectory, trails, water tower.

**19. PALO DURO CANYON STATE PARK,** 11450 Park Road 5, Canyon, TX 79015; 806-488-2227; *www.tpwd.state.tx.us.* **GPS:** N34.57.02/W101.40.08. **Background:** Known as the "Grand Canyon of Texas," Palo Duro is one of the state's most scenic destinations. The park provides access to portions of the 120-mile-long canyon in the heart of the Panhandle. The amphitheater hosts summer productions of *Texas,* the state's official outdoor drama. **Facilities:** Visitor center, RV/tent sites, cabins, picnic areas and shelters, trails, amphitheater, stables, Canõncita Ranch (former Audubon Society property). **CCC**

**Companies:** 1824V, 1828V, 1829V SP-13, 894, 1828V, 2875C SP-14, 1825V, and 1834V SP-15. **CCC Features:** Park entrance and canyon roads, interpretive center, cabins, staff residences and utility buildings.

**20. Possum Kingdom State Park,** Park Road 33, Caddo, TX 76429; 940-549-1803; *www.tpwd.state.tx.us*. **GPS:** N32.52.52/W98.33.66. **Background:** The last park developed by the CCC in Texas occupies land along the shores of Possum Kingdom Lake. Due to WW II, the park did not open until 1950. **Facilities:** RV/tent sites, primitive campground, stone cabins, picnic area, trails, lake and marina. **CCC Company:** 2888 SP-65. **CCC Features:** Park roads and bridges, stonework.

**21. Tyler State Park,** 789 Park Road 16, Tyler, TX 75706-9141; 903-597-5338; *www.tpwd.state.tx.us*. **GPS:** N32.28.56/W95.16.60. **Background:** This park, located in the "pineywoods" of eastern Texas, opened in 1939. **Facilities:** RV/tent sites, group camp with overnight shelters and dining hall, picnic areas, group shelter, 64-acre lake, lakeside amphitheater, trails. **CCC Company:** 2888 SP-54. **CCC Features:** Park roads and stonework, lake and dam, concession building, bathhouse, boathouse, staff residence.

## National Parks

**22. Big Bend National Park,** 1 Panther Drive, Big Bend National Park, TX 79834; 432-477-2251; *www.nps.gov/bibe*. **GPS:** N29.19.65/ W103.12.32. **Background:** Early park advocate Everett Townsend believed that the rugged and remote Chisos Mountain Range along the Rio Grande would be an ideal location for Texas's first national park. A portion of the area was set aside in 1933 as Texas Canyons State Park, while Townsend and others lobbied to designate it a national park. The CCC worked in the area from 1934–1937, constructing the Chisos Mountain Road. When the Texas legislature failed to appropriate funds to purchase land, the CCC relocated to Davis Mountains. A second camp opened in 1940 to carry out projects from surveying boundaries, assisting in archeological work, blazing the Lost Mountain Trail, and erecting structures including administrative buildings, museum, and tourist cottages. In 1944, Big Bend was designated a National Park. **Facilities:** Panther Junction and Chisos Basin visitor centers, RV/tent sites, back-country campsites, lodging and restaurant, picnic areas, trails, interpretive programs. **CCC Companies:** 896 SP-33 and 1856 NP-1. **CCC**

**Features:** Chisos Mountain Road, Chisos Mountain Lodge cottages, Lost Mine Trail, park store.

## Other Parks

**23.** FORT GRIFFIN STATE HISTORIC SITE, 1701 North US Highway 283, Albany, TX 76430; 915-762-3592; *http://www.thc.state.tx.us/index.shtml.* **GPS:** N32.55.45/W99.13.22. **Background:** A true vestige of the "Old West," Fort Griffin is located on the prairie near Clear Fork of the Brazos River. Built in 1867, the fort protected frontier settlers until 1881. CCC enrollees stabilized structures and the park opened in 1938. The park was transferred to the Texas State Historical Commission in 2008. **Facilities:** RV/tent sites, primitive group camp, picnic areas, group shelter, equestrian camps, trails, interpretive center, amphitheater, recreation fields. **CCC Company:** 3803 SP-63. **CCC Features:** Park roads, picnic stoves, stabilized ruins.

# West Region

### CALIFORNIA

### Destination Parks

#### D1. DEATH VALLEY NATIONAL PARK

> *The CCC program at Death Valley National Monument was a success, laying the foundation for all the development that has taken place since. Few areas of the monument were left untouched as enrollees strove to improve access, living conditions, and sightseeing opportunities.*[46]

> — Linda Greene, Historian
> Death Valley National Park

Set aside as a National Monument by President Herbert Hoover in 1933, Death Valley owes its development and early operations to the CCC. Sequoia National Park superintendent John White, serving as the monument's administrator, proposed assignment of two CCC camps in Death Valley — one each in the northern and southern ends of the monument. Engineer T. R. Goodwin urged reconsideration that the camps be sited on either side of Cow Creek Wash near the center of the park. His proposal was accepted and in October, 1933, Company 530 NM-1, "Camp Funeral Range" (Figure 152), arrived to set up two tent camps. The night before the second crew, Company 530 NM-2, "Camp Cow Creek," was to arrive, a windstorm destroyed the camp. Rough wooden buildings were quickly built and occupied by mid-November.

Death Valley's remoteness was difficult for enrollees, many of whom were from Ohio, Kentucky, Indiana, and West Virginia. Despite trips to Los Angeles and Boulder City, many considered themselves "marooned." Morale was low and desertions a problem. Beginning in May, 1935, only California enrollees were assigned to Death Valley. The first group, Company 908 NM-5, relocated from the San Bernardino National Forest and established "Camp Wildrose" in an area of the desert that was habitable all year. Once the camp was erected, enrollees from the Cow Creek camps summered at Wildrose.

**Figure 152.** CCC "Camp Funeral Range" was located near the depths of Death Valley National Park in California. Many of the camp structures today still serve as shops and offices for the park staff.

A fourth camp, NM-7 at "Camp Panamint," was established but served only as a side camp. During their years in Death Valley, the men constructed the park's administrative, residential, maintenance, and visitor facilities. They also took on other tasks from staffing check-in stations and handling radio communications to registering campers and conducting tours. The CCC's legacy at Death Valley, designated a national park in 1994, includes adobe brick administrative structures at Cow Creek; staff residences, experimental plant nursery, and comfort station in Park Village; campground and comfort station at Texas Springs (Plate 15, top); and several buildings at Wildrose. In addition, the CCC graded miles of park roads, blazed trails, and installed water systems essential for staff and tourists to safely work in or visit the park.

Notable CCC-related structures at Cow Creek, Park Village staff residential area, Wildrose, Texas Spring, and Emigrant Junction have been listed on the National Register of Historic Places, recognizing the park's tangible links to the work of the CCC.

***Additional Information:*** CA Highway 190, Death Valley, CA 92328 (Figure 153); 760-786-3200; *www.nps.gov/deva.* **GPS:** N36.27.70/W116.52.0.

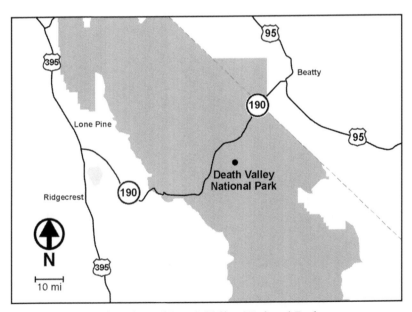

**Figure 153.** The location of Death Valley National Park.

Facilities include Furnace Creek and Scottys Castle visitor centers, Stove-pipe Wells Village, historic sites and structures, RV/tent sites, Furnace Creek Inn (concession), picnic areas, trails, interpretive programs.

---

## D2. SEQUOIA NATIONAL PARK AND KINGS CANYON NATIONAL PARK

*Visitors today who file through Crystal Cave, lean on the parapet at Amphitheater Point, camp at Lodgepole Campground, drive through Tunnel Log, run their hands along the Moro Rock handrail, hike the trails and drive the roads of Sequoia, and enjoy a thousand other little benefits can thank the young men of the Civilian Conservation Corps for their labor.*[47]

— Lary M. Dilsaver and William C. Tweed
*Challenge of the Big Trees*

Established in 1890, Sequoia National Park — along with adjacent General Grant National Park, renamed and designated Kings Canyon National Park in 1940 — were set aside to preserve magnificent stands of sequoias growing on the western slopes of the Sierras. Today the two contiguous parks are managed as one unit.

The park was patrolled by the US Cavalry before it was transferred to the newly created NPS in 1916. To Sequoia's lasting benefit, it was overseen during the early years by English-born Colonel John White, a veteran of the Spanish-American War and WW I. He was appointed superintendent in 1920 and remained, with only a short absence as regional director, until 1947. Under White's supervision, the CCC carried out projects that improved visitor access without compromising the scenic beauty that White jealously guarded. In *Challenge of the Big Trees*, Lary Dilsaver and William C. Tweed wrote that White's "power and skill . . . turned the CCC into the most valuable development tool in the park's history." [3]

Sequoia hosted twelve CCC companies in seven camps, NP-1–5 and NP-9–10, while five additional companies worked from three

**Figure 154.** CCC "Camp Grant" was nestled in the forested hills of Sequoia National Park.

camps — NP-30, 31, and 34 — in Kings Canyon (Figure 154). Typically, five camps were open at any given time with men alternating between high altitude work in summer and foothills work in winter. CCC enrollees in Sequoia and Kings Canyon doubled the road mileage in the parks; blazed or repaired trails; planted thousands of trees; and built rock walls and parapets along park roads, most notably the Generals Highway. The men also followed Dr. E. P. Meinecke's design in developing more than 200 campsites, erected more than 50 comfort stations, and built or renovated 90 administrative or residential buildings.

Three CCC projects remain especially noteworthy. The first is Tunnel Log along Moro Rock Road where innovative enrollees carved a road through a fallen sequoia. Second is the Indian Head Entrance sign, carved by CCC enrollee George Muno. Third is Crystal Cave, discovered in 1918. CCC crews laid out the access road and parking area, developed the cave's trail system, and installed lighting that revealed the cavern's natural wonders. In addition to their work in the parks, CCC men also erected fire lookout towers in the surrounding Sequoia National Forest that remain accessible to visitors.

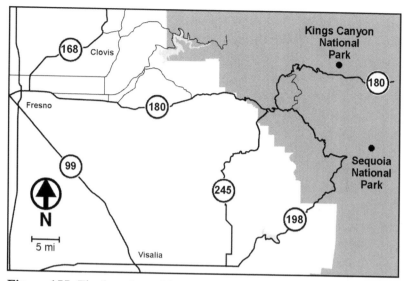

**Figure 155.** The location of Sequoia National Park and Kings Canyon National Park.

*Additional Information:* 47050 Generals Highway, Three Rivers, CA 9321-9700 (Figure 155); 559-565-3341; *www.nps.gov/seki.* **GPS:** N36.29.31/W118.50.20. Facilities include Foothills, Lodgepole, Grant Grove, and Cedar Grove visitor centers; Mineral King Museum; RV/tent sites; lodging; picnic areas; trails; scenic drives and overlooks; interpretive programs; outfitter services.

---

## D3. YOSEMITE NATIONAL PARK

*Yes, I would do it all over again. It was a new life for a nineteen-year-old kid. I, like so many of the others, enlisted as a teenager and came out a man. And it happened in the most beautiful place in the world, Yosemite.*[48]

— Darrell Stover, Enrollee
Company 942 YNP-6

Yosemite Valley, a lush oasis surrounding the Merced River, is the heart of one of the world's stunning landscapes. Carved by wind and water, Yosemite had been home to Native Americans for many centuries before the first European explorers ventured into the valley in 1833. As word spread of its exceptional beauty, residents sought to protect the valley from exploitation. In 1864, President Abraham Lincoln signed a bill deeding Yosemite Valley and the Mariposa Grove of sequoias to California as a preserve. Later, naturalist John Muir urged Congress to extend protection to the surrounding mountains and valley. Finally, in 1890, Yosemite was designated a National Park.

Yosemite became a tourism destination and, by the 1920s, the park was struggling with inadequate campgrounds and picnic areas, commercialism, and lack of staff and visitor facilities. In 1933, creation of the CCC provided the necessary resources to improve conditions at Yosemite by carrying out landscape projects; developing trails, campgrounds, picnic areas, and observation points; and providing needed staff, work, and residential facilities. During the CCC's nine-year existence, more than 8,000 men in 24 companies worked in Yosemite. The park hosted ten CCC camps: YNP-1/NP-15, "Camp Wawona 1," YNP-2/NP-16, "Camp Wawona 2," YNP-3/NP-17, "Camp Crane Flat," YNP-4/NP-18, "Camp Eleven Mile Meadow," YNP-5NP-19, "Camp Merced Grove," YNP-6/NP-20, "Camp Cascades," YNP-7/NP-21, "Camp Wawona 3," YNP-8/NP-22, "Camp Middle Fork," YNP-9/NP-23, "Camp Tamarack Flat," and YNP-10/NP-24, "Camp Empire Meadows." Valley camps operated all year while those in the high country were open only in summer (Figure 156).

Many of the CCC's accomplishments continue to enhance the visitors' experience. Among them are viewing areas at Glacier Point and Henness Ridge; steel cables and steps on the east face of Half Dome (Figure 157); lookout towers at Crane Flat and North Mountain; and the Arch Rock Entrance Station. The men also constructed the Badger Pass ski complex, including ski hut, water tower, comfort station, and original ski trails; the Foresta Bridge between Big Meadow and El Portal; the Fern Spring Rest Area; and a number of ranger cabins and other staff facilities (figures 158 and 159). In addition, enrollees developed or improved campgrounds, picnic areas, and miles

**Figure 156.** First Lady Eleanor Roosevelt poses with CCC enrollees at "Camp Wawona" in the southern part of Yosemite National Park.

**Figure 157.** CCC enrollees installing climbing cables on the slopes of Half Dome in Yosemite National Park.

**Figure 158.** CCC timber crews section downed trees in Yosemite National Park.

**Figure 159.** CCC workers prepare willow tree cuttings for planting in Yosemite National Park.

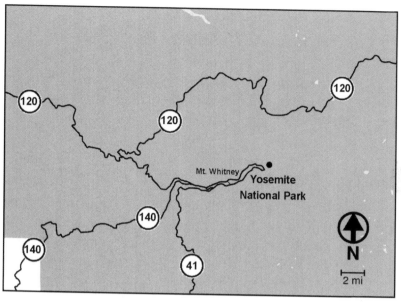

**Figure 160.** The location of Yosemite National Park.

of trails; and a former CCC camp dining hall now serves as the Tuolumne Meadows Visitor Center.

***Additional Information:*** CA Highway 140, Yosemite National Park, CA 95389 (Figure 160); 209-372-0200; *www.nps.gov/yose.* **GPS:** N37.44.78/W119.35.49. Facilities include Valley and Tuolumne Meadow visitor centers, RV/tent sites, back-country campsites, historic lodgings, dining and craft shops, historic sites and structures, picnic areas, botanical and geological features, trails, Badger Pass winter sports facilities, scenic byways, interpretive programs, outfitter services.

## D4. Mount Tamalpais State Park and
## Muir Woods National Monument

*Perhaps the most impressive single CCC construction project in Mount Tamalpais State Park is the open-air theater.*[49]

— Joseph H. Engbeck, Jr.
*By the People, For the People: The Work of the Civilian Conservation Corps in California State Parks, 1933–1941*

Rising more than 2,500 feet above San Francisco Bay, Mount Tamalpais, Miwok for "coastal mountain," has been described as a "sentinel standing guard over the Golden Gate." In the late 19th century, when loggers threatened to cut the area's magnificent redwoods, the Tamalpais Conservation Association was organized to save them. Congressman William Kent, an association member, donated 611 acres to the federal government in 1905. Three years later the site was designated Muir Woods National Monument, honoring Kent's friend, naturalist John Muir.

This action laid the foundation for future efforts to preserve Mount Tamalpais. In 1926, Californians passed legislation providing funds to the California State Parks Commission for new parks development. Mount Tamalpais State Park was established in 1930, just as the Depression descended across the nation. In October, 1933, CCC Company 1920V NM-3, "Camp Muir Woods," arrived in Muir Woods, remaining only a short time before moving to "Camp Tamalpais," SP-23, in the state park. These men were soon joined by Company 1921V SP-36, "Camp Alpine Lake." Enrollees built roads and bridges, trails, picnic areas, and other facilities both in the park and the monument. They also replaced a wooden fire tower on the summit with a steel and concrete structure that still stands.

The most notable CCC structure is the Mountain Theatre located in a natural bowl overlooking San Francisco Bay (Figure 161). In 1913, the Mountain Play Association (MPA) hosted the first performance at the site. Three years later, Kent deeded the land to MPA and landscape architect Emerson Knight was commissioned to design a

**Figure 161.** CCC workers laid one-ton blocks of stone to create the Cushing Theatre overlooking San Francisco Bay at Mount Tamalpais State Park.

permanent facility, envisioning a theater that would appear as part of the native landscape. Work began in 1931 but ceased when funds ran out. In 1936, the land was given to the park and the CCC went to work. Moving massive stones into place using simple hoists and hand-tools, the CCC completed the theater in 1941.

Today, Mount Tamalpais State Park and Muir Woods National Monument have been recognized for their importance as natural preserves so close to the heart of San Francisco; while the magnificent Sydney Cushing Mountain Theatre hosts sold-out performances every summer. Each site remains a tribute to the work of the CCC.

***Additional Information:*** Mount Tamalpais: 801 Panoramic Highway, Mill Valley, CA 94941 (Figure 162); 415-388-2070; *www.parks.ca.gov.* **GPS:** N37.54.25/W122.36.25. Facilities include visitor center, RV/ tent sites, group camps, cabins, picnic areas and shelters, lakes and water activities, trails, Cushing Theatre. Muir Woods National Monument: Mill Valley, CA 94941-2696; 415-388-2596; *www.nps.gov/ muwo.* **GPS:** N37.53.52/W122.34.25. Facilities include visitor center, picnic areas, trails, historic sites.

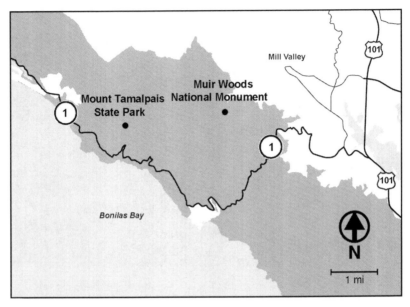

**Figure 162.** The location of Mount Tamalpais State Park and Muir Woods National Monument.

# Other CCC-Related Parks

## State Parks

**1. ARMSTRONG REDWOODS STATE NATURAL RESERVE,** 17000 Armstrong Woods Road, Guerneville, CA 95446; 707-869-2015; *www.parks.ca.gov.* **GPS:** N38.32.03/W123.0.21. **Background:** Originally set aside as a redwoods preserve in the 1870s by Colonel James Armstrong, the land was sold to Sonoma County in 1917. It was acquired by the state and opened as a state park in 1936. **Facilities:** Visitor center, picnic areas, trails. Campground located in adjacent Austin Creek State Recreation Area. **CCC Company:** 2916 P-304 **CCC Features:** Campground, picnic areas, park roads, Mount Jackson lookout tower, Forest Theater, staff residences.

**2. BIG BASIN REDWOODS STATE PARK,** 21600 Big Basin Way, Boulder Creek, CA 95006-9064; 831-338-8860; *www.parks.ca.gov.* **GPS:** N37.10.37/W122.13.26. **Background:** The "Big Basin" redwood grove was first set aside as a preserve in 1902 but little development took place until June, 1933, when the site hosted one of the first CCC camps in the California state parks system. **Facilities:** Visitor center, RV/tent sites, tent cabins, picnic areas, trails (including sections of the Skyline to Sea Trail), Waddell Creek Rancho Del Oso Nature Center trails and beach. **CCC Companies:** 1508 and 1913 SP-15. **CCC Features:** Park roads, campground, restored lodge, trails, amphitheater, fire lookout tower, staff residences.

**3. CALAVERAS BIG TREES STATE PARK,** 1170 East CA Highway 4, Arnold, CA 95223; 209-795-2334; *www.parks.ca.gov.* **GPS:** N38.16.65/W120.18.53. **Background:** Site of the first CCC camp in California's state parks, this land of Giant Sequoia trees has been a tourist destination since the 1850s. CCC enrollees developed park roads and bridges, renovated an old hotel (which burned in 1943), laid out picnic areas and campground, and erected several buildings. **Facilities:** Visitor center, RV/tent sites, group lodge, picnic areas and shelters, trails. **CCC Companies:** 590 SP-1, 1921V, and 2940 SP-22. **CCC Features:** Big Trees Lodge, campground, comfort stations, picnic areas and shelters, trails, park roads, stone bridges (most notably the Fallen Sentinel Bridge).

**4. CASTLE CRAGS STATE PARK,** 20022 Castle Creek Road, Castella, CA 96017; 530-235-2684; *www.parks.ca.gov.* **GPS:** N41.08.91/W122.19.29. **Background:** Located in Shasta-Trinity National Forest, the park features a granite outcrop called Castle Crags which overlooks the Sacramento River. **Facilities:** Visitor center, RV/tent sites, trails (including access to the Castle Crags Wilderness and the Pacific Crest Trail), picnic areas, amphitheater, Castle Rock Spring. **CCC Company:** 998 SP-25. **CCC Features:** Park roads, retaining walls, campground, picnic areas, suspension bridge, trails, staff residences, Castle Rock Spring stonework.

**5. CUYAMACA RANCHO STATE PARK,** 12551 Highway 79, Descanso, CA 91916; 760-765-0755; *www.parks.ca.gov.* **GPS:** N32.55.58/W116.33.82. **Background:** Located in the hills and desert areas east of San Diego, CCC enrollees worked on facilities in this park and in nearby Anza-Borrego Desert State Park. Both parks were damaged in 2003 wildfires and several historic CCC structures were lost. **Facilities:** Visitor center, RV/tent sites, Hual-Cu-Cuish Group Camp, picnic areas and shelters, trails, park roads. **CCC Companies:** 1501 DSP-1/SP-4, 1627 SP-14, and 2921 SP-28. **CCC Features:** Cuyamaca Rancho: Park roads, refurbished old Rancho structures, Pasa Picacho

Campground and support buildings, remaining structures from the Hual-Cu-Cuish Group Camp, picnic areas and shelters, trails, Mount Cuyamaca fire tower and fire suppression station, staff residences, CCC camp buildings (now part of local school system camp complex); Anza-Borrego: Stone picnic shelters (ramadas), facilities.

**6. D. L. BLISS STATE PARK,** 9991 Emerald Bay Road, Tahoma, CA 96142; 530-525-7277; *www.parks.ca.gov.* **GPS:** N38.57.05/ W120.06.37. **Background:** Located above Lake Tahoe, the park was established from a 1929 gift of land on Rubicon Point donated by the Bliss family. **Facilities:** Visitor center, RV/tent sites, group camp, picnic areas, trails, beach. **CCC Companies:** 917, 219, and 1940 SP-18. **CCC Features:** Park roads, visitor center, campground, picnic areas, trails, staff residences, administrative buildings.

**7. HUMBOLDT REDWOODS STATE PARK,** Avenue of the Giants, Weott, CA 95571; 707-946-2409; *www.parks.ca.gov.* **GPS:** N40.18.44/ W123.54.46. **Background:** During the 1920s, the Save the Redwoods League sought protection of redwoods along California's Eel River. They were successful in preserving many acres of land but had no funds for development until the arrival of the CCC. **Facilities:** Visitor center and museum, RV/tent sites, picnic areas and shelters, group lodge, interpretive exhibits. **CCC Companies:** 1507 SP-2 and 5460 SP-32. **CCC Features:** Visitor center, campgrounds and support buildings, park entrance, headquarters, remodeled rental cabins, park roads, recreation building, staff residences.

**8. LA PURISIMA MISSION STATE HISTORIC PARK,** 2295 Purisima Road, Lompoc, CA 93436; 805-733-3713; *www.parks.ca.gov.* **GPS:** N34.40.15/W120.25.26. **Background:** Established in 1787 by Franciscan missionaries, this historic site preserves it as an 1812 mission. The site was made a park in 1933 and structures were reconstructed or restored by the CCC (Figure 163). The historic site was dedicated on December 7, 1941. **Facilities:** Visitor center, historic sites and structures, picnic areas, trails, interpretive programs. **CCC Company:** 1951 SP-29. **CCC Features:** Reconstructed church, bell tower, rectory, shops, garden, and cemetery walls.

**9. MCARTHUR-BURNEY FALLS MEMORIAL STATE PARK,** 24898 Highway 89, Burney, CA 96013; 530-335-2777; *www.parks.ca.gov.* **GPS:** N41.0.80/W121.39.04. **Background:** Tucked into forested slopes of the Cascade Mountains that were once covered by lava, the park is known for Burney Falls and Lake Britton. The land was a 1920 gift

**Figure 163.** CCC artisans are making adobe bricks for the reconstructed La Purisima Mission.

from the family of John and Catherine McArthur. **Facilities:** RV/tent sites, trails, Lake Britton. **CCC Companies:** 977 and 1909 SP-20. **CCC Features:** Park roads, stone entrance pillars and rock walls, campground, trails, staff residence.

**10. MENDOCINO WOODLANDS STATE PARK,** Mendocino Woodlands Camp Association, Little Lake Road, PO Box 267, Mendocino, CA 95460; 707-964-7944; *www.parks.ca.gov.* **GPS:** N39.19.36/ W123.42.05. **Background:** One of only two RDAs west of the Mississippi, and the only one in California, Mendocino Woodlands was jointly developed by the WPA and CCC enrollees from Russian Gulch State Park. The park, developed specifically for organized group camping activities, is a National Historic Landmark. **Facilities:** Lodging, dining, and recreation facilities in three group camps; available only by reservation. **CCC Company:** 572 SP-11. **CCC Features:** Camp One: Administration building, recreation hall, dining hall, infirmary, 36 cabins, shower-houses. Camp Two (youth camp): Administration building, dining hall, infirmary, wash houses, swimming pool, outdoor theater. Camp Three: Tent cabins, dining hall, wash house (all built in collaboration with WPA).

**11. MORRO BAY STATE PARK,** Morro Bay State Park Road, Morro Bay, CA 93442; 805-772-2560; *www.parks.ca.gov.* **GPS:** N35.20.85/ W120.50.60. **Background:** Established in 1934 on the grounds of a bankrupt golf club, the park is nestled between the bay and the Pacific Ocean. Notable features include Morro Rock Ecological Preserve, Morro Estuary Natural Preserve, and Monarch Butterfly Roosting Area. **Facilities:** RV/tent sites, group camp, picnic areas and shelters, trails, marina, 18-hole golf course. **CCC Companies:** 1916V and 5447 SP-17. **CCC Features:** Park entrance road, picnic areas and fireplaces, comfort stations, stone walls, steps and other rockwork, old golf clubhouse (staff housing).

**12. MOUNT DIABLO STATE PARK,** 96 Mitchell Canyon Road, Clayton, CA 94517; 925-837-2525; *www.parks.ca.gov.* **GPS:** N37.52.89/ W121.54.87. **Background:** Rising above San Francisco Bay, Mount Diablo has long been a tourist destination. Beginning in 1933, CCC enrollees from Calaveras Big Trees worked on winter projects at Mount Diablo. The CCC built many park structures, including Mount Diablo Summit Observation Tower. **Facilities:** RV/tent sites, picnic areas, trails, summit tower, Mitchell Canyon Interpretive Center. **CCC Companies:** 590, 1921V, and 2932V SP-9. **CCC Features:** Park entrance and roads, picnic areas, trails, staff residences, fire suppression crew quarters, summit tower with museum exhibits (WPA).

**13. MOUNT SAN JACINTO STATE PARK,** 25905 Highway 243, Idyllwild, CA 92549; 951-659-2607; *www.parks.ca.gov.* **GPS:** N33.45.27/ W116.42.84. **Background:** A favorite destination for naturalist John Muir, the site was acquired for a park in 1930. Nestled in an alpine setting above Palm Springs, the park is accessible by road or from the Palm Springs Tramway. **Facilities:** Campground, trails (including sections of the Pacific Crest Trail), picnic areas, winter sports areas, Top-of-the-Tram Restaurant. **CCC Companies:** 913 and 974 SP-19. **CCC Features:** Park access road, stone entrance pillars, trails, Summit Shelter, Round Valley Ranger Station, staff housing, administrative buildings.

**14. PALOMAR MOUNTAIN STATE PARK,** 19952 State Park Road, Palomar Mountain, CA 92060; 760-742-3462; *www.parks.ca.gov, www.astro.caltech.edu/palomar.* **GPS:** N33.19.95/W116.54.59.

**Background:** This land, on the slopes of Palomar Mountain, was set aside for a park in the early 1930s. Atop the summit is the world renowned Mount Palomar Astronomical Observatory. **Facilities:** Visitor center, campgrounds, picnic areas, trails, pond. **CCC Company:** 904 SP-16. **CCC Features:** Park access roads, campground and support buildings, picnic areas, stone fireplaces, trails, staff residences.

**15. PFEIFFER BIG SUR STATE PARK,** 47225 Highway 1, Big Sur, CA 93920; 831-667-2315; *www.parks.ca.gov.* **GPS:** N36.15.06/ W121.47.18. **Background:** Located on the Big Sur River, inland from the Big Sur coastline of mountains and redwood-lined canyons, the park was developed by the CCC. **Facilities:** Visitor center, RV/tent sites, picnic areas and shelters, trails, Big Sur Lodge. **CCC Company:** 990 SP-12. **CCC Features:** Park roads, bridges, administration buildings, campgrounds and support buildings, picnic areas and shelters, trails, post office, service station, rock-work from former swimming pool, wooden park signs.

**16. PRAIRIE CREEK REDWOODS STATE PARK,** Newton B. Drury Scenic Parkway, Orick, CA 95555; 707-465-7347; *www.parks.ca.gov.* **GPS:** N41.21.32/W124.01.61. **Background:** Nestled amid Redwoods and restored natural prairie lands, this park was first preserved by the Save the Redwoods League in the 1920s. CCC enrollees also developed facilities at nearby Jedidiah Smith Redwoods, Del Norte Coast Redwoods, Patricks Point, and Dry Lagoon State Parks. **Facilities:** Visitor center, RV/tent sites, picnic areas, trails. **CCC Company:** 1908 SP-8. **CCC Features:** Prairie Creek: Park roads, entrance station, visitor center, campground and support buildings, picnic areas and shelters, trails, restored Elk Prairie, staff residence. Jedidiah Smith: Park roads, campground, trails, staff residences. Del Norte Coast Redwoods: Park roads, campground, picnic areas, trails; Patricks Point: Campground, picnic areas, support buildings, staff residences. Dry Lagoon: Park roads, picnic areas.

**17. RUSSIAN GULCH STATE PARK,** Russian Gulch State Park Road, Mendocino, CA 95460; 707-937-5804; *www.parks.ca.gov.* **GPS:** N39.19.89/W123.48.24. **Background:** Located along northern California's Mendocino Coast, Russian Gulch sits amid bluffs overlooking Mendocino Headlands and the Pacific Ocean, cedar lined canyons, and Russian Gulch Creek. CCC enrollees also carried out projects at nearby Van Damme State Park. **Facilities:** RV/tent sites, group camp, picnic areas and shelters, trails, recreation hall. **CCC**

**Company:** 572 SP-11. **CCC Features:** Russian Gulch: Park roads, campgrounds, trails, picnic areas, staff residences, fire-suppression crew quarters, recreation hall (CCC-remodeled older building); Van Damme: Visitor center, campground, picnic areas.

**18. SAN CLEMENTE STATE BEACH,** 3030 Avenida del Presidente, San Clemente, CA 92672; 949-492-3156; *www.parks.ca.gov.* **GPS:** N33.24.30/W117.36.14. **Background:** Sandstone mesas and wide beaches mark this Pacific Ocean-side park established in 1937. **Facilities:** Visitor center, RV/tent sites, group camp, picnic areas with ramadas, trails, amphitheater. **CCC Company:** 916 SP-27. **CCC Features:** Park roads, entrance pillars and retaining walls, campgrounds, picnic areas and ramadas, trails, administrative buildings, superintendent's residence (originally home of San Clemente's first mayor).

**19. SEACLIFF-NEW BRIGHTON STATE BEACH,** 201 State Park Drive, Aptos, CA 95003; 831-685-6442; *www.parks.ca.gov.* **GPS:** N36.58.35/W121.54.78. **Background:** Located on Monterey Bay near Santa Cruz, Seacliff (1931) and New Brighton (1933) were among the first of California's public beaches. New Brighton is also known as China Beach for a 19th-century Chinese fishing village once located here. CCC enrollees carried out development work here and at nearby Natural Bridges, Rio Del Mar, and Sunset state beaches. **Facilities:** Visitor center, RV/tent sites, picnic areas and shelters, trails, beaches. **CCC Company:** 3345 SP-24. **CCC Features:** Park roads and bridges, campground, picnic areas and ramadas, trails, sea walls, staff residences.

# National Parks

**20. LASSEN VOLCANIC NATIONAL PARK,** CA Highway 89, Mineral, CA 96063; 530-595-4480; *www.nps.gov/lavo.* **GPS:** N40.28.47/W121.30.29. **Background:** Before the eruption of Mount Saint Helens in 1980, Mount Lassen was the nation's most recently active volcano, having last erupted in 1915. It was the area's volcanism, combined with its scenic beauty that led to creation of Lassen Peak and Cinder Cone national monuments in 1907. The two were combined into Lassen Volcanic National Park in 1916. The CCC developed many of the park's recreational features and structures (Figure 164). **Facilities:** Visitor center, Loomis Museum, historic sites and structures, geological features, RV/tent sites, group camps, backcountry campsites, picnic areas, trails (including a portion of the Pacific Crest Trail), interpretive programs. **CCC Companies:** 1919V, 1921V, 2869, 2940

**Figure 164.** Superintendent David Madsen (left) is conferencing with an associate at Lassen Volcanic National Park.

LNP-1/NP-26, and 975 LNP-2/NP-27. **CCC Features:** Manzanita, Warner Valley, Sulphur Works, Butte Lake, Summit Lake and Kings Creek campgrounds; picnic areas; Manzanita Lake Campfire Circle and amphitheater; trails; administrative and utility structures.

**21. Lava Beds National Monument,** 1 Indian Wells HQTRS, Tulelake, CA 96134; 530-667-8100; *www.nps.gov/labe.* **GPS:** N41.42.88/W121.30.46. **Background:** The landscape of this park, created by eruptions of Medicine Lake Shield Volcano more than a half-million years ago, is a rugged terrain of cinder cones, craters, lava flows, and more than 500 underground lava tubes. Sites within the park were also battlegrounds during the Modoc War of 1872–1873. The national monument was established in 1925. **Facilities:** Visitor center and museum, RV/tent sites, picnic areas, trails, caves, historic site and structures, geological features, trails, scenic roads, interpretive programs. **CCC Companies:** 1989 and 3879 NM-6 and 6411 NP-32. **CCC Features:** Park roads, campground loop A, picnic tables, trails (surface and within caves), cave ladders and stairs.

**22. PINNACLES NATIONAL MONUMENT,** 5000 Highway 146, Paicines, CA 95043; 831-389-4485; *www.nps.gov/pinn.* **GPS:** N36.29.80/ W121.08.55. **Background:** This unusual geological area, created from the eruption of a volcano more than 20 million years ago, was set aside as a national monument in 1908. **Facilities:** Bear Gulch Visitor Center, RV/tent sites, picnic areas, trails. **CCC Companies:** 1954 NM-4 and 904 NP-25. **CCC Features:** Visitor center, Bear Gulch Creek Dam, trails including carved stone steps and handrails, picnic areas.

# COLORADO

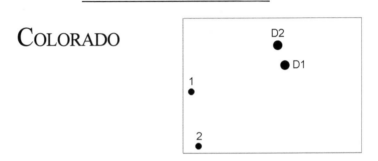

## Destination Parks

### D1. RED ROCKS PARK AND AMPHITHEATRE

*The Beatles, U2, and Joe Caton and the New Dealers all made historic appearances on the stage of Red Rocks Amphitheatre. You read about the Beatles, maybe you saw U2's 'Under the Blood Red Sky' video. Joe Caton and the New Dealers? They built the place.[50]*

— Mark Wolf
"Depression-Era Feats Include Red Rocks, Lowry"
*Denver Rocky Mountain News*

Red Rocks Park, set in the transition zone between the Great Plains and the Rocky Mountains, preserves one of the CCC's most significant achievements. In the heart of this Denver Mountain Park is Red Rocks Amphitheatre, an 8,774-seat outdoor performing-arts venue designed by architect Burnham Hoyt and built by CCC workers between 1936 and 1941. What makes the site remarkable is its natural setting between Ship Rock and Creation Rock, two sandstone monoliths rising high above the surrounding landscape (Figure 165).

The vision for a theater at Red Rocks originated with John Brisben Walker, a wealthy magazine publisher who purchased 4,000 acres near Morrison in the early 1900s. The tract included stone outcrops locals called "Red Rocks" that Walker recognized had remarkable acoustic qualities. He built a temporary stage and hosted concerts at the site. In 1909, Walker supported creation of Denver Mountain Parks, an agency charged with preserving the area's scenic landscapes. Included in the land eventually set aside were 632 acres at Red Rocks, sold by Walker to the city in 1927. Before the Depression halted development, a scenic parkway through Red Rocks was built and the Red Rocks Pueblo constructed. This original concession house is still in use and now known as The Trading Post. In 1935, Mayor Benjamin Stapleton asked parks' manager George Cranmer to recommend improvements projects that might be carried out by ECW workers. Cranmer saw this as the opportunity to bring Walker's vision for a permanent stage at Red Rocks to reality. He requested a CCC company

**Figure 165.** This aerial view shows Red Rocks Amphitheatre, now a prominent feature in what was once called the "Garden of Angels" by early Colorado settlers.

293

to build an amphitheater in the park. A short time later, Company 1848 SP-13/MA-1 arrived and set up camp. The camp complex is now Denver Mountain Parks' district headquarters. The men labored on the project for five years, blasting stone, pouring thousands of yards of concrete, and landscaping the surrounding parklands. The world class performing arts center was dedicated in 1941 (Plate 15, bottom). It was in 1947 that the first annual Easter Sunrise Service was held here. In addition to the amphitheater, Red Rocks Park includes nature trails and picnic areas. The park is also home to a variety of native plants and wildlife from the desert and plains. Nearby Dinosaur Ridge (*www.dinoridge.org*) preserves 100-million-year-old fossils and remarkably preserved footprints.

In 2003, Red Rocks Amphitheatre was renovated and modernized. A new visitor center was built that complements Hoyt's original designs. The center contains exhibits on area history as well as a documentary film about the geology and history of the amphitheater's construction. The Pueblo Trading Post also features an exhibit about the CCC at Red Rocks. The site, called by *Architectural Digest* "an

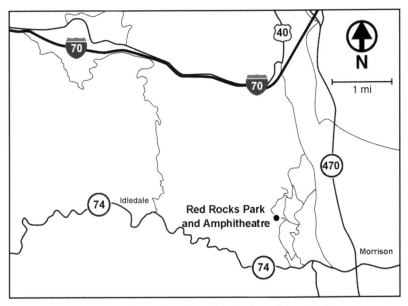

**Figure 166.** The location of Red Rocks Park and Amphitheatre.

architectural and acoustical triumph," has been nominated for designation as a National Historic Landmark.

***Additional Information:*** 18300 West Alameda Parkway, Morrison, CO
80465 (Figure 166); 720-865-2494; *http://www.redrocksonline.com.*
**GPS:** N39.39.90/W105.12.28. Facilities include visitor center,
amphitheatre, Pueblo Trading Post, picnic areas, trails. Note: The old
CCC camp is not regularly open to the public.

---

## D2. ROCKY MOUNTAIN NATIONAL PARK

> *A few months ago I was broke. At this writing I am sit-*
> *ting on top of the world. Almost literally so, because*
> *National Park No. 1 CCC Camp near Estes Park . . . is*
> *9,000 feet up. Instead of holding down a park bench or*
> *pounding the pavements looking for work, today I have*
> *work, plenty of good food, and a view of the sort that*
> *people pay money to see.*[51]

> — Battell Loomis, Camp NP-1
> "With the Green Guard," *Liberty Magazine,* April 29, 1934

Established by President Woodrow Wilson in 1915, Rocky Mountain National Park preserves a stunning landscape featuring more than
50 mountain peaks rising above 12,000 feet. By the late 1920s, hap-
hazard development of the site had yielded disorganized campgrounds,
poorly maintained trails, meadows scarred from earlier grazing and
logging, and an incomplete Trail Ridge Road over the Continental
Divide that had been intended to replace primitive Fall River Road.
Today, Trail Ridge is the highest continuously paved road in the nation. With the onset of the Depression, the park managers despaired
that needed work could not be completed — but this outlook dramatically changed with the creation of the CCC.

The first CCC enrollees arrived in the park on a frigid day in
May, 1933, pitching tents for Camp NP-1 in 18 inches of snow. Within
a few days, they were at work on projects that the park had waiting.
With equipment scarce, recruits traveled to work on red tourist buses

which caused locals to dub them "woodpeckers." Over nine years, Rocky Mountain hosted 14 CCC companies in six camps: NP-1, NP-4, and NP-11 east of the divide; and NP-3, NP-4, and NP-12 west of the divide (figures 167 and 168). Due to harsh winters, most camps were seasonal with the exception of NP-4 on Mill Creek and NP-12 that operated all year just outside the park near Grand Lake.

The CCC carried out an enormous number of projects in the park. They improved existing trails while adding nearly 100 miles more; stocked lakes and streams with 1.5 million trout — carrying them into the back-country in specially-designed insulated packs; and applied Dr. E. P. Meinecke's designs in redeveloping Aspenglen and Glacier Basin campgrounds and laying out Timber Creek campground. Crews also built amphitheaters at Aspenglen and Glacier Basin campgrounds and at Moraine Park. Others laid transmountain telephone lines along Trail Ridge Road; assisted in remodeling Moraine Park Lodge as a museum; and worked with naturalist Dorr Yeager in staffing museums and information stations. Some crews trained as fire fighters and in search and rescue or battled insect infestations in 37,000 acres of ponderosa pines. Crews also built staff housing; landscaped damaged areas and road cuts; constructed the Fall River Ranger Station complex that remains as excellent examples of Rustic design; and cleared timber from planned Shadow Lake and Granby Lake reservoirs.

**Figure 167.** Winters were cold for the CCC men in Rocky Mountain National Park, but many thought they were on top of the world.

**Figure 168.** The first enrollees to arrive at the CCC camp in Rocky Mountain National Park lived in tents until barracks buildings were built.

In a 2005 paper, "The History of the CCC in Rocky Mountain National Park," Julia Brock summed up the impact of the CCC at Rocky Mountain by noting that, "By providing almost limitless manpower, the Corps allowed the Park's landscape architects and engineers to breathe life into their vision for the Park as a viable recreational space."

*Additional Information:* 1000 Highway 36, Estes Park, CO 80517 (Figure 169); 970-586-1206; *www.nps.gov/romo*. **GPS:** N40.21.59/ W105.34.98. Facilities include visitor centers, museums, historic sites, scenic byways, RV/tent sites, amphitheaters, back-country campsites, picnic areas, trails, climbing, interpretive programs, winter sports.

# Other CCC-Related Parks

## National Parks

**1.** Colorado National Monument, Rimrock Drive, Fruita, CO 81521-0001; 970-858-3617; *www.nps.gov/colm*. **GPS:** N39.06.16/ W108.44.17. **Background:** Set atop the Colorado Plateau west of the confluence of the Colorado and Gunnison rivers, Colorado National

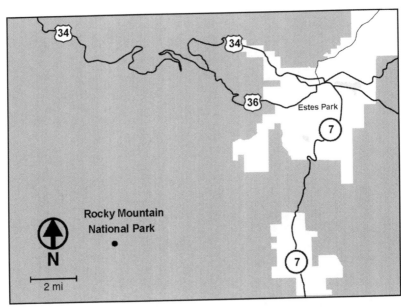

**Figure 169.** The location of Rocky Mountain National Park.

Monument preserves an arid landscape of cliffs, spires, and overlooks along historic Rim Rock Drive. The CCC assisted WPA and PWA workers in constructing this scenic drive (Figure 170). On December 12, 1933, a collapse of the stone "half tunnel" along the drive killed 9 LEMs. This is considered to have been the most tragic accident in CCC history. **Facilities:** Visitor center/museum, RV/tent sites, backcountry campsites, picnic areas, trails, scenic drive and overlooks, interpretive programs. **CCC Companies:** 824 NM-1/NM-2/NP-3, 825 NM-3/NP-10, and 2123 and 3892 NP-8. **CCC Features:** Rim Rock Drive, overlooks, staff residences, utility buildings.

**2. MESA VERDE NATIONAL PARK,** US Hwy. 160, PO Box 8, Mesa Verde, CO 81330-0008; 970-529-4465; *www.nps.gov/meve.* **GPS:** N37.10.28/ W108.28.28. **Background:** One of the best preserved archeological sites in the nation, Mesa Verde, which means "green table" in Spanish, was an ancestral home of Pueblo Indians from 600 to 1300 CE. The area was filled with villages and buildings, the most notable built into the cliffs rising above Montezuma Valley. The site was set aside as the first park of its kind by President Theodore Roosevelt in 1906. During the Depression, two CCC companies developed facilities and

**Figure 170.** CCC workers carry out a road building project at Colorado National Monument.

assisted with archeological excavations and interpretation. **Facilities:** Visitor center, museum, historic sites and structures, scenic roads and overlooks, RV/tent sites, picnic areas, trails, interpretive programs. **CCC Companies:** 861 NP-6 and 1843 NP-5. **CCC Features:** Park roads, trails and walkways, Morefield Village Campground, museum furnishings, fixtures, and exhibits, Spruce Canyon campfire circle, preserved historic sites (notably Pit houses B and C), CCC camp recreation hall and barracks building.

# HAWAII

## Other CCC-Related Parks

## National Parks

**1. HAWAI'I VOLCANOES NATIONAL PARK,** HI Highway 11, PO Box 52, Hawai'i National Park, HI 96718-0052; 808-985-6000; *www.nps.gov/ havo.* **GPS:** N19.24.80/W155.14.31. **Background:** Established in 1916 as Hawai'i National Park, the preserve originally contained two units: one on Hawai'i that protects two of the world's most active volcanoes — Mauna Loa and Kilauea, and the other on Maui that preserves Haleakala volcano. The unit on Maui was designated a separate park in 1951. Hawai'i Volcanoes is renowned for its dynamic geology and varied landscapes — from the summit of Mauna Loa to the Pacific Ocean. The park's historic Volcano House Hotel was established in 1846. CCC enrollees did extensive work in the park (Figure 171), including rebuilding the hotel following a devastating

**Figure 171.** This stone shelter overlooks the Pacific Ocean at Hawai'i Volcanoes National Park.

1940 fire. **Facilities:** Kilauea Visitor Center, Jagger Museum, campgrounds, picnic areas, historic sites and structures, geological features, trails, back-country campsites, shelters, cabins, Crater Rim and Chain of Craters roads, interpretive programs. **CCC Company:** HNP-1. **CCC Features:** Hawai'i Volcanoes: Crater Rim Road retaining walls, Hilina Pali and Mauna Loa trails, Kipuka Puaulu (Bird Park) restoration, Footprints Shelter, Kipuka Nene Fire Cache, rebuilt Volcano House, staff residences, administration building, maintenance facilities. Haleakala: trails, cabins.

# NEVADA

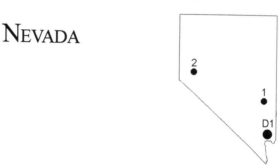

## Destination Parks

### D1. LAKE MEAD NATIONAL RECREATION AREA AND VALLEY OF FIRE STATE PARK

> *In their widely scattered projects throughout the Lake Mead area, the CCC boys proved valuable as scouts for the Park Service naturalists.*[52]
>
> — Dennis McBride
> *Hard Work and Far From Home:*
> *The Civilian Conservation Corps at Lake Mead, Nevada*

In the Mojave Desert near Las Vegas are three landmarks from the Great Depression. The first is massive Herbert Hoover Dam, originally called Boulder Dam, built to harness the Colorado River. The second is Lake Mead, named for Bureau of Reclamation director Elwood Mead and created from the waters impounded by Boulder

Dam. The third is Valley of Fire State Park, set aside in 1935 as Nevada's first park.

As Boulder Dam neared completion in 1935, the state recognized that Lake Mead would become a popular tourist destination, but they had no funds for development. With NPS support, CCC Companies 573 NP-4 and 2536 NP-6 were assigned to the area. The men did not live in barracks but in dormitories recently vacated by dam workers. Each company occupied its own building and the complex was dubbed "Twin Camp." Enrollees carried out projects at Lake Mead on a scale rarely seen elsewhere; building miles of lakeshore roads; improving Boulder City Airport; and traveling by boat to remove piles of driftwood and debris deposited by the rising waters.

In 1936, CCC men began work in the new Boulder Recreation Area. Crews developed bathing facilities, picnic shelters, comfort stations, and other facilities at Boulder Beach; laid out a campground and beach at Vegas Wash; erected and staffed two check-in stations, one west of Boulder City and another in Arizona; and blazed trails, including Red Mountain Trail leading from Boulder City into the surrounding hills. They also assisted in archeological field work at ancient native village sites and abandoned turquoise mines, including Pierces Ferry in Arizona, and the ruins of Lost City Pueblo (Pueblo Grande de Nevada) near Overton (Figure 172). Enrollees built the Lost City Museum that also served as NPS headquarters (Figure 173). Work at some sites was made more urgent as they soon would be lost to rising lake waters.

In addition to work in the recreation area, the CCC also helped develop adjacent Valley of Fire State Park in the sandstone hills northwest of Lake Mead (Figure 174). The park is renowned for its colorful stone, petrified wood, and ancient petroglyphs. Especially notable are cabins, no longer in use, fashioned by the CCC from rough blocks of the native stone (Plate 16, top).

***Additional Information:*** Lake Mead NRA: 601 Nevada Way, Boulder City, NV 89005 (Figure 175); 702-293-8990; *www.nps.gov/lame.* **GPS:** N36.0.60/W114.47.79. Facilities include Alan Bible Visitor Center, Lost City Museum, historic sites, RV/tent sites, picnic areas and shelters, trails, lake with beaches, marinas and water sports facilities,

**Figure 172.** CCC workers assisted in archeological excavations at Lake Mead National Recreation Area.

**Figure 173.** The CCC built the Lost City Museum near Lake Mead National Recreation Area.

**Figure 174.** Picnic ramadas and stone cottages provided visitors a spectacular setting in which to enjoy the beauty of Valley of Fire State Park.

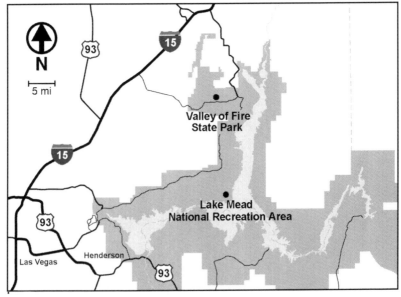

**Figure 175.** The location of Lake Mead National Recreation Area and Valley of Fire State Park.

trails, interpretive programs. Valley of Fire: Valley of Fire Highway, PO Box 515, Overton, NV 89040; 702-397-2088; *http://parks.nv.gov.* Facilities include visitor center, RV/tent sites, picnic areas and armadas, trails, geological features, historic sites.

# Other CCC-Related Parks

## State Parks

**1. CATHEDRAL GORGE STATE PARK,** State Park Road, Panaca, NV 89042; 775-728-4460; *http://parks.nv.gov.* **GPS:** N37.48.70/ W114.24.79. **Background:** During the Pliocene Epoch, this geologically rich region was the bed of an ancient lake. Over millions of years, erosion carved the Bentonite Clay into the gorge that visitors see today. Cathedral Gorge was set aside in 1935 as one of Nevada's first state parks. **Facilities:** Visitor center, RV/tent sites, picnic areas, trails. **CCC Company:** 974 PE-204. **CCC Features:** Campground, picnic areas with ramadas, comfort station, trails, stone water tower.

**2. FORT CHURCHILL STATE HISTORIC PARK,** 1000 Highway 95A, Silver Springs, NV 89429; 775-577-2345; *http://parks.nv.gov.* **GPS:** N39.17.67/W119.16.13. **Background:** Established in 1861, Fort Churchill was an active military post until 1869. The site was deeded to the state of Nevada in 1932. Two years later, the local chapter of the Daughters of the American Revolution was named custodian. CCC assisted with archeological work, in preserving and restoring fort ruins, and constructing the visitor center. **Facilities:** Visitor center, RV/tent sites, group camp, picnic areas, trails, ruins. **CCC Company:** 590 SP-5. **CCC Features:** Visitor center, preserved fort buildings.

# UTAH

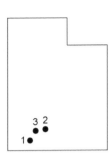

## Other CCC-Related Parks

## National Parks

**1. Zion National Park,** State Route 9, Springdale, UT 84767-1099; 435-772-3256; *www.nps.gov/zion.* **GPS:** N37.12.45/W112.58.84. **Background:** Established in 1909 as Mukuntuweap National Monument and redesignated Zion National Park in 1919, this 229-square-mile park preserves a desert landscape of high mesas and steep sandstone on the Colorado Plateau. The spectacular Zion-Mount Carmel Highway, including a 5,600-foot-long tunnel, is considered an engineering marvel (Figure 176). **Facilities:** Zion Canyon and Kolob Canyon visitor centers, museum, nature center, RV/tent sites, backcountry campsites, picnic areas, trails, scenic drives, interpretive programs. **CCC Companies:** 961 and 1966 NP-2; 962 NP-3 and NP-4; and 2887 NP-4. **CCC Features:** East entrance portals, signage and check-in station, administration building, staff housing (some existing CCC structures), amphitheater, Watchman and Canyon Overlook trails, utility buildings.

**2. Bryce Canyon National Park,** UT Highway 63, Bryce Canyon, UT 84764-0201; 435-834-5322; *www.nps.gov/brca.* **GPS:** N37.38.24/ W112.83.73. **Background:** A landscape of canyons and rock spires called "hoodoos," Bryce Canyon sits on the Paunsaugunt Plateau. Renowned for its beauty and geology, the canyon became a national park in 1928. CCC from Zion National Park spent summer seasons working in Bryce Canyon. **Facilities:** Visitor center, RV/tent sites, back-country campsites, trails, scenic drives, overlooks, Bryce Canyon Lodge, interpretive programs. **CCC Company:** 962 NP-3. **CCC Features:** Park entrance, check station and stonework, campground, comfort station, amphitheater, Under the Rim and Fairyland trails, Sunset Point comfort station, overlook exhibit at Rainbow Point.

**Figure 176.** A CCC camp was perched beneath canyon walls in Zion National Park.

**3. CEDAR BREAKS NATIONAL MONUMENT,** 2390 W. Highway 56, Suite 11, Cedar City, UT 84720; 435-586-9451; *www.nps.gov/cebr.* **GPS:** N37.61.21/W112.83.73. **Background:** Set atop the Colorado Plateau, the park preserves sandstone ravines nearly two miles above sea level. The site was designated a National Monument and transferred to the NPS in 1933. **Facilities:** Visitor center, RV/tent sites, picnic areas, trails, scenic drive, interpretive programs, winter sports activities (park facilities closed in winter). **CCC Company:** 3233 NM-1/NP-5. **CCC Features:** Park roads, trails, wayside exhibits.

# WYOMING

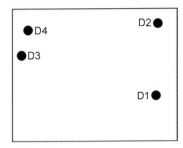

## Destination Parks

### D1. GUERNSEY STATE PARK

*The quality of the architectural and site design at Lake Guernsey . . . made the park a flagship of the CCC state park program.*[53]

— Susan Begley and Ethan Carr
Lake Guernsey State Park
National Historic Landmark Nomination

Located on eastern Wyoming's Hartville Uplift, Guernsey State Park occupies an unusual niche in both state park and CCC history. Set aside in 1903 by President Theodore Roosevelt as part of the Bureau of Reclamation's North Platte River Project, work began on the Guernsey Reservoir in 1925. The project, supervised by Commissioner Elwood Mead, for whom Lake Mead is named, became a model of combined land use for irrigation and recreation. In the late 1920s, locals promoted Lake Guernsey, along with nearby Fort Laramie and traces of the historic Oregon Trail, as tourism destinations — maybe even thinking of a "national park."

With establishment of the ECW program, Commissioner Mead and Interior Secretary Harold Ickes saw Lake Guernsey as the centerpiece for a recreational area to be developed by the CCC. Company 844 BR-9 arrived at Lake Guernsey in May, 1934, and was soon followed by Company 1855 BR-10. Both companies carried out projects of exceptional design and quality (Figure 177). Company 844 built the park museum, a single-story sandstone structure considered among

**Figure 177.** The Skyline Drive follows the shore of Guernsey Reservoir in Guernsey State Park.

the finest examples of CCC architecture in existence (Figure 178). The building blends with the landscape and offers panoramic views of distant Laramie Peak. The museum features natural history exhibits created in the 1930s by University of California-Berkley anthropologist John Ewer. Not to be outdone, Company 1855 erected the "Castle," a medieval fortress-like structure overlooking Lake Guernsey. The building was a combined observation tower, picnic pavilion, and comfort station. Architect C. Eldon Jones described it as the "best latrine I ever saw in the National Park Service;" while the CCC men simply called it the "million dollar biffy." Workers from both companies built park trails and other structures, and Company 1855 enrollees excavated and graded Skyline Drive, which meandered through the hills above the lake, and Brimmer Point Overlook, which offered views of the lake and surrounding landscape.

When Wyoming established its parks system in 1957, Guernsey was transferred from the Bureau of Reclamation to the state. In recognition of the significance and integrity of the CCC work at Guernsey,

**Figure 178.** Guernsey State Park's museum was crafted by CCC artisans with native stone.

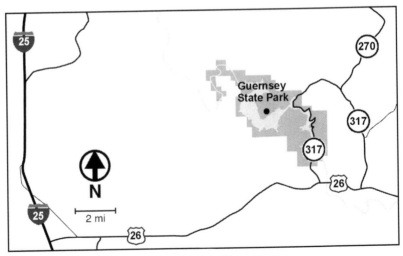

**Figure 179.** The location of Guernsey State Park.

the park has been designated a National Historic Landmark. In the application, the park's development was described as "a unique link between Park Service and state planning, and the planning soon underway for Lake Mead and other national recreation areas."

*Additional Information:* WY Highway 317 and Skyline Drive, Guernsey, Wyoming 82214 (Figure 179); 307-836-2334; *http:// wyoparks.state.wy.us.* **GPS:** N42.16.93/W104.46.14. Facilities include visitor center and museum, historic structures, RV/tent sites, picnic areas and shelters, lake with water sports facilities, trails, and scenic drive.

---

## D2. Devils Tower National Monument

*From 1935–1938, a CCC camp was located here. Practically all the improvements in the area at the present time are the results of their efforts.*[54]

— Ray H. Mattison, NPS Historian
*Devils Tower History: Our First Fifty Years*

Rising more than 1,200 feet above the surrounding landscape, Devils Tower was created over millions of years by erosion of surface sandstone exposing underlying igneous rock that, when molten, had surged up from beneath the earth. Even before it was first described in 1875, by Colonel Richard Dodge, as "one of the most remarkable peaks of this or any country," the tower had long been sacred to the native peoples of the northern plains. Dodge gave the stone tower its present name, noting that the natives called it the "bad gods' tower."

In the early 1890s, Wyoming Senator Francis Warren introduced a bill to create "Devils Tower National Park." The effort failed but the site's significance was not forgotten. On September 24, 1906, President Theodore Roosevelt selected Devils Tower to be America's first national monument. Designation did not spur tourism as the site remained nearly inaccessible until the arrival of automobiles. A primitive road into the monument opened in 1917, but a bridge across the

**Figure 180.** The CCC built the entrance road and check station at Devils Tower National Monument.

Belle Fourche River would not be constructed for another decade. In the early 1930s work began on a permanent road and better visitor facilities, but progress was halted by the Depression. With creation of the ECW program in 1933, resources became available to make Devils Tower more easily accessible. Three CCC companies — 3851, 2555, and 3887 NM-1 — worked in the monument area over a period of three years. The men constructed the park headquarters and a log entrance station (Figure 180). They erected maintenance and utility structures; expanded the superintendent's residence; and installed the park's first water, sewer, and electrical systems. The men blazed trails, including the Tower Trail that encircles the peak, and laid out the first campground and picnic area.

CCC enrollees also built culverts and guard walls and planted native grasses, shrubs, and trees along the entrance road. Of their work, landscape architect Sam Serrano wrote in 1936, "the arrival of

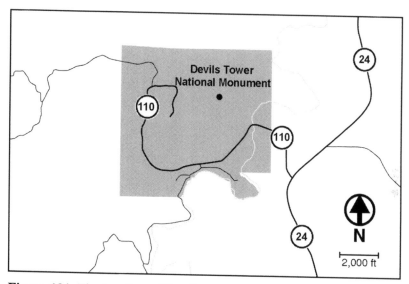

**Figure 181.** The location of Devils Tower National Monument.

the (CCC) . . . marks the beginning of development such as the monument had not previously seen." In recognition of the significance of their work, the monument's Headquarters District and Entrance Road have both been listed on the National Register of Historic Places.

*Additional Information:* WY Highway 110, PO Box 10, Devils Tower, WY 82714-0010 (Figure 181); 307-467-5283; *www.nps.gov/deto.* **GPS:** N44.35.44/W104.43.23. Facilities include RV/tent sites, picnic areas, amphitheater, trails, interpretive programs, concessionaire climbing guides and services.

## D3. GRAND TETON NATIONAL PARK

*Without doubt, the most significant accomplishment of the Civilian Conservation Corps in Jackson Hole was the clean-up of dead and downed trees along the shores of Jackson Lake.*[55]

— John Daugherty
*A Place Called Jackson Hole:*
*A Historic Resource Study of Grand Teton National Park*

The magnificent Teton Range rising nearly 7,000 feet above Jackson Hole was created over millions of years by colliding subterranean plates forming what geologists call "fault block mountains." In 1897, Yellowstone National Park superintendent S. B. M. Young urged that the Teton Range and portions of Jackson Hole be added to his park, but no action was taken. Twenty years later, NPS Director Stephen Mather and Assistant Director Horace Albright called expansion "one of the seven urgent needs facing the Park Service." Despite the urgency, it would take nearly three decades to establish Grand Teton National Park as visitors see it today. It is a story filled with political intrigue and power struggles, arguments over property rights, and secretive land purchases by philanthropist John D. Rockefeller.

With Congressional support, President Calvin Coolidge signed legislation creating Grand Teton National Park in 1929, but the park included only the mountains and the lakes, leaving much of the valley beyond its boundaries. In 1930, Rockefeller's involvement in land sales, through his Snake River Land Company, was made public; setting off local protests and Congressional investigations that ultimately upheld the transactions. Another decade passed and expansion of the park appeared to be at an irresolvable impasse. Rockefeller even confided to Interior Secretary Harold Ickes that he intended to sell the land if the government could not accept the gift. Finally, in 1943, President Roosevelt exercised his powers under the Antiquities Act to and set aside 221,000 acres as the Jackson Hole National Monument. Two years later, the Rockefellers donated nearly 30,000 acres to the monument. For another decade there were repeated, unsuccessful efforts in Congress to abolish the monument. Finally, in 1950, President Harry Truman signed legislation merging the 1929 Grand Teton National Park with Jackson Hole National Monument, creating the park as it exists today. In *Crucible for Conservation*, Robert Righter called creation of the park, "perhaps the most notable conservation victory of the twentieth century."

The park greatly benefited from CCC enrollees who labored there from 1933 to 1942. Thirteen companies operated from six camps: NP-1-5 and NP-12. Enrollees carried out projects including construction of the superintendent's residence, staff housing, and maintenance buildings in what is now the Old Administrative Area Historic District; developments in the Jenny Lake Campground and picnic area; blazing or improving trails, notably the Phelps Lake-Granite Canyon Trail and the Teton Glacier-Garnet Canyon Trail; and erecting Death Canyon and Cascade Canyon patrol cabins. The most significant work the CCC performed may have been clearing of piles of dead trees along Jackson Lake (Figure 182). Over three years, enrollees cleared

**Figure 182.** CCC workers clear debris from the shores of Jackson Lake in Grand Teton National Park.

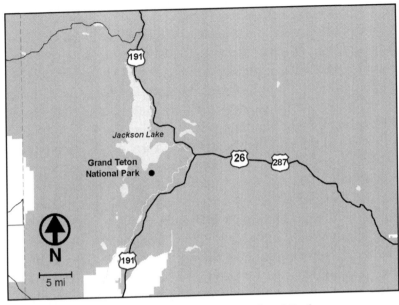

**Figure 183.** The location of Grand Teton National Park.

7,000 acres of shoreline, much of it through difficult manual labor. Today, rare extant CCC buildings from NP-4 at the south end of Jenny Lake remain in use by a park concessionaire.

***Additional Information:*** US 26/89/191 and Teton Park Road, Moose, WY 83012-0170 (Figure 183); 307-739-3300; *www.nps.gov/grte*. **GPS:** N43.39.34/W110.43.10. Facilities include visitor centers, historic sites and structures, RV/tent sites, lodging, picnic areas, trails, interpretive programs, outfitter and guide services, restaurants, winter sports areas.

## D4. YELLOWSTONE NATIONAL PARK

*What the park needed to continue its improvement and protection schedule was a large infusion of money and manpower. It received both from the Civilian Conservation Corps.* [56]

— Kiki Leigh Rydell and Mary Shivers Culpin
*Managing the Matchless Wonders: A History of Administrative Development in Yellowstone National Park, 1872–1965*

In the early 1830s, stories traveling east about boiling springs, geysers, and other geological oddities along the Yellowstone River in the remote western wilderness, were discounted as the ravings of half-crazed "mountain men." In 1871, Dr. F. V. Hayden led the first scientific expedition into the Yellowstone country and confirmed the existence of the remarkable natural features. His reports, combined with the astonishing images provided by photographer William Henry Jackson and artist Thomas Moran, proved instrumental in the preservation of Yellowstone as America's, and the world's, first "national park" a year later.

With the dawn of automobile travel, Yellowstone was "discovered" by thousands of tourists who put enormous strain on the park's facilities. In 1931, despite the deepening Depression, NPS Director Horace Albright instructed park superintendents to review master plans for improvement projects for possible future projects. When the CCC was established in 1933, Yellowstone was ready. In their book *Managing the Matchless Wonders: A History of Administrative Development in Yellowstone National Park*, Kiki Rydell and Mary Culpin wrote, "the government came to the park's rescue in the form of Emergency Conservation Work (ECW) undertaken by the Civilian Conservation Corps."

Initially, Superintendent Roger Toll assigned enrollees work requiring little technical skill, such as roadside clean-up, debris removal, and removal of pine trees infested with blister rust, a devastating disease affecting pine trees. However, as the men gained experience, they tackled more complex tasks. While they did not construct

Yellowstone's landmark museums and lodges, as many of these structures pre-date the program, CCC enrollees — operating from more than 24 companies and nine camps located across the park, NP-1–8 and NP-15 — carried out projects of lasting benefit to the park.

Among the most significant CCC contributions in Yellowstone, and across the country, were campgrounds developed following the designs of Dr. E. P. Meinecke. At Yellowstone, the CCC reconstructed campgrounds at Mammoth, Old Faithful, and Fishing Bridge; built amphitheaters at Mammoth, Madison, Canyon, and West Thumb; and blazed or improved trails, including portions of the 157-mile-long Howard Eaton Trail. Men erected the first boardwalk trails at Norris Geyser Basin and built the path and observation platform at the Upper Falls of the Grand Canyon of the Yellowstone (Figure 184). Enrollees staffed check-in stations, museums, and CCC-built fire towers at Pelican Cone, Observation Peak, and Mount Washburn. The Corps also operated a nursery near the Gardiner, Montana, entrance, raising trees for reforestation and beautification projects in both Yellowstone and Glacier National Park.

**Figure 184.** At the upper end of the Grand Canyon of the Yellowstone in Yellowstone National Park, visitors marvel at the falls of the Yellowstone River from the CCC-built overlook.

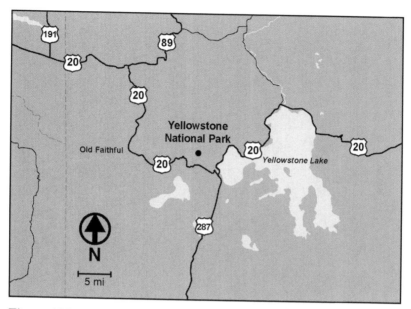

**Figure 185.** The location of Yellowstone National Park.

*Additional Information:* US 89 (Grand Loop Road), Yellowstone, WY 82190-0168 (Figure 185); 307-344-7381; *www.nps.gov/yell.* **GPS:** N44.58.95/W110.41.46. Facilities include visitor centers, museums, RV/tent sites, historic sites, geological features, lodging, picnic areas, trails, boating facilities, winter sports, interpretive programs.

# Northwest Region

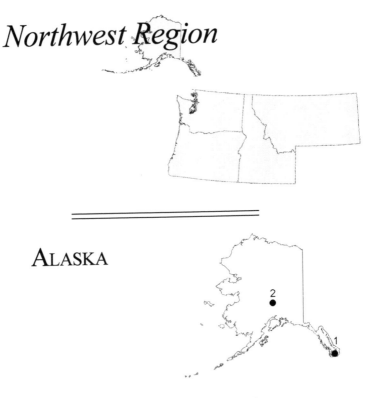

## ALASKA

## Other CCC-Related Parks

## State Parks

**1. TOTEM BIGHT STATE HISTORICAL PARK,** Ketchikan Ranger Station, 9883 North Tongass Highway, Ketchikan, AK 99901; 907-247-8574; *www.dnr.state.ak.us/parks.* **GPS:** N55.25.61/W131.46.57. **Background:** In the early 1900s, the Tlingit and Haida peoples abandoned their villages to seek work in larger communities, leaving behind ornately carved totem poles and other historic structures. In 1938, the Forest Service, using CCC funds, employed natives with carving skills and knowledge of traditions, to reproduce the totems from cedar poles to be displayed at the site of a village once called "Mud Bight" (Figure 186). By 1942, 15 totems, a large clan house, and model village had been reproduced. In 1970, the site was designated a state historical park. Some of the CCC-carved poles have been reproduced again in concrete. **Facilities:** Historic sites, comfort stations, trails. **CCC**

**Figure 186.** Skilled native craftsmen worked for the CCC to reproduce this Clan House at Totem Bight State Historical Park.

**Company:** Local Native Americans. **CCC Features:** Totem poles and other structures.

## National Parks

**2.** DENALI NATIONAL PARK, AK Route 3 (George Parks Highway), Denali Park, AK 99755-0009; 907-683-2294; *www.nps.gov/dena.* **GPS:** N63.43.87/W148.55.23. **Background:** This 6-million-acre park is home to Mount McKinley, called Denali by the natives meaning "the high one," crown jewel of the Alaska Range. Cresting at 20,320 feet, this is the tallest peak in North America. CCC enrollees spent two seasons in the park carrying out a variety of projects. **Facilities:** Visitor centers, RV/tent sites, campgrounds, back-country sites, lodging, trails, fishing, climbing, interpretive programs, guide services. **CCC Company:** NP-1. **CCC Features:** Park headquarters complex (housing, kennels, utility buildings), Wonder Lake Ranger Station complex.

# IDAHO

## Destination Parks

### D1. HEYBURN STATE PARK

*The park is a monument to a generation of young men who helped to stop the abuse of our natural resources and gave America the parks and wildlands that its citizens enjoy today.*[57]

— Mike McKinley
"The Civilian Conservation Corps and
Heyburn State Park Experience, 1934–1942"

Located on the Saint Joseph River where it flows into Chatcolet Lake and Couer d'Alene Lake, Heyburn State Park is rich in scenic beauty and historical significance. For centuries this was home to the Couer d'Alene Indians who fished and hunted the area's forests, marshes, and lakes. In 1859, Lieutenant John Mullan and 150 soldiers began work on the road between Missoula, Montana, and Fort Walla Walla, Washington. Today, traces of the historic Mullan Military Road may still be seen in Heyburn State Park.

Idahoans recognized the scenic value of the Heyburn area and in 1908 land was set aside by Congress for the first state park in the Pacific Northwest. It was named for Idaho Senator, Weldon Heyburn. The site remained undeveloped until 1933, when Idaho requested a CCC camp to improve accessibility and construct visitor facilities. Park Service surveyor Emerson Knight visited the park and reported that Heyburn's "topographic and scenic worth are of high excellence, its historical associations are of much interest and its recreational advantages of high range."

With NPS approval, CCC Company 245 F-141, re-designated Company 1995 SP-1 of "Camp Heyburn," was assigned to the park. The men graded roads, blazed trails; and developed campgrounds, picnic areas, and a lakefront beach area; and built several structures including a caretaker's cottage and a group lodge overlooking Chatcolet Lake at Rocky Point. The lodge, now the Chatq'ele Interpretive Center, features exhibits on the work of the CCC in Heyburn State Park (Figure 187). Several CCC-related structures have been listed on the National Register of Historic Places.

One unique CCC artifact at Heyburn is a large, concrete sign carved in the shape of the state of Idaho (Figure 188). Originally erected at the park entrance in 1935, it was a local landmark for many years. In the 1960s, the sign disappeared after it was struck by a logging truck. Remarkably, in 1991, it was discovered in the woods nearly a mile from its original location. It was recovered and taken to the park's maintenance shop where local CCC veterans restored it. Today, it is back on display, serving as a lasting reminder of the work of the CCC in Heyburn State Park.

**Figure 187.** A log and fieldstone shelter was constructed by CCC workers at Heyburn State Park.

**Figure 188.** CCC enrollees cast this concrete sign for the entrance to Heyburn State Park in the shape of the state of Idaho. After being lost for many years, it was found and returned to a site near the park's entrance.

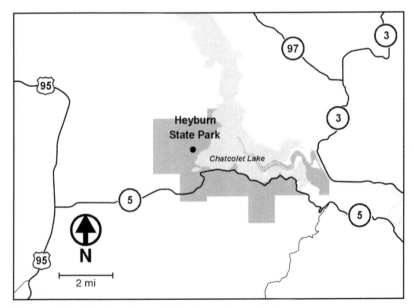

**Figure 189.** The location of Heyburn State Park.

***Additional Information:*** 1291 Chatcolet Road, Plummer, ID 83851 (Figure 189); 208-686-1308; *www.idahoparks.org.* **GPS:** N47.21.21/ W116.46.17. Facilities include Chatq-ele Interpretive Center at Rocky Point, RV/tent sites, picnic areas and shelters, lakes with marina and water sports facilities, trails including sections of the paved Trail of the Couer d'Alenes' Bicycle Trail, winter sports activities, guided boat cruises and outdoor education programs.

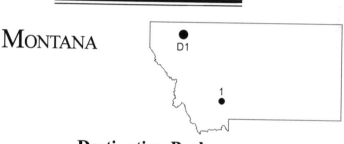

# MONTANA

## Destination Parks

### D1. GLACIER NATIONAL PARK

*There needed to be a proving ground and a show place for those companies, and we provided it. It is of greater note, however, that we had the use of those companies to initiate plans of work that had only been talked about.*[58]

— Eivind Scoyen, Glacier National Park Superintendent
Report to NPS Director Arno Cammerer, 1939

Glacier National Park owes its existence, in large part, to George Grinnell who, as a young man, explored Montana's mountains and became a tireless advocate for a park to save them from exploitation. The Great Northern Railway line over Marias Pass, completed in 1891, brought tourists and increased pressure for preservation. In 1900, the area surrounding Lake McDonald became a forest preserve; a decade later, President William H. Taft signed legislation creating Glacier National Park.

Early visitors arrived by rail, staying at one of the railroad's own hotels and chalets, some of which were only accessible by horseback.

In 1921, work began on the Going to the Sun Road which traversed the Continental Divide at Logan Pass. Completed in 1932, this engineering marvel is now a National Historic Landmark. That same year, the US Congress and Canadian Parliament united Glacier and Canada's Waterton Lakes National Park and formed the world's first "international peace park." Many areas of Glacier remained remote, linked only by a network of footpaths, a circumstance that created difficulties in fighting the frequent forest fires.

With the arrival of CCC crews in the spring of 1933, including some "bewildered" young men from New York City, Glacier's superintendent Eivind Scoyen undertook projects to improve access, communications, and visitor facilities. Over nine years, 29 companies worked from 13 CCC camps: NP-1–6, NP-8–11, and NP-13–15. Permanent camps were established in eastern and western areas of the park, close to roads and park facilities, with back-country side or spike-camps open in the summer (figures 190 and 191). During his August 5, 1934, visit to Glacier, President Roosevelt visited with CCC enrollees of Camp NP-11 at Saint Mary.

Much CCC work involved removal of downed wood, clearing, and replanting of burned-over areas, as well as construction and staffing of lookout towers. Critically important was the stringing of telephone lines linking lookouts, patrol cabins, and headquarters. Especially remarkable was the trans-mountain line requiring placement of seven miles of cable across Logan Pass and along the Going to the Sun Road. The men also developed trails, picnic areas and campgrounds, following the Meinecke design principles. Among CCC features still in evidence are the West Entrance Station, buildings in the Saint Mary utility area, and park headquarters structures, notably residences, garages, and maintenance buildings. All have been nominated to the National Register of Historic Places.

*Additional Information:* Glacier Route 1 (Going to the Sun Highway), West Glacier, MT 59936 (Figure 192); 406-888-7800; *www.nps.gov/glac*. **GPS:** N48.30.49/W113.59.18. Facilities include Apgar, Logan Pass, and Saint Mary visitor centers, RV/tent sites, back-country camping, picnic areas, lodging, scenic drives, lakes and streams, trails, guided tours, interpretive programs, outfitter services.

**Figure 190.** CCC workers pose near their tent side-camp in Glacier National Park.

**Figure 191.** A fortunate group of CCC enrollees enjoy lunch surrounded by the grandeur of Glacier National Park.

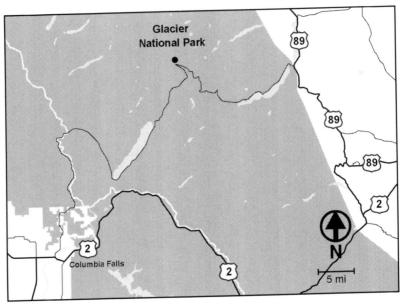

**Figure 192.** The location of Glacier National Park.

# Other CCC-Related Parks

## State Parks

**1. LEWIS AND CLARK CAVERNS STATE PARK,** MT Route 2, Whitehall, MT 59759; 406-287-3541; *http://fwp.mt.gov/parks*. **GPS:** N45.84.31/ W123.24.13. **Background:** First explored in 1898, these caves were operated as a tourist attraction by Dan Morrison until lost in a claim dispute with the Northern Pacific Railroad. Subsequently, the land was given to the federal government and, in May, 1908, President Theodore Roosevelt set it aside as Lewis and Clark Caverns National Monument — although there is no evidence that the explorers visited the site. After the CCC carried out development and improvement work, the land was deeded to Montana for its first state park. **Facilities:** Visitor center, RV/tent sites, picnic areas, tipi and cabins, amphitheater, trails. **CCC Company:** 574 SP-3. **CCC Features:** Visitor center, park roads, chiseled steps and widened cave passages, electric lighting, Paradise Room (discovered by CCC enrollees), cave exit tunnel.

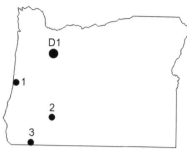

## Destination Parks

### D1. SILVER FALLS STATE PARK

*Forward thinkers of the '30's looked at the spectacular topography and water resources of what is now Silver Falls State Park and envisioned a renewed forest complementing the steep cliffs, deep-cut canyons and dashing waterfalls that awe today's visitors.*[59]

— Fred Delkin
"Silver Falls an Underrated Treasure," *Oregon Magazine*

Silver Falls has been described as the "crown jewel" of the Oregon State Parks system. This area of evergreen forests surrounding Silver Creek on the western slopes of the Cascades contains the largest concentration of waterfalls in North America. Remarkably, before creation of the park in 1933, and arrival of the first CCC enrollees in 1935, the area was a clear-cut wasteland, the result of years of logging.

Despite the devastation, conservationists recognized the site's potential and urged restoration for a park, provided resources could be found. The first 90 acres of land were acquired by the state in 1931 from owners eager to sell property they considered to be of no "economic value." Additional land was added, and the site was dedicated as one of Oregon's first, and still the largest, state parks. Given the park's degraded landscape and its proximity to Salem, it was designated as an RDA, one of only two on the west coast.

Work began when enrollees from CCC Company 611 SP-9 set up camp on the North Fork of Silver Creek in 1935. Crews went to work reclaiming the forest by planting Douglas fir to replace the cut-over cedars. They followed with construction of roads, installation of water and electric lines, and landscaping of picnic and group-camp areas (Plate 16, bottom). Enrollees erected Silver Creek Youth Camp, Smith Creek Youth Camp, Log Cabin shelter, Creasy Lodge, a remnant from the CCC camp; and many other structures in the expanding park. CCC craftsmanship is most evident in the parks largest building, South Falls Lodge, which is noted for its rock walls, metal work, and unique myrtle-wood furniture, all crafted by CCC artisans (figures 193 and 194). In addition, present-day visitors join earlier generations in trekking along the CCC-built Trail of Ten Falls, a seven-mile national recreation trail offering views of stunning cascades. In expressing appreciation for the Corps' contributions, Silver Falls State Park manager Jim Bader has noted that the CCC, with help from WPA workers, built a "full service park from the ground up."

Today, the CCC's legacy at Silver Falls is recognized through the listing of the Silver Creek Youth Camp and South Falls as National Register Historic Districts.

**Figure 193.** This is South Falls Lodge, under construction, at Silver Falls State Park.

**Figure 194.** The historic South Falls Lodge, with its unique myrtle-wood furnishings and hand-crafted fixtures, remains a signature structure at Silver Falls State Park.

*Additional Information:* 20024 Silver Falls Highway, Sublimity, OR 97385 (Figure 195); 503-873-8681; *www.oregonstateparks.org.* **GPS:** N44.52.08/W122.39.25. Facilities include RV/tent sites, horse camps, North Falls and Silver Creek (YMCA) group camps, cabins, yurts, New Ranch and Old Ranch group lodges, Silver Falls Lodge and Conference Center, picnic areas and shelters, historic South Falls Lodge, trails, water activities, interpretive programs.

# Other CCC-Related Parks

## State Parks

1. JESSIE M. HONEYMAN MEMORIAL STATE PARK, 84505 Highway 101, Florence, OR 97439; 541-997-3641; *www.oregon.gov/OPRD/PARKS.* **GPS:** N43.92.99/W124.10.69. **Background:** Located along the coast, the park features freshwater Cleawox and Woahink lakes, trails through stands of Douglas fir, and dunes that are part of Oregon Sand Dunes National Recreation Area (Figure 196). **Facilities:** RV/tent sites, yurts, picnic areas and shelters, water sports facilities, nature center, conference center, trails. **CCC Company:** 1213 SP-10. **CCC Features:** Cleawox Lake Bathhouse (park store), caretaker's cottage, trails.

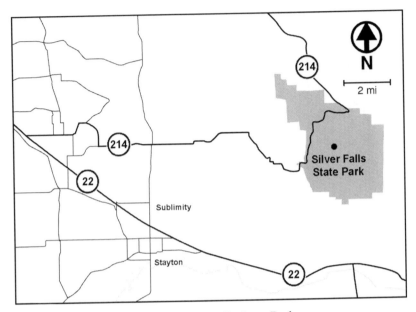

**Figure 195.** The location of Silver Falls State Park.

**Figure 196.** CCC men are working in the Woahink Marshes in Jessie M. Honeyman Memorial State Park.

# National Parks

**2. CRATER LAKE NATIONAL PARK,** Rim Drive, Crater Lake, OR 97604; 541-594-3000; *www.nps.gov/crla.* **GPS:** N42.53.83/W122.08.01. **Background:** Set in the rugged terrain of west central Oregon, Crater Lake is a caldera created by the eruption of Mount Mazama 7,000 years ago. Revered by the Klamath, the site was unknown to Euro-Americans until 1853. Crater Lake became the nation's fifth national park in 1902. **Facilities:** Rim Village and Steel visitor venters, RV/tent sites, Crater Lake Lodge, Mazama Village Motor Inn, trails, scenic Rim Drive. **CCC Companies:** 1555, 1634, 5483 NP-1; 1634, 1989, 544, 3864, 468 NP-2. **CCC Features:** Park roads and trails; Rim Village administration building and comfort station; park headquarters comfort station; maintenance structures; landscaping and stone work; Mount Scott, Crater Peak and Sentinel Point trails.

**3. OREGON CAVES NATIONAL MONUMENT,** 19000 Caves Highway, Cave Junction, OR 97523; 541-592-2100; *www.nps.gov/orca.* **GPS:** N42.05.79/W123.24.13. **Background:** Established in 1909, Oregon Dunes is a small park, rich in botanical and geological diversity. Evergreen forests cover the surface, while the cave preserves remnants of ancient oceanic crust. **Facilities:** Oregon Cave Visitor Center, Valley Visitor Center, Oregon Caves Chateau, picnic areas, surface and cave trails. **CCC Companies:** 1555, 1634, and 5483 NM-1/NP-3. **CCC Features:** Trails, landscaping, stone work, picnic areas, signs, ranger station, check station and restroom building.

# WASHINGTON

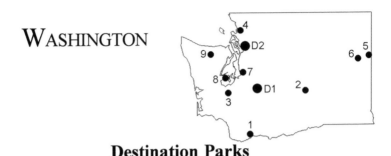

## Destination Parks

### D1. MOUNT RAINIER NATIONAL PARK

*It is difficult to wander very far anywhere in the park
today without encountering their handiwork. Their era
marks a high point in our country's shared commitment
to social reform and natural resource protection.*[60]

— Tim McNulty
*Washington's Mount Rainier National Park: A Centennial Celebration*

On his 1792 expedition, Captain George Vancouver sailed into
Puget Sound and saw a distant, snow-capped mountain. He named it
"Mount Rainier" for his friend, Admiral Peter Rainier. To the native
Yakama, the peak was Tahoma — "sacred mountain that is god." Ris-
ing more than 14,000 feet, Mount Rainier is the tallest peak in the
Cascades and one of many volcanic peaks lining the Pacific coast.
Rainier last erupted nearly 6,000 years ago but could awaken at
any time, as evidenced by the 1980 eruption of nearby Mount Saint
Helens.

In 1888, James Longmire established a hotel and spa near hot
springs on Rainier's southern slopes and, from the hotel, blazed a
trail to a meadow he called Paradise. That same year, naturalist John
Muir, after climbing the mountain, urged designating it a "national
park." Rainier was set aside as the Pacific Forest Reserve in 1893
and, on March 2, 1899, President William McKinley signed legislation establishing it as the nation's fifth national park. In 1904, work
on a "pleasure road" to Paradise began. After six years of construction, the road opened with President Taft journeying to Paradise in an

open touring car. The Paradise Inn opened in 1917 and the park's Longmire headquarters was established a few years later.

Following creation of the CCC in 1933, Rainier's superintendent, Owen Tomlinson, a former military officer, recognized that camps would serve a dual purpose of developing park facilities and "man building." Working with NPS planners, he identified locations for CCC camps and the projects each camp would undertake (Figure 197). Over nine years, 20 CCC companies worked from seven camps: NP-1 at "Tahoma Creek," NP-2 at "Narada Falls," NP-3 at "Carbon River," NP-4 at "Saint Andrews," NP-5 at "White River," NP-6 at "Ohanapecosh," and NP-8 at "Sunshine Point." All camps, except NP-8, were seasonal.

**Figure 197.** A primitive CCC tent camp is nestled in the shadow of Mount Rainier at Mount Rainier National Park.

**Figure 198.** Two CCC enrollees are blazing a back-country trail in Mount Rainier National Park.

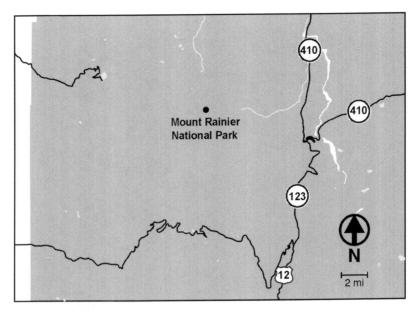

**Figure 199.** The location of Mount Rainier National Park.

Today, many CCC features remain at Rainier. These include entrance gateways at Carbon and Mowich Lake; Ski Hut at Paradise; Ohanapecosh campground; Mount Fremont, Shriners Peak and Gobblers Knob fire towers; White River mess hall and staff housing; North Mowich, Summerland, and Indian Bar trail shelters; Huckleberry Creek ranger cabin; Narada Falls parking area; the latrine at Camp Muir; several administrative and maintenance structures at Longmire; picnic tables with carved "CCC" at White River; and miles of hiking trails (Figure 198). Today, several of the park's CCC-era structures have been designated as National Historic Landmarks.

***Additional Information:*** 55210 238th Avenue East, Ashford Park, WA 98304-2211 (Figure 199); 360-569-2211; *www.nps.gov/mora*. **GPS:** 46.47.21/W121.44.10. Facilities include Paradise, Ohanapecosh, and Sunrise visitor centers; Longmire Museum; RV/tent sites; back-country campsites; Historic Longmire and Paradise inns; picnic areas; trails; winter sports facilities; interpretive programs; guide and outfitter services.

---

## D2. Deception Pass State Park

*Here in Washington, the CCC helped our young state park system emerge fully developed, ready to meet the needs of a growing population. Many of the facilities built by the CCC men . . . are still in use by park visitors and staff today.*[61]

— Brochure
Washington State Parks and Recreation Commission, July 1997

While named for a navigational "mistake," there is nothing mistaken about the beauty of the cliffs, lakes, forests, and Puget Sound shoreline that make up Deception Pass State Park. In 1792, British Captain George Vancouver anchored outside what he believed was a passage between Whidbey and Fidalgo islands, only to discover that Fidalgo was a peninsula separated from the mainland by a channel too narrow to navigate. Exasperated, he called the site "Deception Pass."

**Figure 200.** A CCC crew is installing distinctive log and stone guard-rails along a road in Deception Pass State Park.

In 1866, a military post was built near the pass, strategically positioned to protect Puget Sound. Fortunately, the fort's presence preserved the woodlands around Deception Pass from logging. In 1925, the fort closed and, with urging of conservationists, land was donated to the state for a park. While locals enjoyed the lakes and beaches, it took the arrival of the CCC to improve accessibility and develop tourism facilities.

In 1933, Park Service landscape architects and designers developed a master plan for Deception Pass, identifying projects to be completed by CCC enrollees and local contractors. CCC Company 266 SP-3 arrived in June, 1933, and was followed later by men from Company 4263 SP-4. The men laid out roads, including State Highway 20 in the park, and bridges; set log and stone guard rails blazed trails; developed picnic areas and campgrounds; and erected shelters, bathhouses and comfort stations (Figure 200). In addition, they planted trees, built staff residences and administrative structures, and turned Deception Pass into what has been called a "National Park caliber" preserve and recreation area. CCC crews, laboring alongside local Oak Harbor men, helped to build the beautiful Deception Pass Bridge.

**Figure 201.** A bathhouse built by Corps workers at Deception Pass State Park now serves as the Washington State CCC Museum.

This arched, twin span structure, rising nearly 200 feet above the water, spans tiny Passage Inlet linking Whidbey and Fidalgo islands. Dedicated on July 31, 1935, the bridge has become an iconic symbol of Washington tourism and is listed on the National Register of Historic Places.

Deception Pass State Park retains the rustic flavor of the era in which it was developed. More than 25 CCC-built structures remain, including picnic shelters, the Cranberry Lake and Bowman Bay campgrounds, and the stone and log Bowman Bay Bathhouse that now houses the Washington CCC Museum (Figure 201). Today, the entire park has been recognized by the state as a Legacy of CCC Design and Construction.

***Additional Information:*** 41229 State Route 20, Oak Harbor, WA 98277 (Figure 202); 360-675-2417; *www.parks.wa.gov.* **GPS:** N48.25.10/W122.39.07. Facilities include RV/tent sites, group camps, freshwater lakes, saltwater beaches, trails, picnic areas and shelters, boating facilities, CCC Interpretive Center and Museum (seasonal).

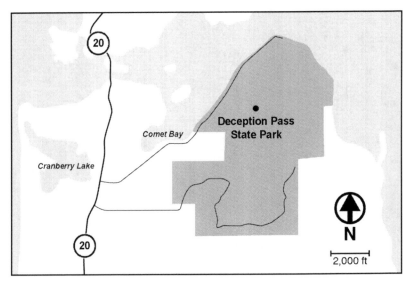

**Figure 202.** The location of Deception Pass State Park.

# Other CCC-Related Parks

## State Parks

**1.** BEACON ROCK STATE PARK, 34841 State Route 14, Skamania, WA, 98648; 509-427-8265; *www.parks.wa.gov*. **GPS:** N45.37.75/ W122.01.30. **Background:** Created by Ice Age floods through the Columbia River gorge, the rock is the remnant of the basalt core of an ancient volcano. It was dubbed "Beacon Rock" by Lewis and Clark who first saw it in October, 1805. In the early 1900s, the rock was purchased by Henry Biddle who built a tourist trail to the summit. His heirs gave the land for a park in 1935 and development work was carried out by the CCC. **Facilities:** RV/tent sites, picnic areas and shelters, kitchen shelters, trails, boating facilities. **CCC Company:** 2643 SP-13. **CCC Features:** Park roads, original campground, picnic areas, kitchen shelters, trails.

**2.** GINKGO PETRIFIED FOREST / WANAPUM RECREATIONAL AREA, 4511 Huntzinger Road, Vantage, WA 98950; 509-856-2700; *www.parks.wa.gov*. **GPS:** N46.57.25/W119.59.29. **Background:** This park preserves one of the most unusual fossilized forests in the world.

Rare ginkgo trees, ferns, and other remains reveal this area as a tropical forest 15 million years ago. The site was unearthed by a highway construction crew in 1931 and a small tract was set aside to preserve the fossils. Beginning in 1936, CCC enrollees assisted in extensive excavations and erected several park buildings. The greatly expanded park now borders Columbia River's Wamapum Reservoir. **Facilities:** Visitor center/museum, Native American petroglyphs, fossils, RV/tent sites, picnic areas and shelters, reservoir. **CCC Companies:** 3224 and 4271 SP-15. **CCC Features:** Park roads, stonework, caretaker's cottage, excavated fossils.

**3. MILLERSYLVANIA STATE PARK,** 12245 Tilley Road South, Olympia, WA 98512; 360-753-1519; *www.parks.wa.gov.* **GPS:** N46.54.58/ W122.54.41. **Background:** In the mid-1800s, John Miller acquired this property near Olympia, calling it Millers Glade. His descendants changed the name to Millersylvania, meaning "wooded glade." In 1921, the family donated old growth fir and cedar forests on Deep Lake for a park. **Facilities:** RV/tent sites, group camping area, group cabin camp, Lakeside Cottage, picnic areas and shelters, Environmental Learning Center, trails, lake with bathhouse and water sports facilities. **CCC Companies:** 1232, 2935V and 938 SP-6. **CCC Features:** Park roads, campground, picnic areas, combination buildings, beach area and bathhouse, superintendent's residence, other administrative structures (Figure 203).

**4. MORAN STATE PARK,** 3572 Olga Road, Eastbound, WA 98245; 360-376-2326; *www.parks.wa.gov.* **GPS:** N48.38.93/W122.50.37. **Background:** Located on Orcas Island, land for the park was donated in 1921 by former Seattle mayor Robert Moran. The park's centerpiece is the CCC-built stone observation tower atop Mount Constitution, highest point in the San Juan Islands. **Facilities:** RV/tent sites, Vacation House cottage, picnic areas and shelters, group shelters, trails, water sports facilities on five freshwater lakes, Moran Environmental Learning Center. **CCC Companies:** 1233 and 4768 SP-1. **CCC Features:** Park roads and bridges, picnic areas and fireplaces, trails, Log Kitchen Shelter, Mount Constitution Tower.

**5. MOUNT SPOKANE STATE PARK,** North 26107 Mount Spokane Park Road, Spokane, WA 99021; 509-238-6845; *www.parks.wa.gov.* **GPS:** N47.55.10/W117.06.62. **Background:** Dominating Spokane's skyline, the park preserves forests and granite outcroppings along the slopes of Mount Spokane, southernmost peak in the Selkirk Range.

**Figure 203.** This 1930s photo shows a log and stone building under construction in Millersylvania State Park.

In 1927, the mountain became the first Washington state park east of the Cascades. The CCC built the mountain-top Vista House and other structures. **Facilities:** RV/tent sites, group camp, picnic areas and shelters, kitchen shelter, winter sports areas, more than 200 miles of trails, Vista House shelter. **CCC Companies:** 611 SP-10 and 949 SP-7. **CCC Features:** Park roads, picnic areas, kitchen shelter, trails, improved Cooks Road (summit road), Vista House.

**6. RIVERSIDE STATE PARK,** 9711 West Charles Road, Nine Mile Falls, WA 99026; 253-288-2572; *www.parks.wa.gov.* **GPS:** N47.46.97/ W117.33.33. **Background:** This park preserves wooded hills and waters of the Spokane and Little Spokane rivers. The Spokane River is lined with basalt boulders, evidence of ancient volcanic activity. **Facilities:** RV/tent sites, group camp, picnic areas and shelters, kitchen shelter, trails, boat launch, Spokane House Interpretive Center. **CCC Company:** 949 SP-7. **CCC Features:** Park roads, trails, campground, picnic areas and shelters, kitchen shelter, trails.

**7. SALTWATER STATE PARK,** 25205 8th Place, Des Moines, WA 98198; 253-661-4956; *www.parks.wa.gov.* **GPS:** N47.22.51/W122.19.29. **Background:** This shore-side park opened in 1933 as a symbol of cooperation between the two rival cities of Seattle and Tacoma, and the two communities later buried a hatchet here to symbolize the end of their competition. **Facilities:** RV/tent sites, picnic areas and shelters, kitchen shelter, artificial diving reef, trails. **CCC Company:** 935 SP-11. **CCC Features:** Park roads, kitchen shelter, superintendent's residence and workshop, trails.

**8.** TWANOH STATE PARK, 12190 East Highway 106, Union, WA 98592; 360-275-2222; *www.parks.wa.gov.* **GPS:** N47.22.66/W122.58.37. **Background:** Located on Hood Canal, a natural fjord flowing into Puget Sound, the park's name comes from the Skokomish for "gathering place." The area was logged in the 1890s, and the CCC carried out reforestation, landscaping, and park development. **Facilities:** RV/tent sites, picnic areas and shelters, kitchen shelters, water sports facilities, beach, trails. **CCC Companies:** 4270 and 4728 SP-18. **CCC Features:** Park roads, picnic areas and shelters, kitchen shelters, comfort stations, bathhouse, concession building.

# National Parks

**9.** OLYMPIC NATIONAL PARK, 600 East Park Avenue, Port Angeles, WA 98362; 360-565-3130; *www.nps.gov/olym.* **GPS:** N48.02.31/W123.25.81. **Background:** Some of the most rugged and remote forests and mountains in the nation, the area was set aside as a forest preserve in 1897. It was named a national monument in 1909, but designation as a park was opposed by timber companies. After President Roosevelt visited in 1937, he declared, "This must be a park!" A year later, Olympic National Park was established. **Facilities:** Olympic, Hurricane Ridge, Hoh Rain Forest visitor centers; RV/tent sites; picnic areas; Crescent Lake; Sol Duc Hot Springs; trails; interpretive programs. **CCC Companies:** 936 F-17/NP-9, 946 F-19, 948 F-20, 982 F-21, and 3569 NP-10. **CCC Features:** Park headquarters complex; Elwha Ranger Station; Moose Lake, Hoh Lake, Happy Four, Three Forks, Felton Creek shelters; Sol Duc Campground; Altair and Elwha Campground kitchens; La Poel Picnic Area; Eagle, Elkhorn, Graves Creek, North Fork Quinault guard stations; Deer Park winter sports area; trails; roads (including first scenic drive to Hurricane Ridge).

# Endnotes for Section II

[1] Isabelle Story, *The National Parks and Emergency Conservation Work.* Washington, DC: Government Printing Office, 1936. *www.nps.gov/history/history/online_books/ecw/1936/sec4.htm*

[2] O. R. Head, Acting Superintendent, Camp Report, CCC Camp 7, 1934. National Archives and Records Administration, Record Group 79.

[3] C. R. Vinten, "The Civilian Conservation Corps at Highlands Hammock State Park." Sebring: Highlands Hammock State Park Archives, 2.

[4] Lucy Ann Lawless, "The Civilian Conservation Corps and the State Park: An Approach to the Management of the Designed Landscape Resources at Franklin Delano Roosevelt State Park, Pine Mountain, Georgia." Master's thesis in Landscape Architecture, The University of Georgia, 1992, 2.

[5] Pamela McRae, *Tishomingo County News*, September 12, 1996.

[6] Eric Nygard, Superintendent, Hanging Rock State Park. Correspondence with authors, 2006.

[7] Tommy Sims, South Carolina Department of Archives and History. Correspondence with authors, 2006.

[8] James P. Jackson, quoted in Harley Jolley, *The CCC in the Smokies.* Gatlinburg: The Great Smoky Mountains Association, 2001, 14.

[9] District C Annual Report, Fourth Corps Area, 1937. National Archives and Records Administration, Record Group 79.

[10] Waverly Groves, address to President Bill Clinton at the inauguration of the Americorps Program, 1994.

[11] Forest Gladden, District VI Manager, Virginia Department of Conservation and Recreation. Correspondence with authors, 2006.

[12] Laura Cohen, Chief of Interpretation, Prince William Forest Park. Correspondence with authors, 2006.

[13] Earlyn "Stubbie" Wheeler, Foreman CCC Co. 1130 SP-4, CCC Camp Reports, National Association of Civilian Conservation Corps Alumni Archives.*

[14] Warren Kasper, Park Ranger, Chesapeake and Ohio Canal National Historical Park. Interview with authors, 2006.

[15] George O'Hearn, Superintendent, CCC Co. 107 SP-7, National Association of Civilian Conservation Corps Alumni Archives.*

[16] James L. Garvin, "Notes on the Development of Bear Brook State Park." New Hampshire Division of Historical Resources, September, 2003.

[17] Tom Davis, CCC Enrollee Co. 1268 SP-5, Voorhees State Park. Quoted in "Learning a Trade," *Happy Days,* April 4, 1934. National Archives and Records Administration, Record Group 79.

[18] C. Larsen, *Happy Days*, March 24, 1934. National Archives and Records Administration, Record Group 79.

[19] Eric Rensel, Environmental Education Specialist, Parker Dam State Park, "Civilian Conservation Corps at Parker Dam State Park." Report to Pennsylvania Department of Conservation and Natural Resources, December 11, 2003.

[20] Caption of photograph, *Happy Days*, September 8, 1934.

[21] Kelly Smith, Naturalist, Cacapon State Park. Interview with authors, 2006.

[22] Harry Collier, ECW Special Investigator, 1938 Supplemental Report. National Association of Civilian Conservation Corps Alumni Archives.*

[23] Kay Rippelmeyer-Tippy, "A Brief History of the Civilian Conservation Corps at Giant City State Park, 1933–1941." Illinois Department of Natural Resources, March, 2003.

[24] "CCC Youths Bare Heads at Nancy Lincoln's Grave," *Indianapolis News*, February 12, 1934. Lincoln State Park Archives.

[25] Clyde "Tubby" Littrell, CCC Veteran, CCC Co. 1540 SP-9, Audubon State Park. Interview with authors, 2005.

[26] T. J. McVey, ECW Special Investigator, CCC Camp Report 1934, National Archives and Records Administration, Record Group 79.

[27] Roger N. Rosentreter, "Roosevelt's Tree Army: Michigan's Civilian Conservation Corps." *Michigan History Magazine*, June, 1986. *www.michigan.gov/dnr*

[28] David R. Benson, *Stories in Log and Stone: The Legacy of the New Deal in Minnesota State Parks*. Saint Paul: Minnesota Department of Natural Resources, 2002, 97.

[29] Ibid, 91.

[30] Rachel Stout-O'Connor, Historian, John Bryan State Park. Correspondence with authors, 2005.

[31] Mary Schueller, *Rustic Reflections of Copper Falls State Park.* Richfield: Rustic Books LLC, 2005, 98.

[32] Editorial, *Backbone Lyre*, April 25, 1934. National Archives and Records Administration, Record Group 79.

[33] Lynn Morrow, Preservation Corner, "Grand Buildings of the Thirties: Missouri Public Parks." *Ozarks Watch Magazine*, 1(4): 2005, 2. *http://ozarkswatch.missouristate.edu*

[34] Eric Haugland, Park Ranger, Scotts Bluff National Monument. Correspondence with authors, 2005.

[35] George Warren, CCC Enrollee, CCC Co. 794 SP-1, International Peace Garden. From exhibit in International Peace Garden visitor center.

[36] Jack Krank, CCC Veteran, quoted in "Proud to be a CCC Boy" by Kathy Tandberg, *The Common: Supplement to the Beulah Beacon and The Hazen Star*, June 17, 1999.

[37] Bradley Block, Chief of Interpretation, Custer State Park. Correspondence with authors, 2005.

[38] M. R. Tillotson, CCC-era Superintendent, Grand Canyon National Park, National Archives and Records Administration, Record Group 79.

[39] M. K. Maierhauser and Lendell Cockrun, "The Intertwined History of Colossal Cave and La Posta Quemada Ranch," 2000. *www.colossalcave.com/ccc*

[40] *1937 Yearbook: Parks and Recreation Programs.* US Department of the Interior, National Park Service, Washington, DC: Government Printing Office, 1938, 5.

[41] T. J. Priehs and Therese Burton, eds., *Bandelier National Monument.* Tucson: Western National Parks Association, 1990, 35.

[42] Kris Marek, quoted in "Oklahoma's State Parks — Rich in Beauty and History," by Keli Clack. *www.americasstateparks.org/article_20_ok*

[43] Suzanne H. Schrems, *Encyclopedia of Oklahoma History and Culture.* Oklahoma City: Oklahoma Historical Society, 2007. Online edition published as *Oklahoma Historical Society's Encyclopedia of Oklahoma History and Culture* at *http://digital.library.okstate.edu/encyclopedia*

44 Jim Fox, "CCC: Fond Memories from a Time of National Hardship," *Texas Parks and Wildlife Magazine*, September, 1978.

45 James Wright Steely, *Parks for Texas: Enduring Landscapes of the New Deal.* Austin: University of Texas Press, 1999, 114.

46 Linda Greene, Historian, Death Valley National Park, "Death Valley National Park National Register of Historic Places, Multiple Property Documentation Form, Section E." Denver: United States Department of the Interior, National Park Service, 1988, 9.

47 Lary M. Dilsaver and William C. Tweed, *Challenge of the Big Trees: A Resource History of Sequoia and Kings Canyon National Parks.* Three Rivers: Sequoia Natural History Association, 1990, 5. *www.cr.nps.gov/ history/online_books/dilsaver-tweed/chap6a.htm*

48 Darrell Stover, CCC Enrollee, Co. 942 YNP-6, quoted in "The Civilian Conservation Corps (CCC) in Yosemite." *Yosemite Journal*, 67(4): 2005, 6.

49 Joseph Engbeck, Jr., *By the People, for the People: The Work of the Civilian Conservation Corps in California State Parks, 1933–1941.* Sacramento: California State Parks, 2002, 67.

50 Mark Wolf, "New Deal Leaves Imprint on Colorado, Depression-Era Feats Include Red Rocks, Lowry," *Rocky Mountain News*, 1999. Online version Highbeam Research, December 23, 2010; *www.highbeam.com/doc/ 1G1-67424846.html*

51 Battell Loomis, CCC Co. NP-1, Rocky Mountain National Park, "With the Green Guard," *Liberty Magazine*, April 29, 1934, 52–53. Quoted in Lloyd K. Musselman, *Rocky Mountain National Park: Administrative History, 1915–1965, Chapter VII: The Depression and the CCC.* Washington, DC: National Park Service, Office of History and Historic Architecture, Eastern Service Center, Washington, DC, July, 1971.

52 Dennis McBride, *Hard Work and Far from Home: The Civilian Conservation Corps at Lake Mead, Nevada.* Boulder City: Boulder Images, 1995, 44.

53 Susan Begley and Ethan Carr, "National Historic Landmark Nomination, National Register of Historic Places Registration Form." National Park Service, 1997, 4.

54 Ray H. Mattison, Historian, Devils Tower, "The First Fifty Years," 1955. *www.nps.gov/deto/historyculture/places.htm*

[55] John Daugherty, *A Place Called Jackson Hole: A Historic Resource Study of Grand Teton National Park.* Moose: Grand Teton Natural History Association, 1999. *www.nps.gov/history/history/online_books/grte2/hrs.htm*

[56] Kiki Leigh Rydell and Mary Shivers Culpin, *Managing the Matchless Wonders: A History of Administrative Development in Yellowstone National Park, Historic Resources Study, Volume III, Park Administrative History, Part I.* Yellowstone National Park: Yellowstone Center for Resources, YCR-CR-2006-03, 2006.

[57] Mike McKinley, "The Civilian Conservation Corps and the Heyburn State Park Experience, 1934–1942." Heyburn State Park Archives, 18.

[58] Eivind Scoyen, CCC-era Superintendent, Annual Report to the National Park Service Director, 1939.

[59] Fred Delkin, "Silver Falls an Underrated Treasure." *Oregon Magazine,* December, 2001, 2. *www.oregonmag.com/silverfalls1201.htm*

[60] Tim McNulty, *Washington's Mount Rainier National Park: A Centennial Celebration.* Seattle: The Mountaineers, 1998, 59.

[61] Washington State Department of Parks and Recreation, brochure, July 1997.

---

\* The National Association of Civilian Conservation Corps Alumni (NACCCA) ceased operations in 2008. A portion of their archives was acquired by the Smithsonian Institution, while another portion was sent to the succeeding organization, CCC Legacy (*ccclegacy.org*).

# Section III

## Perspectives and Resources

*The CCC lives on in spirit. It has left its heritage for America in the preservation of its natural resources for the enjoyment of all generations.*

— Inscription on a plaque
Red Rocks Park and Amphitheatre, Colorado.

# Afterword

A common question that arose in our many conversations with CCC veterans was "Would the CCC work today?" Almost without exception, these men — many now in the ninth decade of their lives — answered, "Yes!"

Their experiences as young men in the Corps, unemployed and desperate to help themselves or their families, proved to be a defining moment in many of their lives. More than just a job, life in the CCC instilled discipline and teamwork, an appreciation and understanding of others from vastly different backgrounds, an opportunity to learn a skill and further their education, and, in the process, develop an enduring love of the outdoors. For thousands, the CCC was a training ground for future careers — as well as preparing them for the challenges they would face in WW II.

In addition to the personal benefits to the men who served, the CCC provided an enormous service to the nation. The projects they undertook in forests and parks across the country represented an unprecedented triumph of environmental stewardship for which we, as a nation, still benefit.

In this second decade of the 21st century, we are again feeling the effects of a severe financial downturn, high unemployment, devastating natural disasters, and declining funds for parks and forests. To many there has never been a more appropriate time to reconsider a program like the CCC to address the dual concerns of wasted human resources and threatened natural resources. Programs like the Student Conservation Corps (SCC), California Conservation Corps (CCC), Americorps, and other initiatives have been established and are providing benefits. Now an organization, We Can Take It (*www.wecantakeit.org*) has undertaken to promote reactivation of the national CCC through grassroots support for proposed legislation (HR 4318: 21st Century Civilian Conservation Corps Act) currently before Congress.

Reflect on the words of President Franklin D. Roosevelt to CCC enrollees in 1933:

"You are part of a great national movement for the improvement and protection of vast wooded resources of the country. The nation will owe you a debt of gratitude a hundred years hence." We owe it to ourselves and the generations to follow, to honor the legacy of the Civilian Conservation Corps by preserving and protecting the lands, parks, and forests that they have bequeathed to us.

## Appendix I

# A Glossary of Selected Agencies, Legislation, and the Times

**Civilian Conservation Corps (CCC):** An agency created by the Emergency Conservation Work Act passed by Congress and signed into law by President Roosevelt on March 31, 1933. Despite the advocacy of Roosevelt and other members of the administration, the CCC was never a permanent organization and was funded through Congressional appropriations. Following America's entry into WW II, Congress appropriated no future funds for the CCC and the camps closed on July 1, 1942.

**Emergency Conservation Work (ECW) Act:** The parent legislation creating the Civilian Conservation Corps, the ECW Act was enacted on March 31, 1933. At the time, the terms "Emergency Conservation Work" and "Civilian Conservation Corps" were often used interchangeably. On June 28, 1937, Congress passed new legislation formally establishing the CCC as the official agency to carry out the conservation work.

*Happy Days*: The weekly CCC newspaper, published from 1933 to 1942 and distributed to all CCC camps. It featured news and human interest stories, often written by enrollee reporters, about camp life and company accomplishments.

**National Park Service (NPS):** Created by the Organic Act of 1916, the NPS is the agency within the Department of the Interior charged with oversight of America's national parks and historic sites. The expansion of the NPS in 1933 brought most national monuments, national battlefields and military parks, and national cemeteries under management of the NPS. The overwhelming majority of work performed by the CCC in national and state parks was carried out under the direct supervision of planners, architects, landscape designers, engineers, and project managers employed by central or district offices of the NPS.

**New Deal:** First explicitly mentioned as a "new deal for the American people" in Roosevelt's acceptance speech at the 1932 Democratic National Convention, the term came to represent the broad range of governmental initiatives and programs of the Roosevelt Administration that were intended to reverse the effects of the Great Depression.

**Recreational Demonstration Area (RDA):** Often described as the parks that most truly represented the egalitarian ideals of the New Deal, RDAs were parks created from marginal or abandoned lands, usually close to urban areas, with group camping facilities for use by civic, charitable, or other non-profit organizations. The underlying intent was to provide opportunities for outdoor recreation and enjoyment for youth or families of modest means who could not easily access more remote state or national parks. RDAs were developed on land purchased by the federal government. Upon completion, the management of nearly all RDAs was turned over to state parks agencies. Many of these parks continue their original mission of offering group camping facilities and activities. *Alternative term:* Recreation Demonstration Areas.

**Resettlement Administration (RA):** Created in 1935, the Resettlement Administration utilized relief funds to provide support for destitute families living in once-thriving farming, mining, and lumbering communities, either by offering assistance to these families where they lived or, in extremely devastated areas, by purchasing the land and relocating the people to more productive areas. In 1937, the RA was superseded by the Farm Security Administration (FSA) that carried out a number of ambitious farm programs. A number of Recreation Demonstration Area projects were funded in part by land purchases from RA funds. An excellent example of coordination of RA work and the CCC is at Tennessee's Cumberland Mountain State Park and nearby Cumberland Homesteads community built for families financially wiped out by the failure of a mining company.

# Appendix II

# CCC Enrollee Oath

(Upon entering the CCC, each enrollee subscribes to the following oath. It is a contract between the enrollee and the US Government, and should be lived up to in each respect.)

I, _____ , do solemnly swear that the information given above as to my status is correct. I agree to remain in the Civilian Conservation Corps for the period terminating at the discretion of the United States between ..................... unless sooner released by proper authority, and that I will obey those in authority and observe all the rules and regulations thereof to the best of my ability and will accept such allowances as may be provided pursuant to law and regulations promulgated pursuant thereto. I understand and agree that any injury received or disease contracted by me while a member of the Civilian Conservation Corps cannot be made the basis against the government, except such as I may be entitled to the Act of September 7, 1916 (39 Stat. 724) ( an act to provide compensation for employees of the United States suffering injuries while in the performance of their duties and for other purposes), and that I shall not be entitled to any allowances upon release from camp, except transportation in kind to the place at which I was accepted for enrollment. I understand further that any articles issued to me by the United States Government for the use while a member of the Civilian Conservation Corps are, and remain, property of the United States Government and that willful destruction, loss, sale, or disposal of such property renders me financially responsible for the cost thereof and liable to trial in the civil courts. I understand further that any infraction of the rules or regulations of the Civilian Conservation Corps renders me liable to the expulsion therefrom. So help me God.

*— Your CCC: A Handbook for Enrollees,* 1940

# Appendix III

# **Civilian Conservation Corps — Selected Facts**

Duration of the program: April 5, 1933, to June 30, 1942

Nicknames: "Roosevelt's Tree Army," "Tree Troopers," "Soil Soldiers," "Cees," "3 Cs," "Colossal College of Calluses," "Woodpecker Warriors"

Total men enrolled: 3,463,766

Juniors, veterans, and Native American enrollees: 2,876,638

Territorial enrollees: 50,000 (estimated)

Non-enrolled personnel: 263,755

Average enrollee: 18 to 19 years old, 147 pounds, 5 feet 8¼ inches tall

Average weight gain of enrollees in first 3 months: 11.5 pounds

Number of illiterate enrollees taught to read: 40,000

Average number of camps operating in US per year: 1,643

Total number of different camps: 4,500

Highest elevation of a CCC camp: 9,200 feet above sea level — Rocky Mountain National Park, Colorado

Lowest elevation of a CCC camp: 270 feet below sea level — Death Valley, California

Camp locations: Every state in the union, plus Alaska, Hawaii, Puerto Rico, US Virgin Islands

Total cost: $3 billion

Approximate cost per enrollee in 1940 for food, clothing, overhead, and allotments to dependents: $1,000

Allotments to dependents: $662,895,000

Number of people directly benefited from enrollees' checks: 12 to 15 million

Value of work in 1942 dollars: $2 billion

Miles of roads built: 125,000 miles

Miles of telephone lines strung: 89,000 miles

Miles of foot trails built: 13,000 miles

Farmland benefited from erosion control projects: 40 million acres

Stream and lake bank protection: 154 million square yards

Range revegetation: 814,000 acres

Firefighting man-days: More than 6 million

Number of enrollees who died fighting fires: 29

Overall death rate: 2.25 per thousand

State parks developed: 800

Public campground development: 52,000 acres

Mosquito control: 248,000 acres

Number of fish stocked: 972 million

Historic restoration: 3,980 structures

Number of trees planted: Between 2 and 3 billion

Number of federal government agencies participating in some capacity: 25

Unofficial motto: "We can take it!"

— James Justin CCC Museum, CCC Legacy Foundation
*www.ccclegacy.org*

# Appendix IV

## The Nine Civilian Conservation Corps Areas

**First:**    Connecticut, Maine, Massachusetts, New Hampshire, Rhode Island, Vermont

**Second:**    Delaware, New Jersey, New York

**Third:**    District of Columbia, Maryland, Pennsylvania, Virginia

**Fourth:**    Alabama, Florida, Georgia, Louisiana, Mississippi, North Carolina, South Carolina, Tennessee

**Fifth:**    Indiana, Kentucky, Ohio, West Virginia

**Sixth:**    Illinois, Michigan, Wisconsin

**Seventh:**    Arkansas, Iowa, Kansas, Minnesota, Missouri, Nebraska, North Dakota, South Dakota

**Eighth:**    Arizona, Colorado, New Mexico, Oklahoma, Texas, Wyoming (excluding western Wyoming and Yellowstone National Park)

**Ninth:**    Alaska, California, Hawaii, Idaho, Montana, Nevada, Oregon, Utah, Washington, and western Wyoming and Yellowstone National Park

# Appendix V

# "What We Did for a Dollar a Day"

*In the depth of the Great Depression in 1933,*
*President Roosevelt created the CCC.*
*For our nation, he had a plan —*
*to give young men jobs, improve our forests, and build state and*
*federal parks*
*throughout the land.*
*From the country, villages, towns, large cities, and the ghettos, by*
*the*
*thousands we came.*
*We were eager to participate in FDR's CCC game.*
*Our uniforms and equipment were 1917 army style.*
*And every time we went to town, the girls would point to our pistol-*
*legged*
*trousers and smile.*
*We lived in tents and barracks and had to sweep the floors and*
*make our bed.*
*We shined our shoes, brushed our teeth, and combed our head.*
*To heat the barracks, we built our own fires and cut our own wood.*
*The need for dry kindling was well understood.*
*They taught us to lay rock, pour cement, and build lakes for geese*
*and ducks,*
*to operate bulldozers and drive trucks.*
*We dug ditches, built roads, and sloped banks,*
*built campgrounds, log cabins, and water tanks.*
*We worked in the rain, the snow, and the mud,*
*to crush rock, cut logs, and rescue people from the Mississippi*
*flood.*

*Our camps were located all across the land,*
*from Alaska to Death Valley's burning sand.*
*We were often stationed far from home in places we had never been,*
*to perform hard work with little money to spend.*
*When in town, if we asked girls for a date they would say, "No*
*thanks, we go out*
*with railroad men,*
*because you CCC boys only have five dollars to spend."*
*With axes, rakes, saws, and leaking fire pumps on our back,*
*we climbed mountains to fight fire all day with only a sandwich in a*
*paper sack.*
*If we ever went home for a visit, we always had a short time to stay,*
*because we had to hitch-hike or walk all the way.*
*Working in the kitchen would have been a good deal,*
*but they had too many pots and pans to wash and spuds to peel.*
*In the evening before we could eat,*
*we lowered the flag and had retreat.*
*We did our work well all across the land;*
*our forest roads are still lined with our shrubs and trees.*
*And as people ride by and enjoy the scenery, they always say,*
*"These roads and trees were put here by the CCC's."*
*And we are proud to say,*
*we did this all for just a dollar a day.*

— John Derden, CCC Enrollee, 1937–1939

# Appendix VI

# **Acknowledgements**

In researching and writing this book, we have benefited from the enthusiastic support of and assistance from dozens of individuals and groups who have shared our passion for preserving the legacy of the CCC in the parks. Below, we have attempted to list everyone who helped us in this undertaking but, inevitably, we may have left someone out. For this we apologize in advance.

**Alabama:** Carl Scardina, Alabama State Parks; Connie Roberson and David Odom, Cheaha State Park; Vivian Cooper, Chewacla State Park; Tim Whitehead, De Soto State Park; Kent Wilborn, Monte Sano State Park. **Alaska:** Jane Lakeman, Denali National Park. **Arizona:** J. J. Lamb, Colossal Cave Regional Park; Pam Cox, Grand Canyon National Park. **Arkansas:** Sharon Shugart, Hot Springs National Park. **California:** John Arnold, California State Parks; Blair Davenport and James Reynolds, Death Valley National Park; Cari Kreshak, Lassen Volcanic National Park; Alexandra Picavet and Ward Eldredge, Sequoia and Kings Canyon national parks; Lois Orr, Yosemite National Park. **Colorado:** Jerry Tripp-Addison and Ron C. Garrison, Red Rocks Park and Amphitheatre; William Butler and Sybil Barnes, Rocky Mountain National Park. **Connecticut:** Gary Nasiatka, Macedonia Brook State Park. **Florida:** William M. Stanton, Florida State Parks; Dorothy Harris, Highlands Hammock State Park. **Georgia:** Gail DeLoach, Georgia Archives; Kim Hatcher, Georgia State Parks; David Foote, Vogel State Park. **Hawaii:** Jadelyn Monitz-Nakamura, Hawai'i Volcanoes National Park. **Idaho:** Ron Hise, Heyburn State Park. **Illinois:** Mike Kelly and Richard Kelly, Giant City Lodge; Jenny Skufca, Giant City State Park; Marge Shroeder and Hal Hassen, Illinois State Parks; David Hedrick, Lincoln's New Salem State Historic Site. **Indiana:** Glory June Grieff, Paul Diebold and Ginger Murphy, Indiana State Parks; Mike Capps, Lincoln Boyhood National Memorial; Peggy

Brooks, Lincoln State Park; Fred Wooley, Pokagon State Park. **Iowa:** Mary Shea, Backbone State Park; Angela Corio, Iowa State Parks; Deborah Coates, Pilot Knob State Park. **Kentucky:** Mary Dee Miller, Audubon State Park; Cindy Lynch, Columbus-Belmont State Park; Bret Smitley and Lisa Davis, Cumberland Falls State Park; Vickie Carson, Joy Lyons, Bob Ward, Ted Messenger and Terry Langford, Mammoth Cave National Park; Brian Gasdorf, Natural Bridge State Park; Dean Henson, Pine Mountain State Park. **Louisiana:** Nicole Adams, Chemin-a-Haut State Park; Rita MacMurray, Fontainbleau State Park; Raymond Berthelot, Louisiana State Parks. **Maine:** Brooke Childrey and Lee Terzis, Acadia National Park; Bill Elliott, Camden Hills State Park; Rich Bouchard and Cindy Dunham, Tanglewood 4-H Camp and Learning Center. **Maryland:** Sally Griffin, Catoctin Mountain Park; James Perry and Warren Kasper, Chesapeake and Ohio Canal National Historical Park; Steve Robertson, Fort Frederick State Park; Lt. William Thomas, Herrington Manor and Swallow Falls State Parks; Ross Kimmell, Robert Bailey, and Diane B. Feheley, Maryland State Parks; Sgt. Al Preston, South Mountain Recreation Area. **Massachusetts:** Martin Beveridge and Ellen Fitzpatrick, Massachusetts Department of Conservation and Recreation; Donna Stimpson, Mount Greylock State Reservation. **Michigan:** Lisa Gamero, Michigan State Parks; Mike Montgomery and Rob Burg, North Higgins Lake State Park. **Minnesota:** Retta James-Gasser, Gooseberry Falls State Park; Connie Cox, Itasca State Park; Bryce Anderson, Minnesota State Parks. **Mississippi:** Robbie Neely and Mark Mason, Mississippi State Parks; Bill Brekeen, Tishomingo State Park. **Missouri:** Dan Wedermeyer and Ramona Beckmann, Meramec State Park; Kim Dillon, Missouri State Parks; Jim Newberry, Washington State Park. **Montana:** Deidre Shaw and Ann Fagre, Glacier National Park. **Nebraska:** Jeff Fields, Ponca State Park; Eric Haugland, Scotts Bluff National Monument. **Nevada:** Cody Tingey, Cathedral Gorge State Park; David Morrow and Barbara Rohde, Nevada State Parks. **New Hampshire:** Carol Martel, Jim Garvin and Ed Mussey, Bear Brook State Park. **New Jersey:** Dean Cramer, Parvin State Park; Patricia Kallesser, Voorhees State Park. **New Mexico:** Chris Judson and Gary Roybal, Bandelier National Monument; Bob Hoff, Carlsbad Caverns

National Park. **New York:** Michael Miecznikowski, Allegany State Park; Jim Gold, Bureau of Historic Sites; Ed Winslow, Gilbert Lake State Park; Brian Scriven, Letchworth State Park; John Feeney, Mills-Norrie State Park; Christine Robinson, Saratoga National Historical Park. **North Carolina:** Jody Merritt, Fort Macon State Park; Eric Nygard and Jason Anthony, Hanging Rock State Park; Joanne Clendinning, William B. Umstead State Park. **North Dakota:** Jeff Hoffer, Fort Abraham Lincoln State Park; John McQueen, International Peace Garden; Annette Schilling, North Dakota Tourism; Bruce M. Kaye, Theodore Roosevelt National Park; Steve Crandall, Turtle River State Park; **Ohio:** Rachel Stout-O'Connor, John Bryan State Park; Michael Williams, Ohio Department of Natural Resources. **Oklahoma:** Michelle Finch-Walker, Beavers Bend State Park; Ken Ruhnke, Chickasaw National Recreation Area; Mark Teders, Lake Murray State Park. **Oregon:** Craig Ackerman and Steve Mark, Oregon Caves National Monument and Crater Lake National Park; Chris Havel and Jim Bader, Silver Falls State Park. **Pennsylvania:** James Davis, Blue Knob State Park; Dale Luthringer, Cook Forest State Park; John Heiser, Gettysburg National Military Park; Eric Rensel, Parker Dam State Park; David Heiney, Promised Land State Park. **South Carolina:** Joanna White and Traci Bash, Oconee State Park; Al Hester, South Carolina State Parks; Paul Knowland, Table Rock State Park. **South Dakota:** Brad Block, Custer State Park. **Tennessee:** Kim Moore, Cove Lake State Park; Meredith Mullen, Cumberland Falls State Park; Annette Hartigan, Great Smoky Mountains National Park; Derrick L. Miller, Harrison Bay State Park; Michelle Carpenter-Forbess, Montgomery Bell State Park; James Cox, Reelfoot Lake State Park; Jack Gilpin, Tennessee State Parks. **Texas:** Bill Brock, Big Bend National Park. **Utah:** Ron Terry, Zion National Park. **Vermont:** William Cobleith, CCC Veteran; Nate McKeen, Mount Ascutney State Park; Raymond Toolan, Lamoille Forest; Greg Western, Vermont CCC Alumni Association; Rochelle Skinner and Ed O'Leary, Vermont State Parks. **Virginia:** Jackie Holt and Peter Givens, Blue Ridge Parkway; Forrest Gladden and Ellen Reynolds, Douthat State Park; Bessie Weber, Fairy Stone State Park; Laura Cohen, Prince William Forest Park; Robert E. L. Krick, Richmond National Battlefield Park; Reed

Engle, Shenandoah National Park. **Washington State:** Jack Hartt, Deception Pass State Park; Deborah Osterberg, Mount Rainier National Park; Jacilee Wray, Olympic National Park; Steven Wang, Washington State Parks. **West Virginia:** Kelly Smith and Thomas Ambrose, Cacapon Resort State Park. **Wisconsin:** Kent Goeckerman, Jill Crom, Rosemary Greenlee (Atlanta photographer), and Mary Schueller, Copper Falls State Park; Kerry Isensee, Pattison State Park; Michelle Fischer, Wisconsin Department of Tourism;  Paul Kosir, Wyalusing State Park. **Wyoming:** Christine Czazasty, Devils Tower National Monument; Pam Holtman, Grand Teton National Park; Todd Thibodeau, Lake Guernsey State Park; Mary Hopkins and Ashley Bruner, Wyoming State Historic Preservation Office; Lee Whittlesey and Elaine Hale, Yellowstone National Park. **National Park Service:** Bruce Farabee (retired), Glacier National Park; David Gilbert, Wade Myers and David Nathanson, Harpers Ferry Center.

# Appendix VII

# Credits for Figures[1]

**Foreword:** ix: National Park Service (NPS)

**Section 1:** 6: Great Smoky Mountains National Park Archives (GSMNP); 9: Library of Congress; 15 top and bottom: National Park Service Historic Graphics Collection (NPSHGC); 17: Georgia Secretary of State, Archives and History Division (GSAHD); 20, 23, 25, 26, 27 (top and bottom): NPSHGC; 28 top and bottom: National Archives and Records Administration (NARA); 29 top: CCC Legacy Foundation (CCCLF), bottom: Minnesota Department of Natural Resources (MNDNR); 30: GSAHD; 32 top: CCCLF, bottom: Terry Langford, Mammoth Cave National Park Museum; 43, 46, 49: NPSHGC; 50: GSMNP; 52: NARA; 54: NPSHGC

**Section II:** pp. 68, 69: Ren Davis (RD); 70: NARA; 72, 74: RD; 76: GSAHD; 79, 81, 82: NPSHGC; 85: RD; 90: Hanging Rock State Park; 92–94, 99: RD; 101, 102: GSMNP; 104, 107, 108: RD; 110: NPSHGC; 111, 113: RD; 115: Prince William Forest Park; 118: NARA; 120 top and bottom: NPSHGC; 124: RSD; 126: NPSHGC; 130: RD; 137: Ed Mussey, Bear Brook State Park; 140: Patricia Kallesser, Voorhees State Park; 142 top and bottom: NPSHGC; 144: Gilbert Lake State Park; 147: NPSHGC; 150: RD; 156: Ascutney State Park; 162: RD; 166: NPSHGC; 172, 179, 180: RD; 182: Terry Langford, Mammoth Cave National Park Museum; 187 top and bottom: Michigan Department of Natural Resources; 191: Minnesota Department of Natural Resources (MNDNR); 194: NPSHGC; 196, 197: MNDNR; 199: Ohio Department of Natural Resources; 204: Rosemary Greenlee; 208: NPSHGC; 215: CCCLF; 216: Helen Davis 221: NPSHGC; 224, 225, 227, 228, 229, 230: RD; 232, 233: NPSHGC; 237 top and bottom: NARA; 240, 241, 242, 243, 245, 247, 250, 252: NPSHGC; 254: Chickasaw National Recreation Area; 255 top and bottom: NPSHGC; 257: Beavers Bend State Park; 260, 261, 263, 268, 273, 276, 279 top and bottom, 280 top and bottom: NPSHGC; 283: RD; 287, 291: NPSHGC; 293: Red Rocks Park; 296: NARA; 297, 299,

---

[1] Credits are presented here first by the section of the book in which they appear, then by page number upon which they occur, and lastly by the person or other entity to which credit is extended. The full name of the credited entity is given upon first use and thereafter is identified by an abbreviation.

bottom, 304, 307, 309: NPSHGC; 310: Wyoming Travel and Tourism; 312, 315, 318: NPSHGC; 321: Historic American Buildings Survey; 323: Heyburn State Park; 324: CCCLF; 327 top and bottom: NPSHGC; 330, 331: Oregon Parks and Recreation; 332, 335, 336: NPSHGC; 338: Washington Department of Transportation; 339: RD, 342: NPSHGC.

**Color Plates:** Plate 1 top and bottom: RD; Plate 2: RD; Plate 3: RD; Plate 4 top and bottom: RD; Plate 5: RD; Plate 6 top and bottom: RD; Plate 7 top and bottom: RD; Plate 8 top: Monica Sosnowski, bottom: RD; Plate 9 top and bottom: RD; Plate 10: RD; Plate 11 top: RD, bottom: MNDNR; Plate 12: RD; Plate 13 top and bottom: RD; Plate 14 top: RD, bottom: NPSHGC; Plate 15 top: RD, bottom: Rod Tanaka, Denver Theaters and Arenas; Plate 16 top: RD, bottom: Oregon Parks and Recreation.

# Selected References

Benson, David R. *Stories in Log and Stone: The Legacy of the New Deal in Minnesota State Parks.* Duluth: Minnesota Department of Natural Resources, 2002.

Brock, Julia. *A History of the CCC in Rocky Mountain National Park.* Estes Park: Rocky Mountain Nature Association and Rocky Mountain National Park, 2005.

*http://www.nps.gov/history/history/online_books/rmno/ccc.pdf*

Carr, Ethan. *Wilderness by Design: Landscape Architecture and the National Park Service.* Lincoln: University of Nebraska Press, 1998.

Cohen, Stan. *The Tree Army: Pictorial History of the Civilian Conservation Corps, 1933–1942.* Missoula: Pictorial Histories Publishing Co., 12th Printing, 2009.

Cole, Olen, Jr. *The African-American Experience in the Civilian Conservation Corps.* Gainesville: University of Florida Press, 1999.

Cutler, Phoebe. *The Public Landscapes of the New Deal.* New Haven: Yale University Press, 1985.

Daugherty, John. *A Place Called Jackson Hole: A Historic Resource Study of Grand Teton National Park.* Moose: Grand Teton Natural History Association, 1999.

*http://nps.gov/history/history/online_books/grte2/hrs.htm*

Dilsaver, Lary M., and William C. Tweed. *Challenge of the Big Trees: A Resource History of Sequoia and Kings Canyon National Parks.* Three Rivers: Sequoia Natural History Association, 1990.

*http://www.nps.gov/history/history/online_books/dilsaver-tweed/chap6.htm*

Dudley, Harold M., and A. C. Oliver. *The New America: The Spirit of the Civilian Conservation Corps.* New York: Longmans, Green and Co., 1937.

Engbeck, Joseph H., Jr. *By the People, for the People: The Work of the Civilian Conservation Corps in California State Parks, 1933–1941.* Sacramento: California State Parks, 2002.

Engle, Reed L. *Everything Was Wonderful: A Pictorial History of the Civilian Conservation Corps in Shenandoah National Park.* Luray: Shenandoah National Park Association, 1999.

Fechner, Robert. *What about the CCC? Emergency Conservation Work.* Washington: Government Printing Office, 1937.

Good, Albert H., ed. *Park and Recreation Structures.* Washington: National Park Service, 1938.

Harrity, Richard, and Ralph G. Martin. *The Human Side of FDR.* New York: Duell, Sloan and Pearce, 1960.

Hoyt, Ray. *Your CCC: A Handbook for Enrollees.* Washington, DC: Happy Days Publishing Company, 1940.

Graham, Otis L., Jr., and Meghan Robinson Wander. *Franklin D. Roosevelt: His Life and Times.* New York: G. K. Hall and Co., 1985. Republished: Da Capo Press, New York, 1990.

Henderson, Henry L., and David B. Woolner, eds. *FDR and the Environment.* New York: Palgrave MacMillan, 2005.

Jolley, Harley E. *The CCC in the Smokies.* Gatlinburg: Great Smoky Mountains Association, 2001.

Landrum, Ney C. *The State Park Movement in America: A Cultural Review.* Columbia: University of Missouri Press, 2004.

Lawless, Lucy Ann. "The Civilian Conservation Corps and the State Park: An Approach to the Management of the Designed Landscape Resources at Franklin Delano Roosevelt State Park, Pine Mountain, Georgia." Master's thesis in Landscape Architecture, The University of Georgia, 1992.

Maher, Neil M. *Nature's New Deal: The Civilian Conservation Corps and the Roots of the American Environmental Movement.* New York: Oxford University Press, 2008.

Mattison, Ray H. "The First Fifty Years." Washington, DC: National Park Service, 1955.
*http://www.nps.gov/deto/historyculture/places.htm*

McBride, Dennis. *Hard Work and Far from Home: The Civilian Conservation Corps at Lake Mead, Nevada.* Boulder City: Boulder Images, 1995.

McClellan, Linda Flint. *Presenting Nature: The Historic Landscape Design of the National Park Service, 1916 to 1942.* Washington: National Park Service, 1993.

Morgan, Ted. *FDR: A Biography.* New York: Simon and Schuster, 1985.

Paige, John C. *The Civilian Conservation Corps and the National Park Service, 1933–1942: An Administrative History.* Washington: National Park Service, 1985.

Parent, Laurence. *Official Guide to Texas State Parks*. Austin: The University of Texas Press, 1997.

Perkins, Frances. *The Roosevelt I Knew*. New York: Viking Press, 1946.

Rauch, Basil. ed. *The Roosevelt Reader: Selected Speeches, Messages, Press Conferences, and Letters of Franklin D. Roosevelt*. New York: Rinehart and Co., 1957.

Righter, Robert. *Crucible for Conservation: The Creation of Grand Teton National Park*. Boulder: Colorado Associated University Press, 1983.

Roosevelt, Franklin D. *The Public Papers and Addresses of Franklin D. Roosevelt*. Volume two, *The year of crisis, 1933*. New York: Random House, 1938.

Rydell, Kiki Leigh , and Mary Shivers Culpin. *Managing the Matchless Wonders: A History of Administrative Development in Yellowstone National Park, 1872–1965*. Yellowstone: National Park Service, 2006. http://www.nps.gov/yell/historyculture/admindevel.htm

Salmond, John A. *The Civilian Conservation Corps, 1933–1942: A New Deal Case Study*. Durham: Duke University Press, 1967.

Schlesinger, Arthur M., Jr. *The Age of Roosevelt: The Coming of the New Deal*. Boston: Houghton Mifflin, 1958.

Schueller, Mary J. *Rustic Reflections of Copper Falls State Park*. Richfield: Rustic Books, LLC, 2005.

Steeley, James Wright. *Parks for Texas: Enduring Landscapes of the New Deal*. Austin: The University of Texas Press, 1999.

Story, Isabelle. *The National Park Service and Emergency Conservation Work*. Washington: Government Printing Office, 1936. http://www.nps.gov/history/online_books/ecw/1934/sec4.htm

Unrau, Harlan D., and Frank G. Willis. *Administrative History: Expansion of the National Park Service in the 1930s*. Washington: National Park Service, 1983. http://www.nps.gov/history/onlinebooks/unrau-willis/adhi.htm

Watkins, T. H. *The Great Depression: America in the 1930s*. New York: Little, Brown and Co., 1993.

———. *The Hungry Years: A Narrative History of the Great Depression in America*. New York: Henry Holt and Co., 1999.

Wirth, Conrad L. "Civilian Conservation Corps Program for the United States Department of Interior, March 1933 to June 30, 1943: Report to Interior Secretary Harold L. Ickes." Washington: Government Printing Office. 1945.

———. *Parks, Politics, and the People*. Norman: University of Oklahoma Press, 1980.

# Index[1]

---

[1] Bold numbers indicate the page number upon which a photograph of the subject is located.